Shakespeare and Latinidad

For Terry Boffone and Trina Della Gatta, who ardently supported our work and who passed away before this book came to print.

Shakespeare and Latinidad

Edited by Trevor Boffone and
Carla Della Gatta

EDINBURGH
University Press

Edinburgh University Press is one of the leading university presses in the UK. We publish academic books and journals in our selected subject areas across the humanities and social sciences, combining cutting-edge scholarship with high editorial and production values to produce academic works of lasting importance. For more information visit our website: edinburghuniversitypress.com

Edinburgh University Press Ltd
The Tun – Holyrood Road
12(2f) Jackson's Entry
Edinburgh EH8 8PJ

Typeset in 10.5/13pt Bembo by
Servis Filmsetting Ltd, Stockport, Cheshire

A CIP record for this book is available from the British Library

ISBN 978 1 4744 8848 8 (hardback)
ISBN 978 1 4744 8850 1 (webready PDF)
ISBN 978 1 4744 8851 8 (epub)

Contents

Part III: Shakespeare in Latinx Classrooms and Communities

Part IV: Translating Shakespeare in Ashland

Acknowledgements

This book would not be possible without the creativity and artistry of the many Latinx theatre-makers that fill these pages. Without their work, there are no intersections between Shakespeare and Latinidad and, put simply, we wouldn't be able to have such a robust conversation about the myriad ways that the US Latinx community interacts with the work of William Shakespeare.

Like so many edited collections, this book was born out of conversations engendered at a scholarly gathering. In this case, the 'Latinx Shakespeares: A Borderlands Drama Symposium' at Texas A&M University–San Antonio served as our spark. Co-organised by Adrianna M. Santos and Katherine Gillen, the symposium stimulated several of the chapters in this book. We thank them for providing space for like-minded theatre and literature scholars to come together and advance the conversation on Shakespeare and Latinidad. Convenings hosted by the Latinx Theatre Commons (LTC) provided the space that, along with fostering conversations on theatre-making, also was the setting of our initial meeting in 2015 and many subsequent occasions for working together as advocates for Latinx theatre. Moreover, we would like to recognise Katherine Gillen who helped get this book off the ground as well as Jessica Hinds-Bond for championing our work through both her friendship and her extraordinary feedback on our writing.

Throughout this process, our editor Michelle Houston has been a fervent supporter of this project. The entire staff at Edinburgh University Press has exceeded all expectations and has been a joy to work with. We thank the anonymous peer reviewers whose insight greatly improved the shape and scope of this collection.

The final stages of this book came together during the Covid-19 pandemic. We would like to extend a special thanks to our contributors and our various support networks that helped us finalise this collection. With the myriad of challenges and priorities in our homes, our work and the world, we are indebted to the perseverance of all involved in seeing this collection through to completion.

Carla would like to thank Bruce Avery for encouraging her to write performance reviews on Shakespeare productions when she lived in London during her MA programme, which sparked her interest in performance theory and her decision to enter a PhD programme in Theatre; and Henry Godinez, who always made time to discuss Latinx theatre with Carla during her doctoral studies, with the necessary perspective informed by practice and doing the work in the theatre.

Trevor would like to thank Steward Savage for igniting his interest in Shakespeare. Savage's work in tandem with Trevor's first visit to the Oregon Shakespeare Festival proved to be turning points in Trevor's relationship with Shakespeare, moving the needle from indifferent to fully engaged believer in all things Shakespeare. He also thanks his spouse Kayla who answered many questions about Shakespeare and offered much feedback on his writing.

And last, but certainly not least, we owe much gratitude to our research assistants Lady Ophelia, Hamlet, Teddy Honeybear and Pickles whose cuddles and purrs kept us on track during editing and writing days.

Contributor Biographies

Frankie J. Alvarez is best known as the passionate artist Agustín on HBO's critically adored series *Looking* and its companion *Looking: The Movie*. His film credits include *Rockaway*, *Vandal* and *The Drummer*. His television credits include *New Amsterdam*, *Law & Order: SVU*, *The Good Wife*, *Blindspot*, *Controversy*, *The Brides*, *Madam Secretary*, *Smash*, *It's Freezing Out There* and *Aphasia*. His theatre credits include *Othello* (workshop, NYTW), *Those Lost Boys: The Ten-Year Reunion* (co-creator, Ars Nova), *twenty50* (Denver Theatre Center), *Bathing in Moonlight* (McCarter Theatre), *The Whipping Man* (Actors Theatre of Louisville), *Hamlet: Prince of Cuba / Hamlet: Príncipe de Cuba* (Asolo Rep), *Measure for Measure* and *Julius Caesar* (Oregon Shakespeare Festival). Frankie is also an accomplished audiobook narrator, and is best known for his work on the acclaimed debut novel by Justin Torres, *We the Animals*. He has a BFA from Florida State University and an MFA from The Juilliard School.

Trevor Boffone is the founder of the 50 Playwrights Project and a member of the National Steering Committee for the Latinx Theatre Commons. He is a Lecturer in the Women's, Gender & Sexuality Studies Program at the University of Houston. He is the author of *Renegades: Digital Dance Cultures from Dubsmash to TikTok* (Oxford University Press, 2021). He is the co-editor of *Encuentro: Latinx Performance for the New American Theater* (Northwestern University Press, 2019), *Teatro Latino: Nuevas obras de los Estados Unidos* (La Casita Grande Press, 2019) and *Nerds, Goths, Geeks, and Freaks: Outsiders in Chicanx and Latinx Young Adult Literature* (University Press of Mississippi, 2020).

Diana Burbano is a Colombian immigrant, a playwright, an Equity actor and a teaching artist at South Coast Repertory and Breath of Fire Latina Theatre Ensemble. Diana's play *Ghosts of Bogota* won the Nu Voices festival at Actors

Theatre of Charlotte in 2019. *Ghosts* was commissioned and debuted at Alter Theater in the Bay Area in February 2020. She was in Center Theatre Group's 2018–19 Writers Workshop cohort and is in the Geffen's Writers Lab in 2020–21. She has worked on projects with South Coast Repertory, Artists Repertory Theatre, Breath of Fire Latina Theatre Ensemble and Center Theatre Group. She is the 2020 Dramatists Guild Representative for Southern California.

Migdalia Cruz is a Bronx-born, award-winning, multi-platform playwright, lyricist, translator and librettist of more than sixty works for stage, radio, film, TV and podcast, performed in 150 venues in forty cities in twelve countries. An alumna of New Dramatists, she received seven major US grants, and was named the 2013 Helen Merrill Distinguished Playwright. María Irene Fornés nurtured her voice at INTAR, and Latino Chicago Theater Company helped Migdalia hone it as their playwright in residence. She is co-chair of the DGF Playwriting Fellows 2020–21 with Lucy Thurber; mentors the NYC Latinx Playwrights Circle; and was commissioned in 2020 by Nylon Fusion, Planet Connections, The Homebound Project, Clubbed Thumb, The Flea and INTAR. Recent live productions: *Lives of the New Kind of Saints: a geo-located piece* with music/sound design by Cristian Amigo @INTAR/Battery Park (November 2020), and PlayON!*Richard III* (August 2020) in Sunderland, England @TheatreSpaceNorthEast. Her PlayOn!*Macbeth* will soon be a podcast.

Cynthia Santos DeCure is a bilingual actor and dialect coach with more than twenty years of professional experience. She is an Assistant Professor Adjunct of Acting at the Yale School of Drama. Certified as an Associate Teacher of Fitzmaurice Voicework and as a teacher of Knight-Thompson Speechwork, Cynthia was the dialect coach for *El Huracán* at Yale Repertory Theatre in 2018. She has also coached productions at Children's Theatre of Minneapolis, Phoenix Theatre, Long Beach Shakespeare Company and REDCAT, and was the on-set dialect coach for the Netflix series *Orange is the New Black*. Cynthia is on the steering committee of the Latinx Theatre Commons and on the board of the Voice and Speech Trainers Association, where she is Director of Equity, Diversity, and Inclusion. She is a member of Actors' Equity Association and the Screen Actors Guild. Cynthia is co-editor of the book *Scenes for Latinx Actors: Voices of the New American Theatre* (Smith & Kraus, 2019).

Carla Della Gatta is Assistant Professor of English at Florida State University. She has published essays and reviews, dramaturged professionally, and worked as a scholar and adviser for various theatres. She has been awarded fellowships from the Woodrow Wilson Foundation, the Folger Shakespeare

Library, the New York Public Library and the American Society for Theatre Research. Della Gatta received the J. Leeds Barroll Dissertation Prize from the Shakespeare Association of America for the best dissertation in 2016. Her first monograph, *Latinx Shakespeares: The Staging of Intracultural Theatre*, is in process. It explores the intersection of Shakespeare and Latinidad through dramaturgical and textual analysis of cultural adaptations.

Alejandra Escalante is an actress who has performed in *Love's Labor's Lost, Henry IV, Part I, Henry IV, Part II, The Tempest, A Wrinkle in Time, The Tenth Muse, Romeo and Juliet, As You Like It* and *Measure for Measure* at Oregon Shakespeare Festival; *The Trestle at Pope Lick Creek* at Rapscallion Theatre Collective; *Hey Mary!* at Midtown International Theatre Festival; *A House Full of Dust* at Wings Theatre; *Sense and Sensibility* at Guthrie Theater; *2666, The Upstairs Concierge, Measure for Measure* and *Song for the Disappeared* at Goodman Theatre; *Another Word for Beauty* and *Fingersmith* at New York Stage and Film; *Darwin in Malibu* at Washington Stage Guild; *A New Day* at Boston Center for American Performance; and *Quark Victory* at Piven Theatre. She has a BFA in Acting from Boston University and has also been trained at the London Academy of Music and Dramatic Art.

Micha Espinosa is an Arizona-based interdisciplinary performing artist, activist, teacher, and voice, speech and dialect coach who has performed and taught globally. She is a professor (BFA, Stephens College; MFA Acting, University of California San Diego) at Arizona State University, master teacher and trainer of Fitzmaurice Voicework (FV) and Director of Global Outreach for FV Institute; award-winning editor of the books *Monologues for Latino Actors* and *Scenebook for Latinx Actors*; and an affiliate artist with performance art collective La Pocha Nostra. Her scholarship, artivism and creative research all seek to challenge systems of inequity and Eurocentrism. She is passionate about global and feminist perspectives and the cultural voice.

Joe Falocco is an Associate Professor of English at Texas State University. He is the author of *Reimagining Shakespeare's Playhouse: Early Modern Staging Conventions in the Twentieth Century* (Boydell & Brewer, 2010), along with articles in several major journals including *Shakespeare Bulletin* and *Upstart Crow*. His essay 'Tommaso Salvini's Othello and Racial Identity in Late Nineteenth-Century America' (*New England Theatre Journal* 23, 2012) won the American Theatre and Drama Society's Vera Mowry Roberts Outstanding Essay Award. Falocco has worked as an actor and director at regional theatres and Shakespeare festivals around the United States and recently made his Spanish-language debut as Hernan Cortez in *Mexico 499* for Proyecto Teatro in Austin.

Katherine Gillen is Associate Professor of English at Texas A&M University-San Antonio. She is the author of *Chaste Value: Economic Crisis, Female Chastity, and the Production of Social Difference on Shakespeare's Stage* (Edinburgh University Press, 2017). Her essays appear in several collections and in journals such as *Studies in English Literature, Shakespeare Studies* and *Exemplaria*. Her current work focuses on race in early modern drama and on Shakespeare appropriation, particularly Latinx Shakespeare, and her monograph in progress is tentatively titled *Race, Rome, and Early Modern Drama: The Whitening of England and the Classical World*.

Henry Godinez, born in Havana, Cuba, is Professor of Theatre at Northwestern University and the Resident Artistic Associate at the Goodman Theatre, where he is the director of the Latino Theatre Festival. Most recently, for the Goodman, he has fostered the co-production of *Pedro Paramo* with Teatro Buendia of Cuba. Also at Goodman he has directed *The Sins of Sor Juana, Boleros for the Disenchanted* (and world premiere at Yale Repertory Theatre), *Millennium Mambo, Straight as a Line, The Cook, Mariela in the Desert, Electricidad, Zoot Suit* and the Goodman/Teatro Vista co-production of *Cloud Tectonics*. He has directed and acted in theatres across the country. Godinez is the co-founder and former artistic director of Teatro Vista. In 2010, he was appointed by Governor Pat Quinn to the Illinois Arts Council, where he serves on its Executive Committee. He serves on the Editorial Board of the Northwestern University Press and the Board of Directors of Albany Park Theatre Project.

José Cruz González's plays include *American Mariachi, Under a Baseball Sky, Among the Darkest Shadows, The Astronaut Farmworker, The Long Road Today, The San Patricios, Sunsets and Margaritas, The Sun Serpent, Invierno, The Heart's Desire, Tomás and the Library Lady, September Shoes, Odysseus Cruz* and *The Highest Heaven*. A collection of his plays, *Nine Plays by José Cruz González: Magical Realism & Mature Themes in Theatre for Young Audiences*, was published by the University of Texas Press in 2009. González has written for *Paz*, the Emmy Award nominated television series produced by Discovery Kids for The Learning Channel. *The Astronaut Farmworker* was a 2016 PEN Center USA Literary Award Finalist. He is a Professor Emeritus at California State University at Los Angeles, and a member of The Dramatists Guild of America and TYA/USA, and the College of Fellows of the American Theatre, John F. Kennedy Center for the Performing Arts.

Marissa Greenberg is Associate Professor of English at the University of New Mexico. She is the author of *Metropolitan Tragedy: Genre, Justice, and the City in Early Modern England* (University of Toronto, 2015) and the recipient of fellowships from the Folger Shakespeare Library and the National Endowment for the Humanities. Greenberg has published articles in journals including *English Literary Renaissance, Genre, Modern Language Quarterly, Renaissance Drama* and *Shakespeare Bulletin*, and her essay in *Shakespeare and Latinadad* is one in a series on Shakespeare and adaptation. Currently she is at work on projects related to teaching for social justice in the online classroom and embodiment, movement and history in the writings of John Milton.

Michelle Lopez-Rios is a teatrista, teacher and activist. Together with Alvaro Saar Rios, she co-founded the Royal Mexican Players in 2004. Selected coaching credits include *Mojada, Julius Caesar* (Oregon Shakespeare Festival); *Measure for Measure, Father Comes Home from the Wars* (Goodman Theatre); *Familiar* (Steppenwolf); *Othello, Hamlet, Comedy of Errors, Taming of the Shrew* (Houston Shakespeare Festival). Selected directing credits include *Luchadora!* (The Theatre School at DePaul), *The Mole Hill Stories* (First Stage) and *Enfrascada* (Renaissance Theaterworks). She appeared in the world premiere of *Luchadora!* by Alvaro Saar Rios and the Mark Taper PLAY production of *Bocón* by Lisa Loomer. She is an Associate Professor of Voice and Speech at The Theatre School at DePaul.

David Lozano serves as the Executive Artistic Director of Cara Mía Theatre Co. and specialises in writing, directing, and producing bilingual plays for the Latinx community in north Texas. Notable productions include *To DIE:GO in Leaves, by Frida Kahlo* (devised by Cara Mía's artistic ensemble), *Nuestra Pastorela* (co-written with Jeffry Farrell), *Crystal City 1969* (with Raul Treviño), *The Dreamers: A Bloodline* (devised by Cara Mía) and *Deferred Action*.

Daniel José Molina is an actor from Santo Domingo, Dominican Republic. He has performed on Broadway in *Fish in the Dark* (Cort Theatre), Off-Broadway in *Terra Firma* (BIPAC), and in *Othello* at the A.R.T. He spent three seasons at Utah Shakespeare Festival. At the Oregon Shakespeare Festival, he has performed as Henry V in *Henry V*; Ferdinand in *Love's Labor's Lost*; Hal in *Henry IV, Parts I* and *II*; Ferdinand in *The Tempest*; Elliot in *Water by the Spoonful*; Posthumus in *Cymbeline*; and Romeo in *Romeo and Juliet*. He appeared in the film *The Yellow Birds*. Daniel is the 2011 recipient of the National Irene Ryan Acting Award. He holds a BFA from Savannah College of Art and Design.

Jerry Ruiz's directing credits include the world premiere of *Fade* by Tanya Saracho (Denver Center for the Performing Arts Theatre Company, Primary Stages), *Twelfth Night* (Old Globe, PlayMakers Repertory Company, and Chalk Rep), *Mala Hierba* (Second Stage Theatre), *Basilica* by Mando Alvarado

(Rattlestick Playwrights Theater), *Philip Goes Forth* and *Love Goes to Press* (Mint Theater Company), *Enfrascada* (Clubbed Thumb), *Mariela in the Desert* by Karen Zacarías (Repertorio Español), *The King is Dead* by Caroline V. McGraw, *Rattlers* by Johnna Adams (Flux Theatre Ensemble), and *Waiting for the Hearse* (Mixed Blood Theatre). Ruiz has developed work at Playwrights Horizons, Soho Rep, The Public Theater, Atlantic Theater Company, Oregon Shakespeare Festival and the Playwrights Realm. From 2011 to 2015 he served as curator for the Crossing Borders Festival of New Plays at Two River Theater in New Jersey. He is Assistant Professor of Theatre and Head of MFA Directing at Texas State University.

Olga Sanchez Saltveit is Assistant Professor of Theatre at Middlebury College and Artistic Director Emerita of Milagro, the Northwest's premier Latino arts and culture organization where she served as the company's Artistic Director from 2003 to 2015. She is an actor, director, writer, educator and arts activist. Her directorial work has been seen in Portland, Seattle, New York City, Washington, DC, Martha's Vineyard, Peru, Venezuela, Honduras and Cuba. Olga served as co-artistic director of the People's Playhouse in New York City, artistic director of Seattle Teatro Latino, and co-founder of La Casa de Artes, a Seattle-based non-profit organisation dedicated to celebrating the beauty of Latino arts and cultural heritage. She is a founding member of the Portland-based Latinx writers' group Los Porteños. Olga served on the Executive Committee and the Diversity Task Force on TCG's (Theatre Communications Group) board of directors. She serves on the Advisory Committee of the Latinx Theatre Commons.

Adrianna M. Santos earned a BA in English from University of Texas at Austin, and an MA and PhD in Chicana/o Studies with an emphasis in Feminist Studies from University of California, Santa Barbara. She teaches classes on Chicanx/Latinx Literature as an Assistant Professor of English at Texas A&M University-San Antonio where she acts as faculty adviser for the Mexican American Student Association and co-coordinator of the Mexican American, Latinx, and Borderlands Studies Minor. She was a member of the National Women's Studies Association's Women of Color Leadership Project and has volunteered at Santa Barbara Rape Crisis Center, Martinez St. Women's Center, and Child Advocates of San Antonio. She has published and spoken on anti-violence advocacy and writing as resistance in *El Mundo Zurdo*, *Aztlán*, *Chicana/Latina Studies*, *Latina Critical Feminism* and the conferences of NACCS, MALCS, MLA and ALA, and is working on a book manuscript titled *Chicanx Poetics, Trauma and Healing in the Literary Borderlands: Beyond Survival*.

Roxanne Schroeder-Arce is Associate Dean of Fine Arts Education in the College of Fine Arts and Associate Professor in the Department of Theatre & Dance at the University of Texas at Austin. In addition to teaching, Schroeder-Arce is a scholar, director and playwright. Her plays, including *Mariachi Girl* and *Señora Tortuga*, are published by Dramatic Publishing. She has published articles in journals such as *Youth Theatre Journal, International Journal for Education & the Arts* and *Theatre Topics* and chapters in books such as *Latinos and American Popular Culture* (ed. Patricia M. Montilla) and *Nerds, Goths, Geeks, and Freaks: Outsiders in Chicanx and Latinx Young Adult Literature* (ed. Trevor Boffone and Cristina Herrera). She was also artistic and youth director of Teatro Humanidad, a bilingual theatre company in Austin. A first-generation college student, she is also an alumna of the Keene State College Upward Bound Program.

Daphnie Sicre is an Assistant Professor of Theatre Arts at Loyola Marymount University, where she teaches directing, solo performance, Latinx theatre, and theatre for social change. She shares a deep passion for discovering multiple Latinx and African American perspectives in theatre. Her latest publication is a chapter in *The Routledge Companion to African American Theatre and Performance* (ed. Kathy A. Perkins et al.), titled 'Afro-Latinx Themes in Theatre Today'. Other publications include '#UnyieldingTruth: Employing the Culturally Responsive Pedagogy', from the book *Black Acting Methods* (ed. Sharrell D. Luckett with Tia M. Shaffer), and the forthcoming book chapter, 'A Time of Protest; Exploring Activism through Newspaper Theatre and Hip Hop Pedagogy', in *Dynamic Bodies, Emerging Voices: Racializing and Decolonizing Actor Pedagogy*. Engaging in anti-racist and culturally competent theatre practices, Daphnie facilitates Theatre of the Oppressed workshops remixed with Hip Hop Pedagogy to teach about equity, diversity and inclusion in theatre. When she is not writing, teaching or conducting workshops, she can be found directing.

Octavio Solis is a playwright and author whose works *Mother Road, Quixote Nuevo, Se Llama Cristina, John Steinbeck's The Pastures of Heaven, Ghosts of the River, Lydia, June in a Box, Lethe, Gibraltar, Bethlehem, Dreamlandia, El Otro, Man of the Flesh, Prospect, El Paso Blue, Santos & Santos, La Posada Mágica and Cloudlands* (with music by Adam Gwon) have been mounted in theatres across the country such as the Oregon Shakespeare Festival, the California Shakespeare Theatre, the Center Theatre Group, Yale Repertory Theatre, the Denver Center for the Performing Arts, the Magic Theatre, South Coast Repertory Theatre, El Teatro Campesino, Campo Santo, INTAR and Cornerstone Theatre. His short stories have been published in *Zyzzyva, Catamaran, Huizache* and the *Chicago Quarterly Review*. Solis has received numerous awards including the United States Artists Fellowship for 2011 and the 2014 Pen Center USA Award for Drama. His new book *Retablos* is published by City Lights Publishing.

James M. Sutton is an Associate Professor of English at Florida International University (FIU), Miami. He is the author of *Materializing Space at an Early Modern Prodigy House: The Cecils at Theobalds, 1564–1607* (Ashgate, 2005) and related articles. He acted as department chair from 2008 to 2016. In February 2016, he served as project lead when FIU exhibited a Folger Shakespeare Library First Folio (as part of 'The Book that Gave us Shakespeare' national tour of the Folio). His current research foregrounds 'local Shakespeares' in both Slovenia and South Florida. This work bridges Shakespeare to issues of exile, transplantation, immigration and (in Miami) Latinx identities. With his FIU colleague Asher Z. Milbauer, he has co-edited *Exile in Global Literature and Culture: Homes Found and Lost* (Routledge, 2020).

Caridad Svich received the 2012 OBIE for Lifetime Achievement and the 2018 Ellen Stewart Award for Career Achievement in Professional Theatre from the Association of Theatre in Higher Education and the 2018 Tanne Foundation Award for her body of work. She is co-screenwriter of *Fugitive Dreams*, which premiered at the 2020 Fantasia Film Festival and Austin Film Festival. She is the author of over eighty plays, among them *12 Ophelias, Iphigenia, Crash Falls...*, *Red Bike* and *The House of the Spirits*. She has edited several books on theatre, among them *Audience Revolution* (Theatre Communications Group, 2016). She is author of *Mitchell and Trask's Hedwig and the Angry Inch* (Routledge, 2019). She is founder of NoPassport theatre alliance & press.

José Luis Valenzuela is the Artistic Director of the Latino Theater Company (LTC), and The Los Angeles Theatre Center (LATC) and is also a Distinguished Professor at UCLA's School of Theater, Film & Television. Valenzuela is an award-winning theatre director, and has been a visionary and an advocate for Chicanx/Latinx Theater for over thirty years. He has directed critically acclaimed productions at major theatres both internationally and nationally, including the LATC where he created the Latino Theatre Lab in 1985 and the Mark Taper Forum where he established the Latino Theater Initiative in 1991. He has directed *The Mother of Henry, Solitude, Premeditation, Dementia* and *A Mexican Trilogy* for the LTC. Most recently he directed *Macbeth* at Oregon Shakespeare Festival, and Karen Zacarias's *Destiny of Desire* at Arena Stage, South Coast Rep, The Goodman Theatre and Oregon Shakespeare Festival. He produced the national *Encuentro Festival* in 2014 and national and international *Encuentro de las Américas* in 2017.

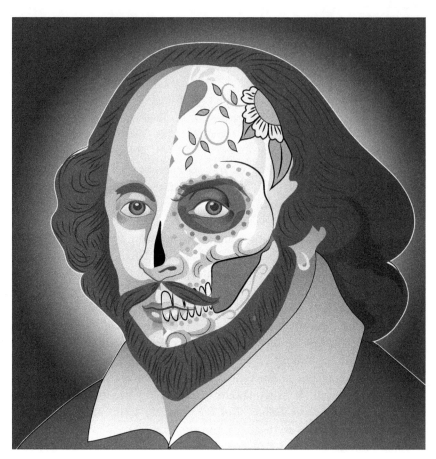

Calaveraspeare by José Rivera

Introduction: Shakespeare and Latinidad

Trevor Boffone and Carla Della Gatta

In 2012, visual artist José Pulido introduced the world to an image that would fully encompass how Shakespeare has been remixed with Latinidad – the Calaveraspeare. Riffing off a portmanteau of *calavera* (the Spanish word for skeleton) and Shakespeare's name, Calaveraspeare is a contradiction in and of itself. The image, which graces the cover of this book, is at once familiar and new and exciting. The image features Shakespeare holding a skull, with his mouth open as if in mid-speech, reciting his iconic 'To be or not to be' monologue from *Hamlet*. He is dressed in traditional Elizabethan costume, much like one would expect of Shakespeare. But something is off about this image. The Bard is a skeleton, modelled on José Guadalupe Posada's famed Day of the Dead calaveras. His hands are bones sans flesh. His face is adorned with colourful marigolds and wavy lines. Even his eyes are yellow marigolds. The *Hamlet* skeleton is also a calavera.

This is Calaveraspeare, that later resonates in the de facto logo of Oregon Shakespeare Festival's Latinx Play Project (LxPP), which grew out of the Latino/a Play Project. Echoing Pulido's image, the artist José Rivera created a portrait of Shakespeare for LxPP that is even more true to canonical images of the Bard, but in this rendering half of Shakespeare's face is covered in Day of the Dead-style artwork. This 'make-up' is *on top* of his skin, as if to say that this is a costume that he wears. He is the same William Shakespeare that everyone read in high school; the same playwright whose work has been adapted into the films we know and love today; the same playwright that theatre companies all across the globe continue to produce year in and year out. But this time, the Bard is celebrating the Latinx community. He is acknowledging that there are cultures and identities outside of his own experience that must be placed on equal footing with his own.

These two images – of a kind and yet each unique in its own right – are at once iconic, British and worldwide, while also being explicitly Mexican and

Latinx. Calaveraspeare is an image of cultures that shouldn't go together so seamlessly, but here they appear to have always gone hand in hand. Pulido and Rivera's work become visual examples of the phenomenon of what follows in this book – the intersection of Shakespeare and Latinidad.

Shakespeare and Latinidad is born out of the recent groundswell of Shakespearean performance generated by Latinx theatre practitioners. 'Latinx' is the gender-non-binary term for people from a shared colonial heritage of the Américas who reside in the United States; 'Latinidad' is Latinx culture. It is a term that encompasses everyone from the Indigenous peoples of Spanish-language dominant countries to the racially white and Black Latinx peoples from over twenty countries. The productions we attend to include adaptations of Shakespearean plays by Latinx playwrights, Latinx performers in Shakespearean productions that are sometimes asked to perform a role as a Latinx character and sometimes not, and Latinx Shakespeares – productions where Latinidad is integrated into Shakespearean stories and plays so that they are made Latinx.[1]

Since the turn of the millennium, events, conversations and productions have occurred across the United States in distinct and discrete spaces that convey the significant role that Shakespeare is playing in Latinx theatre. Latinx theatre spaces and festivals have expanded exponentially in the last decade, but an ongoing connection between Shakespeare and Latinidad remains challenging. This book addresses this challenge by bringing artists and scholars together, in conversation on the page. Our understanding of Latinx theatre is informed by foundational Chicanx theatre historian Jorge Huerta, who advocates:

> Neither the ancestry of its author, not the fact that it is written in a particular language, determines whether or not a play is Chicano. If the theme explores the nature of being Chicano, I would call it Chicano and more particularly, ethno-specific theatre.[2]

Given that Latinx theatre includes any theatre that addresses Latinx themes, Latinx-themed Shakespeare productions are included in the Latinx theatre canon. The diversity of Latinx culture – and theatre for that matter – demands a conversation across regions, dramaturgies, national heritages, uses of Spanish and scholars and practitioners. Shakespeare is the most performed playwright in the United States (and worldwide), and the United States has more Shakespeare festivals than any other country in the world. Latinx theatre is American theatre, and any conversation about American theatre must attend to Shakespeare. Shakespeare and Latinidad is not merely a field worthy of inquiry because it was previously unstudied until the last decade; it is a productive avenue for how we can stage a conversation about theatre and identity.

While Shakespeare as it relates to Central America, South America and the non-US Caribbean is a robust field in its own right, this book is not about theatre-making in those places. A shared aesthetics and dramaturgy – not just of Shakespeare but of any production – between Central and South America and Latinx in the United States varies by country of origin, shared linguistic cartographies and generational and theatrical influences. Latinx peoples in the United States remain in a marginalised position due to linguistic, immigration and racial politics that affect and inform theatre-making. While different national and cultural histories of translation into Spanish may link the performance of Shakespeare by Latinx people in the United States and those in Central and South America, there is otherwise not a strong parallel that unites the hemispheric Shakespeares.

The work of Shakespeare and Latinidad is explicitly US-based, recognising how a marginalised community in the United States has engaged with the world's most iconic playwright. This work might seem unlikely, but, as this book testifies, Latinx theatre-makers, audiences and advocates have been entangled in the web of Latinx Shakespeares long before Carla Della Gatta addressed this means of adaptation in a crucial early career plenary at the Shakespeare Association of America meeting in 2015, when she named Latino Shakespeares as a field.[3] Even so, as this collection demonstrates, the larger scope of this book, the various connections between Shakespeare and Latinidad, predates this conversation. The US Latinx community has been intersecting with Shakespeare for decades, from Spanish-language productions of Shakespeare plays in the 1800s to Latinx-themed productions and adaptations that became increasingly common with the formation of Hispanic/Latino as an ethnic category in the 1950s–1980s, and the growth of the Latinx population from the 1990s onward. In recent years, Latinx scholars have taken up its implications for the performance of identity. As such, the field of Latinx Shakespeares is a recovery project for American theatre in the first two decades of the twenty-first century, and this book begins that process.

Although the majority of Latinx theatre artists do not regularly engage with Shakespeare, very few have been able to avoid him altogether. Shakespeare is so thoroughly ingrained in the worldwide theatre community that nearly every theatre artist has collaborated on a production, adaptation, remix or riff of Shakespeare. The range of intersections highlight how this phenomenon is not relegated to simply one region. There is not just one motivation. It is not even linguistically singular. Shakespeare is more than just a playwright in the United States and throughout most of the world; the singularity of his name does not encompass the vast influence of his cultural status, place in American education and theatre, and his influence on storytelling. Hence, we pluralise his name in Latinx Shakespeares to reflect the variety of possibilities for performance.

Rather, Shakespeare and Latinidad exhibits the plurality of dramaturgies and approaches to adapting Shakespeare for Latinidad. In the 1970s and 1980s, several attempts to incorporate Latinx culture into Shakespeare performance took the form of a Latinx concept layered on top of a Shakespearean play. Several themed productions of *Julius Caesar*, for example, included Cuban and South American motifs that commented on the role of dictatorships, including productions at The Guthrie in 1969 (dir. Edward Payson Call), the American Shakespeare Company in Connecticut in 1979 (dir. Gerald Freedman) and the Philadelphia Drama Guild in 1988 (dir. Michael Murray). The non-Latinx directors and primarily non-Latinx casts invoked Central and South American politics as a thematic concept rather than attempted to represent Latinx culture in a more nuanced way.

Other productions sought to include the Spanish language, invoking partial translation as a form of Shakespearean adaptation. Strategies included sprinkling in Spanish words and phrases to signal Latinx culture, and oftentimes Latinx culture was pitted in opposition to whiteness, or what Carla Della Gatta has termed 'the *West Side Story* effect', or the 'the re-inscribing of Shakespearean representations of difference of various kinds – class, locale, familial – as a cultural-linguistic difference'.[4] 'The *West Side Story* effect' dramaturgy extended to productions such as Interart Theater in New York in their 1979 *Antony and Cleopatra* (dir. Estelle Parsons) that set Latinx (or the Spanish language) in opposition to whiteness (or Shakespearean English), to the New Brunswick Theater Festival in New Jersey and their 2010 production of *Romeo and Juliet* (dir. Daniel Swern) that set Latinx and African American culture in opposition. In both cases, these shows had white directors and employed Latinx translators or Central and South American translations for the Spanish words. There is no one form of adaptation of Shakespeare into Latinx culture.

These productions have also played fundamental roles in theatre companies' engagement with Latinx audiences as well as in the career trajectories of Latinx playwrights. Some efforts have been successful; others have not. Latinx playwrights have translated the Greeks, Spanish Golden Age plays, Lorca, Shakespeare and others, shifting between contemporary English and Spanish, español antiguo and Elizabethan/Jacobean English, depending on the audience. Despite the range of what is included within the scope of Shakespeare and Latinidad, there are two commonalities: a consistent desire to engage with Shakespeare on the Latinx stage and a growing desire to include Latinidad on the Shakespearean stage.

Latinx Theatre: From Ashlandia to San Antonio

In September 2015, Ashland, Oregon – the site of the Oregon Shakespeare Festival (OSF) – became known to Latinx theatre artists and scholars as Ashlandia. This moment was immortalised in a photograph that continues to make the rounds on social media, recognising this critical juncture in contemporary theatre history.[5] The photograph shows over fifty Latinx directors, actors, playwrights, dramaturgs, scholars, designers and producers smiling brightly inside OSF's Allen Elizabethan Theatre. In the photograph, those who typically stand onstage or in front of a classroom are privy to take the audience's role, in the solitude of a space that accommodates almost twelve hundred people. These theatre-makers, who are typically captured in motion, sit appropriately smiling for the picture.

This group of Latinx theatre artists and advocates had convened in Ashland for the OSF's Latino/a Play Project (LPP), an event that was made possible largely due to the presence of Luis Alfaro, OSF's first-ever playwright in residence, and Associate Artistic Director and scenic designer Christopher Acebo.[6] At the LPP, audiences witnessed staged readings of new work by Alfaro and by Isaac Gomez.[7] Neither play was an adaptation of Shakespeare, and none of the LPP programming addressed adaptation or Shakespeare. Nonetheless, Shakespeare dominated in presence. In Brian Sonia-Wallace's recap of the event for *HowlRound*, quotations from Shakespearean plays signal section themes, even though Shakespeare is nowhere to be found in the write-up itself.[8] Attendees could see OSF productions of *Antony and Cleopatra* and *Pericles*, as well as *The Happiest Song Plays Last*, the third play in Quiara Alegría Hudes's Pulitzer Prize-lauded trilogy.[9] There were formal panel discussions with scholars and dramaturgs and informal lunches and dinners. The weekend closed with a celebration at the ranch home of playwright Octavio Solis in nearby Medford.

LPP came on the heels of the first Carnaval of New Latina/o Work, hosted by the nascent Latinx Theatre Commons (LTC) and held at the Theatre School at DePaul University in Chicago in July 2015.[10] Of the eight new plays that premiered at this festival, none were adaptations of Shakespeare. In fact, even though the previous year's offering from LTC, the October 2014 Encuentro in Los Angeles, *did* feature one Shakespearean production (*Julius Caesar*), the canonical playwright was not prominently featured in what was, as Carla Della Gatta has noted, 'an unprecedented one-month Latino Theatre festival with seventeen productions'.[11] By any measure, anyone looking at the state of Latinx theatre in 2015 might miss Shakespeare's connections to the field, but the relationship had already begun.[12]

In the following years, OSF, the largest repertory theatre in the United States, would launch a greater intersection between Shakespeare and Latinx artists and themes. These efforts, in tandem with Alfaro's position and the work of then artistic director Bill Rauch, would encourage a more diverse American theatre that more thoroughly included the Latinx community. They produced works by Latinx playwrights Quiara Alegría Hudes with both *Water by the Spoonful* (2014) and *The Happiest Song Plays Last* (2015), Marisela Treviño Orta's *The River Bride* (2016), Luis Alfaro's *Mojada: A Medea in Los Angeles* (2017) directed by Juliette Carrillo, Karen Zacarías's *Destiny of Desire* (2018), and Octavio Solis's *Mother Road* (2019). They began to cast more Latinx actors in lead roles in non-Latinx Shakespearean productions of *The Tempest* (2014), *Henry IV, Parts I and II* (2017) and *Henry V* (2018), including contributors to this collection Alejandra Escalante and Daniel José Molina. Further, OSF employed Latinx directors for non-Latinx Shakespearean productions of *Much Ado About Nothing* (2015), *Henry IV, Part I* (2017), *Henry V* (2018) and *Macbeth* (2019), including José Luis Valenzuela, a contributor in this collection.[13] In 2018, a Latina directed a non-Latinx show, and a production of *Romeo and Juliet* had a Latinx production team, including Latinx director Dámaso Rodríguez, dramaturg Tiffany Ana López, as well as a Latinx scenic designer, lighting designer and composer/sound designer. This groundswell of Shakespeare and Latinidad in the unlikely location of rural Oregon is the subject of this book's fourth section.

While these changes occurred on the Shakespearean stage, over the next few years, the movement to produce more Latinx works prompted the Latinx Theatre Commons to produce a number of convenings, and in the Encuentro de las Américas in Los Angeles in 2017, Latinx and South and Central American adaptations and appropriations of Homer, Cervantes and Ibsen were programmed alongside original works. On Broadway, *Hamilton* skyrocketed to unprecedented acclaim and made a household name of Lin-Manuel Miranda while solidifying the integration of hip-hop and multi-ethnoracial casts onto musical theatre stages. Some Shakespeare theatres and practitioners continued their commitment to equity, diversity and inclusion, and well-known Latinx actors nabbed lead roles at high-profile theatres, among them Guatemalan-born Oscar Isaac, who played Hamlet at The Public Theater in 2017; Afro-Latina actress Ariana DeBose, who played Disco Donna in *Summer: The Donna Summer Musical* on Broadway in 2018; and Robin de Jesús, who was Tony-nominated for playing the role of Emory in the high-profile Broadway revival of *The Boys in the Band* in 2018. Meanwhile, conversations about Latinx Shakespeares were brewing in other parts of the country and in the academic landscape.

Much like the aforementioned theatre happenings, the present collection was born out of conversation and collaboration. In April 2018, we gathered at 'Latinx Shakespeares: A Borderlands Drama Symposium', a one-day event that sought to build momentum around the emerging field of Latinx Shakespeares.

Held at Texas A&M University–San Antonio and led by Katherine Gillen and Adrianna M. Santos, the symposium brought together scholars, teachers and theatre practitioners for conversations, workshops and performances that examined the varying ways that Shakespeare intersects with Latinidad, with a focus on how this phenomenon materialises in Texas.[14] Participants shed light on the nuanced ways that Latinx theatre artists engage with Shakespeare and the innovative and culturally relevant ways that this work can enter both classroom and performance spaces. The event included a keynote from Carla Della Gatta on dramaturgies of Latinx *Romeo and Juliet* and a keynote by playwright Josh Inocéncio followed by a performance of his short play *Ofelio*, that reimagines *Hamlet*'s Ophelia in a contemporary queer context during the #MeToo movement.[15] According to Gillen and Santos.

> The event also enriched our regional community of teachers and theater practitioners by providing new ways of drawing connections among texts and imagining canonical literature in new cultural contexts. Just as importantly, it provided space for thinking critically about how we can best serve our students and communities when we teach or produce Shakespeare and how we can do so in ways that don't affirm colonialist and white-supremacist ideologies.[16]

Although Della Gatta and Inocéncio focused on theatre history and theatre-making, respectively, a number of the papers that were presented focused on advocacy and outreach. The symposium demonstrated the growing need for these conversations to take place. For instance, the event featured a large number of high school theatre arts teachers in Texas who yearn for more ways to link canonical theatre such as Shakespeare with the public educational system's growing Latinx population. Moreover, the symposium demonstrated that the very notion of Latinx Shakespeares is still a 'new' concept and, as such, the present volume forges a place in both scholarship and artistic practice for Latinx Shakespeares to take centre stage and be recognised as something greater than the sum of its parts, Shakespearean performance and Latinx theatre.

Shakespeare and Race

Shakespeare and Latinidad brings together twenty-five Latinx artists and scholars. Our methodology is informed by our work with the Latinx Theatre Commons, a movement that prioritises scholarship alongside advocacy, art making and convening. Forward movement requires both aesthetic and critical work, often in conversation, and so this book redefines what, and who, can be included in scholarship. Over two-thirds of the contributors are university professors, and many teach directing, acting and voice. Many wear multiple hats as actors, directors, writers and, of course, educators. This book also redefines how Shakespearean performance is studied and theorised, not only making space for the voices of practitioners, but also demonstrating how theory infuses practice, just as, for scholars, practice infuses theory.

Much like *Weyward Macbeth: Intersections of Race and Performance*, edited by Scott L. Newstok and Ayanna Thompson, the present volume focuses on those 'weyward' moments in which Shakespeare's work speaks to the plurality of ways that the US Latinx community devises and performs ethnic and racial identities. As Ayanna Thompson notes, '"Weyward" – as weird, fated, fateful, perverse, intractable, willful, erratic, unlicensed fugitive, troublesome, and wayward – is precisely the correct word for *Macbeth*'s role in American racial formations.'[17] Indeed, just as *Macbeth* has been a fundamental site for adaptations and appropriations that comment on Blackness and contemporary racialisation in the United States, the Shakespeare canon at large has done similar work within the Latinx community.

The question of Shakespeare and racial and ethnic identities is not unique to the Latinx or Black community. For instance, Alexa Huang's *Chinese Shakespeares: Two Centuries of Cultural Exchange* demonstrates how this phenomenon has worked in China.[18] While China and Shakespeare would seem to be at odds with each other in global culture, *Chinese Shakespeares* demonstrates how the notion of cultural exclusivity is indeed a myth. As Huang asserts, there is transformative power in how the Shakespearean canon has been adapted, appropriated and remixed within Chinese culture.

Ayanna Thompson, in her role as editor for both the collection *Colorblind Shakespeare: New Perspectives on Race and Performance* and *Weyward Macbeth*, puts artists in conversation with scholars.[19] Artists and scholars have also been in conversation on Latinx and Latin American theatre works such as for the critical edition of *The Panza Monologues* by Virginia Grise and Irma Mayorga, as well as *Theatre and Cartographies of Power: Repositioning the Latina/o Americas*, edited by Analola Santana and Jimmy Noriega. Likewise, essays by numerous scholars make up *Latin American Shakespeares*, which addresses non-US performance of Shakespeare in other cultures and languages.[20] The present collection builds on these approaches, effectively bridging the work of artists and scholars and giving them equal importance.

The Shakespeare canon is more often than not read as white, and the legacy of Shakespeare as a tool of coloniality and English-language linguistic terrorism imbues the reception of his canon. Further, the widespread notions for his presence in education range from literary great to 'universal' ideas of humanity, which do not acknowledge the absence and subjugation of most marginalised people. His work does include several characters who are specifically written as people of colour (e.g. Othello and Aaron the Moor) and characters who represent marginalised communities (e.g. Caliban and Shylock). Naturally, these figures can become emblematic of oppressed peoples and communities, as has been the case with Caliban. Within the realm of Latinx and Latin American literary studies, perhaps there is no better example of this phenomenon than Cuban writer Roberto Fernández Retamar's 1971 essay 'Caliban: Notes towards a Discussion of Culture in Our America', in which he argues that Caliban is a symbol of the Américas and shows how European colonisers painted Indigenous peoples in a negative light. Yet, as Fernández Retamar notes, this pejorative image can be reclaimed, embraced and animated for a revolutionary politics that sees Latin America's marginalised communities gain power.[21]

Nearly fifty years later, creative writer and literary scholar Marcos Gonsalez remarks on the complicated relationship many people of colour have to Shakespeare's work. In 'Caliban Never Belonged to Shakespeare', Gonsalez details his experiences studying Shakespeare in school and reveals how he became Caliban when white educators reinforced racial power dynamics seen in plays such as *The Tempest*. Gonsalez writes:

> Something becomes clear to me throughout the years taking these many classes in the United States education system. Something becomes clear to me while writing from the margins, as a poor and gay and mentally ill and fat and Mexican-Puerto Rican person existing in the margins of the United States. I, Caliban, am meant to be in awe of, always under the tutelage and auspices of, an imitation of and a foil to, never, dare I even say it, to surpass, these many Prosperos.[22]

In this world, Prospero holds the power, and Shakespeare, in a larger sense, becomes the language of whiteness. Gonsalez proposes that a primary motivation for studying Shakespeare is to learn the language of whiteness.

Much of Gonsalez's essay speaks to the complexity of Shakespeare and Latinidad. Shakespeare is so prevalent in American education, worldwide theatre, Western storytelling and the cultural imaginary that in many ways he has been removed from his colonial British heritage into something different. But the legacies of racism, cultural and religious bigotry, and colonialist literary practices that have shaped perceptions and editions of Shakespeare's works remain. What then is there to do for Latinx artists with Shakespeare? Gonsalez writes, 'And here we are, the various generations of thinkers and creators, identifying with Caliban, this name and character and idea belonging to a white man. Do we break free from it? Should our intent be to craft new characters, new ideas, new Calibans?'[23]

Scholars have come to this conversation through different theoretical lenses. *Shakespeare and Latinidad* takes its frame from the discipline of theatre. Germane to theatre is the performance of identity, the embracing of a character and perspective outside oneself. All performances are adaptations, even if the sole change that marks the adaptation is a knowing glance, a simple gesture or a set design that alters the tenor of the play. It is something that Latinx practitioners have been doing for years to re-envision myth, canonised plays and Western and non-Western stories for their audiences. As the ethnic category of Hispanic/Latinx has changed in definition, public perception, and in theatrical representation over the decades, so have the possibilities for Shakespeare and Latinidad.

A number of contributors in this collection foreground ethnicity; others do not. Latinx identity and experience is heterogeneous across national and cultural backgrounds, regions, languages, accents and generations. Even in the second decade of the twenty-first century, Latinx indigeneity, queerness and Afro-Latinidad are sorely under-represented onstage, though that is changing across the country. As Latinx production teams take more prominent positions in theatres across the country, notions of Latinx design and dramaturgy, and perhaps even a Latinx Shakespearean aesthetic for both, may take shape. Seemingly contrary to this book's title, the collection as a whole does not take race, or rather ethnicity, as the lens through which to analyse Shakespearean productions. Rather, this is a book of one portion of Latinx theatre and one portion of American Shakespearean performance history, both an archive of what people have done and insights into new directions for Shakespeare and Latinidad. It is predicated on the notion that Latinx artists are always engaged with their culture, even if it is not apparent to an audience or reader. How Latinx culture informs their art is always part of the analysis of theatrical production. This book begins the conversation.

Book Structure and Chapter Overview

As part of the mode of conversation that Shakespeare and Latinidad entails, we offer two road maps for the connections between the essays in this book, the first by theme and the second by production element. The book is organised thematically in four sections, each constituting what we argue are fundamental conversations pertinent to the field of Shakespeare and Latinidad. The first addresses hybridity and borderlands epistemologies, the second strategies for Latinx Shakespeares, the third pedagogy and community engagement, and the fourth, a case study of the *Play on!* initiative at the Oregon Shakespeare Festival. Within each section are traditional scholarly essays that attend to different modes of theatre engagement. A number of the contributors wear multiple hats as scholar/dramaturg, actor/director or playwright/translator, and, as such, the work that follows reflects this plurality of making theatre. These essays and conversations embody theory in the practice and practice in the theory.

The first section of the book, 'Shakespeare in the US Latinx Borderlands', situates liminality and borderlands thinking as two fundamental components of Latinx Shakespeares. Each author addresses various and multiple borderlands epistemologies. Linguistic code-switching includes varieties of language play, from intersplicing Shakespearean words and phrases with Spanish and bilingual, semi-bilingual theatre, and in some cases, multilingual theatre. The physical border between the United States and Mexico makes an appearance in two of the essays, and each of the productions the authors in this section attend to challenges borders of theatrical genres. In this way, the multiplicity of epistemologies of the border – linguistic, dramaturgical and political – pose options for decolonising the historically white dramaturgies of 'realism' of contemporary American Shakespearean performance. As 'decolonisation' has become widely used, and often metaphorically, these authors demonstrate how Latinx theatre-makers challenge hegemonic structures that value Shakespeares, words, stories and theatrical modes.

The section begins with 'Staging Shakespeare for Latinx Identity and Mexican Subjectivity: *Marqués: A Narco Macbeth*', in which Carla Della Gatta challenges the dramaturgies for foregrounding Latinx culture in adaptation, including the incorporation of indigeneity, gender subversion and multimedia platforms. In '¡O Romeo!: Shakespeare on the Altar of Día de Muertos', Olga Sanchez Saltveit examines her role as director and deviser of *¡O Romeo!*, a devised, musical play based on the life, work and imagined death of William Shakespeare, created for Milagro's annual Día de los Muertos celebration in 2014. The production situated Shakespeare in conversation with the history of Aztec culture, Spanish colonisation, and the languages of Spanish and Nahuatl, to create a literary celebration of Día de los Muertos in the Bard's imaginary final play.

In 'Passion's Slave: Reminiscences on Latinx Shakespeares in Performance', Frankie J. Alvarez details his experiences as a Latino actor while working on *Measure for Measure* and *Julius Caesar* at Oregon Shakespeare Festival, as well as one of the most challenging and rewarding roles of his acting career: the titular role in the 2012 bilingual production of *Hamlet: Prince of Cuba* at the Asolo Repertory Theatre. Finally, scholars Katherine Gillen and Adrianna M. Santos, in 'The Power of Borderlands Shakespeares: Seres Jaime Magaña's *The Tragic Corrido of Romeo and Lupe*', employ the borderlands theory of Gloria Anzaldúa to analyse how retelling Shakespeare through a Tejanx lens that makes concrete references to life along the Texas–Mexico border can become a subversive remixing of Shakespeare. This work can negotiate questions of identity, place, language and difference and, in so doing, forge collective responses that centre Latinx voices and borderlands ways of knowing. As the chapters in this section demonstrate, the Shakespearean canon lends itself to a form of remixing that takes into account Latinx insider/

outsider liminality and borderlands sensibilities that imagine a new hybrid space for Latinx Shakespeares.

The following section, 'Making Shakespeare Latinx', engages the possibility of a Latinx dramaturgy. These artists and scholars draw upon first-hand experiences and archival research to imagine the myriad ways that racial and ethnic identities are juxtaposed with Shakespearean texts. Although Shakespeare and the US Latinx community may seem at odds with each other, the chapters in this section convey how Shakespeare is, in fact, ever present in the United States and, as such, Latinx artists wrestle with his legacy as they remix, reimagine and even reject Shakespeare in their work.

The section begins with Caridad Svich, whose chapter, 'In a Shakespearean Key', recounts the playwright's childhood curiosity with *A Midsummer Night's Dream*, which eventually led to her *Hamlet*-inspired *12 Ophelias*. Next, in '*Caliban's Island*: Gender, Queerness and Latinidad in Theatre for Young Audiences', Diana Burbano details how her own borderlands positionality influenced her to write *Caliban's Island*, a TYA play that intertwines characters from *Twelfth Night* and *The Tempest* within a context that is adaptable to multiracial casting. As Burbano proposes, because she is Latina, Latinidad permeates the work, and, as such, renders her Shakespeare Latinx. In 'La Voz de Shakespeare: Empowering Latinx Communities to Speak, Own and Embody Shakespeare's Texts', Cynthia Santos DeCure uses her experiences with vocal coaching and directing *The Tempest* to predominantly Latinx students to unpack how feelings of embarrassment when working on Shakespeare's text can transform into a powerful way to declare vocal rights.

Next, in 'Shakespeare's Ghosts: Staging Colonial Histories in New Mexico', scholar Marissa Greenberg examines Shakespeare's impact across a seventy-five-year period in New Mexico, a region shaped by legacies of colonialism. Greenberg argues that Shakespeare makes audible the ghosts of empire building while also contributing to the suppression of spectral voices. The section continues with a *diálogo* between renowned directors Henry Godinez and José Luis Valenzuela, who consider the various ways that their Latinidad has influenced their approaches to adapting and translating Latinx Shakespeares. In 'Shakespeare Through the Latinx Voice', voice and text director Michelle Lopez-Rios introduces the term 'Latinx voice' to reflect the influence of Latinx artists as actors, directors, playwrights, designers and producers. As such, Lopez-Rios considers the ways that Latinx voice affects the production of Latinx Shakespeares. As the work in this section reveals, the question of identity is always present when Latinx theatre-makers engage with Shakespeare, effectively demonstrating a new, perhaps more inclusive Shakespearean dramaturgy.

The book's third section, 'Shakespeare in Latinx Classrooms and Communities', presents artistic and scholarly attempts to forge Latinx

Shakespeares in educational and community-centred spaces. These chapters reveal how access, advocacy, outreach and pedagogy factor into the larger conversation of Shakespeare and Latinidad. As this section demonstrates, Shakespeare can become a powerful tool for culturally responsive community engagement, be it in a theatre company, a public park or in a classroom.

In 'Shakespeare With, For and By Latinx Youth: Assumptions, Access and Assets', artist-scholar Roxanne Schroeder-Arce explores the intersections of Shakespeare, Latinx youth identity, and arts education by shedding light on efforts in theatre education settings, where teachers and directors employ culturally responsive pedagogy and artistry while they write, teach and direct plays by, for and with Latinx youth. In the following chapter, 'Celebrating Flippancy: Latinas in Miami Talk Back to Shakespeare', scholar James M. Sutton includes the voices of his former students and brings this conversation into a higher education setting to highlight how he has used Shakespeare to engage and empower Latinx college students in South Florida. What follows is a *diálogo* between veteran theatre artists José Cruz González and David Lozano, who discuss ways they have made Shakespeare relevant to Latinx communities in California and Texas over the past three decades.

Chapters by Daphnie Sicre, Jerry Ruiz and Joe Falocco present three detailed case studies that tease out this type of community-centred work. In '*Romeo y Julieta*: A Spanish-Language Shakespeare in the Park', Daphnie Sicre details the challenges she faced in summer 2006 when mounting a Spanish adaptation and translation of Shakespeare for Latinx audiences in Miami. Next, Jerry Ruiz, in 'Politics, Poetry and Popular Music: Remixing Neruda's *Romeo y Julieta*', unpacks his experience directing a staged reading of Neruda's play in 2016 as part of The Public Theater's Mobile Unit Shakespeare programme, which tours to correctional facilities, homeless shelters and community centres throughout New York City. Ruiz explains how interpolating well-known Spanish-language songs by Violeta Parra and Luis Alberto Spinetta helped blossom the play into 2018's *Mala Estrella*, an evening of music and excerpts from *Romeo y Julieta*. Finally, in '"Lleno de Tejanidad": Staging a Bilingual *Comedy of Errors* in Central Texas', director Joe Falocco explores how playful language became an entry point into the bilingual community at a 2014 production at Texas State University. Much like the whole of this collection, as the work in this section exhibits, language often becomes an access point into community-engaged Latinx Shakespeares, whether working with youth, college students or community audiences.

The final section, 'Translating Shakespeare in Ashland', uses the Oregon Shakespeare Festival's *Play on!* initiative (2016–18) as a point of departure to explore the diverse ways that Latinx artists map new linguistic realities within the Shakespearean canon. This section offers a specific case study on

Shakespeare and Latinidad. These chapters synthesise many of the book's preceding themes – namely hybridity, the US Latinx borderlands, identity, community outreach and making Shakespeare Latinx. By focusing on a hyper-local case study of how Latinidad intertwines with Shakespeare, this section offers various road maps on how individual communities and theatre companies can engage with Shakespeare to create meaningful culturally responsive work with the Latinx community. Notably, *Play on!* did this through a new – and controversial – form of translation from Shakespearean English to contemporary English, which this section discusses in depth.

In 'Creating a Canon of Latinx Shakespeares: The Oregon Shakespeare Festival's *Play on!*', Trevor Boffone focuses on OSF's much-debated *Play on!* initiative, which commissioned thirty-six playwrights to translate the Shakespeare canon into contemporary English. *Play on!* led to the groundbreaking *La Comedia of Errors*, a bilingual community engagement project that saw OSF move from equity and diversity measures to legitimate inclusion of previously marginalised communities in Oregon's Rogue Valley. The remaining chapters examine the work of Latinx artists at OSF who have engaged in these Latinx Shakespeares. In 'What I Learned from My Shakespeare Staycation with *Macbeth* and *Richard III*', playwright Migdalia Cruz unpacks her process of translating *Macbeth* and *Richard III* into contemporary English as part of *Play on!* As a Puerto Rican woman from the Bronx, Cruz was eager to become part of the Western canon in such a subversive way, enhancing Shakespeare's drama. Likewise, in '*Will*ful Invisibility: Translating William Shakespeare's *The Reign of King Edward III*', playwright Octavio Solis unpacks what it means for a Latinx playwright to share authorship with Shakespeare and, specifically, considers how choosing a lesser known play offered him more impunity and creative freedom.

This section then transitions to performance, specifically looking at the work of actors and voice coaches. OSF company actors Alejandra Escalante and Daniel José Molina discuss their approaches for working with the language of Shakespearean productions, both in English and in Spanish. Finally, in 'What's with the Spanish, Dude? Identity Development, Language Acquisition and Shame while Coaching *La Comedia of Errors*', voice and text coach Micha Espinosa discusses how OSF's *La Comedia* allowed Espinosa's bilingual identity to be seen in a way she had previously never encountered despite working professionally in the field for over two decades. As this section highlights, these artistic and scholarly perspectives present how OSF has become a cultural centre for new possibilities of Latinx Shakespeares, even in rural Oregon, perhaps the unlikeliest of settings.

Alternative Roadmap

Actors will find useful the essays and interviews by Frankie J. Alvarez, Daniel José Molina and Alejandra Escalante. Alvarez and Molina discuss how playing the role of Hamlet and the role of Romeo, respectively, changed when played in Spanish versus English. All three actors compare their methods for performing in Latinx theatre, Latinx Shakespearean productions and non-Latinx themed Shakespearean productions.

Those interested in how playwrights approach adapting and translating Shakespeare can look to the essays by Migdalia Cruz, Octavio Solis, Caridad Svich and Diana Burbano. Both Cruz and Solis approach their translations for OSF's *Play on!* initiative in fundamentally different ways. Svich, who has adapted Shakespeare, Lorca, Greek and Spanish Golden Age plays, writes of her connection with canonised literatures and her motivations for adaptation and translation. Burbano writes of her personal trajectory in developing a Latinx-themed Shakespearean appropriation for young people.

Approaches to directing range from devised theatre, collaboration and the physical spaces for Latinx Shakespearean performance. As actors, directors and professors, José Luis Valenzuela and Henry Godinez discuss their experience directing Shakespeare in non-Latinx theatres versus their experiences as directors in Latinx theatres. Scholars Daphnie Sicre and Joe Falocco address their work as directors of Spanish and bilingual productions, respectively. Playwright, professor and director José Cruz Gonzalez converses with director David Lozano to explore strategies of engagement with Latinx communities in southern California and in Texas. Scholar Olga Sanchez writes about her experience devising a Shakespeare appropriation with Day of the Dead themes during her long-time position as Artistic Director of Milagro Theatre in Portland.

Methods for voice and dialect training are detailed by Michelle Lopez-Rios, Micha Espinosa and Cynthia Santos DeCure. Espinosa details her process for coaching a semi-bilingual production of *La Comedia of Errors* at OSF in 2019 and Lopez-Rios compares her approaches and the directors' visions for Latinx actors and Latinx Shakespeares in productions at OSF and Chicago's Goodman Theatre. Santos DeCure compares her approaches to coaching for Latinx accents in Shakespeare versus Latinx theatre productions.

Scholars focused on performance analysis can look to the essays of Marissa Greenberg, Carla Della Gatta, and Adrianna M. Santos and Katherine Gillen. Trevor Boffone theorises OSF's *Play on!* initiative that employed contemporary playwrights and dramaturgs to translate Shakespeare's plays into modern-day English. James Sutton's essay on pedagogy at a Hispanic-Serving Institution (HSI) is ultimately a collaboration with his Latinx students that gives voice to their experiences engaging with Shakespeare as well as his strategies for the classroom. Marissa Greenberg employs a local-historical approach to detail how Shakespeare resonates in New Mexico. Gillen and Santos use performance studies to define and analyse a production of borderlands Shakespeares, and Della Gatta takes a holistic approach as to how a Latinx-themed *Macbeth* adaptation can challenge representation along and south of the border.

Although *Shakespeare and Latinidad* is the first comprehensive record of artistic and scholarly work on Latinidad and Shakespeare, it is only a snapshot. Much like the OSF 2015 photo, there are artists and scholars attending to these productions all over the country. Moreover, theatre companies such as the Old Globe in San Diego and The Public Theater have also been key allies in this work. University productions, devised pieces, and the creativity of designers, playwrights and dramaturgs reveal that the intersection of Shakespeare and Latinidad is a bigger phenomenon than these pages manifest. It simply can't be confined to just one book, and, quite frankly, it shouldn't have to be.

Notes

1. Carla Della Gatta, 'From *West Side Story* to *Hamlet, Prince of Cuba*: Shakespeare and Latinidad in the United States', *Shakespeare Studies*, 44 (2016): 151.
2. Jorge Huerta, 'Looking for Magic: Chicanos in the Mainstream', in *Negotiating Performance: Gender, Sexuality, and Theatricality in Latin/o America*, ed. Diana Taylor and Juan Villegas (Durham, NC: Duke University Press, 1994), 39.
3. Carla Della Gatta's early career plenary was published in *Shakespeare Studies* in 2016. See Della Gatta, 'From *West Side Story* to *Hamlet, Prince of Cuba*'.
4. Della Gatta, 'From *West Side Story* to *Hamlet, Prince of Cuba*', 152.
5. That photograph from 2015 shows the group of Latinx artists and scholars seated in the empty Elizabethan stage at OSF. But like many photographs of significant events, it doesn't capture the relationships. Everyone in the photograph knew a few of the people there, but unlike the deliberate curating and comprehensive list of attendees at LTC convenings such as Carnaval, this was more of a social event with inadvertent meetings and chance run-ins. The photograph is a false memory of cohesion and unity, but one that makes sense more in hindsight than it did in its present moment.
6. The Latina/o Play Project (LPP) was rebranded as the Latinx Play Project (LxPP) in 2017.
7. Alfaro's play, *Delano*, became *The Golden State Part I: Delano*, and Gomez's play, *The Women of Juárez*, would later become *La Ruta*, the play that jump-started his career.

8. Brian Sonia-Wallace, 'Moving from Event to Tradition: A Report from the Latino/a Play Project at Oregon Shakespeare Festival', *HowlRound*, 3 November 2015. Available at https://howlround.com/moving-event-tradition (last accessed 10 November 2020).

9. Hudes was the second Latinx playwright to win the Pulitzer Prize for Drama, following Nilo Cruz for *Anna in the Tropics* (2003). Hudes won the Pulitzer for *Water by the Spoonful* (2012), the second play in her trilogy, and she was nominated for *Elliot, A Soldier's Fugue* (2007), the first in the trilogy. Later, Lin-Manuel Miranda became the third Latinx stage writer to win the Pulitzer, doing so for *Hamilton* in 2016.

10. Shakespeare is also linked to the Latinx Theatre Commons, arguably one of the most visible US-based theatre movements of the twenty-first century thus far. It was founded in response to a problematic staging of *Much Ado about Nothing* by the Shakespeare Theatre Company in 2011, when the so-called DC 8, a group of eight Latinx theatre-makers, gathered under the auspices of what would later become *HowlRound*. The DC 8 brainstormed ways to reinvigorate Latinx theatre-makers all across the country, and in this moment the seeds for the LTC were planted.

11. Della Gatta, From *West Side Story* to *Hamlet, Prince of Cuba*', 155.

12. We, the co-editors, met at the LTC Carnaval in 2015, when we serendipitously sat beside one other at the Scholars' Pod session. The photographer took a picture of the two of us in conversation as if we were old friends catching up. While this image became immortalised by the LTC as a recurring stock photo of sorts, it was another false memory of a chance first meeting of future collaborators: we had never met before that moment.

13. Lisa Loomer's *Roe* premiered in 2016 at OSF. While Loomer has a long history with the Latinx theatre community, especially in the 1980s and 1990s, she is of Spanish and Romanian descent.

14. For more on the symposium, see Katherine Gillen and Adrianna M. Santos, 'Latinx Shakespeare in the Texas–Mexico Borderlands', *Shakespeare Newsletter*, 67.2 (2019): 112–13.

15. For more on Josh Inocéncio's *Ofelio*, see Katherine Gillen, 'Shakespeare Appropriation and Queer Latinx Empowerment in Josh Inocencio's *Ofelio*', in *The Routledge Handbook of Shakespeare and Global Appropriation*, ed. Christy Desmet, Sujata Iyengar and Miriam Jacobson (London: Routledge, 2019), 90–101.

16. Gillen and Santos, 'Latinx Shakespeare', 112–13.

17. Ayanna Thompson, 'What Is a "Weyward" *Macbeth*?' in *Weyward Macbeth: Intersections of Race and Performance*, ed. Scott L. Newstok and Ayanna Thompson (New York: Palgrave Macmillan, 2010), 3.

18. Alexa Huang, *Chinese Shakespeares: Two Centuries of Cultural Exchange* (New York: Columbia University Press, 2009).

19. Ayanna Thompson (ed.), *Colorblind Shakespeare: New Perspectives on Race and Performance* (New York: Routledge, 2006).

20. Virginia Grise and Irma Mayorga, *The Panza Monologues*, 2nd edn (Austin: University of Texas Press, 2014); Analola Santana and Jimmy A. Noriega (eds), *Theatre and Cartographies of Power: Repositioning the Latina/o Americas* (Carbondale: Southern Illinois University Press, 2018); Bernice W. Kliman and Rick J. Santos (eds), *Latin American Shakespeares* (Madison, NJ: Fairleigh Dickinson University Press, 2005).

21. Roberto Fernández Retamar, 'Caliban: Notes Toward a Discussion of Culture in Our America', *Caliban and Other Essays*, trans. Edward Baker (Minneapolis: University of Minnesota Press, 1989).

22. Marcos Gonsalez, 'Caliban Never Belonged to Shakespeare', *Literary Hub*, 26 July 2019. Available at https://lithub.com/caliban-never-be-longed-to-shakespeare/ (last accessed 10 November 2020).

23. Gonsalez, 'Caliban Never Belonged to Shakespeare'.

Part I: Shakespeare in the US Latinx Borderlands

1

Staging Shakespeare for Latinx Identity and Mexican Subjectivity: *Marqués: A Narco Macbeth*

Carla Della Gatta

Eduardo Marqués ushers his wife, Amaranta, into the hospital and begs for help as she is in labour. His wife is taken to the operating room; he checks his cellphone and lights a cigarette. Doña Marqués's offstage screams turn to sobs, and a nurse (wearing scrubs and a painted skull-face) appears with dead baby in arms. A rapid scene change: a group of henchmen, another scream, a man shot in the stomach. The person in charge, David Ibarra, interrogates this bleeding man, then orders him killed. A skull-faced woman walks towards the body of the dead man. He rises, she smears blood on his forehead, and they walk away. Scene change: Marqués and his friend Paco, bare-chested and barefooted, 'their designer shirts [. . .] tied around their heads into makeshift turbans'.[1] As they walk through the desert heat, their exchange remains amiable and teasing. Only when Marqués says 'So foul and fair a day I have not seen'[2] does this play explicitly connect to its source text, Shakespeare's *Macbeth*.

Marqués: A Narco Macbeth, by Stephen Richter and Mónica Andrade, adapts Shakespeare's play about an eleventh-century Scottish king, setting it among narcotraficantes in contemporary Mexico. Modern-day drug lords replace Shakespeare's feudal lords, both of them warring figures, emblematic of economic systems that subjugate and harm everyone in their communities. *Marqués* was first mounted by Richter and Andrade in 2016, when they were graduate students at the University of California (UC), Santa Cruz.[3] This bilingual adaptation of a canonised play challenges depictions of Mexican identity and problematises American subjectivity.

Shakespeare is used for outreach and access initiatives, but often his status as the (white) canonised author – representative of coloniality and hegemony – precludes his inclusion as a possible conduit for nuanced and non-stereotyped depictions of Latinx identity. In contrast, when Shakespeare is fully adapted for Latinidad, as in the case of *Marqués*, the production enters the realm of Latinx

Shakespeares, simultaneously serving as both Shakespearean play and Latinx theatre, and integrating the Latinx culture and themes into the Shakespearean story while avoiding cultural stereotypes. In this essay, I utilise both Patricia A. Ybarra's work on the dramaturgies of neoliberalism present in Latinx theatre and Walter Mignolo's application of phagocytosis to interculturalism to illuminate how *Marqués* comments on the (post) colonial violences – economic, political, gendered – of the United States towards Mexico.

Adapting *Macbeth* for Latinidad: Latinx Signifiers and the (Un)natural Order

Loosely historically based, *Macbeth* involves the clashing of feudal lords in Scotland. Unlike many of Shakespeare's other plays, it does not contain racial, cultural, religious or even national division between its primary characters. And yet, in the last one hundred years, it has often been racialised in performance, in part due to references to Blackness in the text. For example, Malcolm, the king's son, says, 'when they shall be opened, black Macbeth / Will seem as pure as snow',[4] associating pejorative ideas of Blackness with an immoral and threatening Macbeth. Ayanna Thompson argues that 'the play's very rhetoric of blood and staining informs – or seeps into – early American racial rhetoric as well'.[5] With themes of literal and figurative darkness, including many scenes set at night, the play invites transposition onto other cultures.[6]

Adaptations of *Macbeth* are many. The play has been transposed to various locales, from Orson Welles's 1936 'Voodoo Macbeth' for the Federal Theatre Project (which involved an all-Black cast and was set in the Caribbean), to the 1970 *Umabatha: The Zulu Macbeth* (part of Lincoln Center Festival in New York), to the 1972 *Black Macbeth* in London (set in Africa), to the 2012 film *Macbett (The Caribbean Macbeth)* with Blair Underwood, Harry Lennix and Danny Glover, to Akira Kurosawa's *Throne of Blood* (1957), which translated the action to feudal Japan. But it also has been used to explore a gang motif, from Ken Hughes's film *Joe Macbeth* (1955), which depicted Chicago gangs, to William Reilly's film *Men of Respect* (1991), which engaged the Mafia in New York. Sande N. Johnsen's film *Teenage Gang Debs* (1966) involved New York gangs, Vishal Bhardwaj's *Maqbool* (2003) showcased the Mumbai underworld, and Geoffrey Wright's *Macbeth* (2006) depicted gangs in Melbourne.

Richter and Andrade retain the primary elements and order of the *Macbeth* storyline in their adaptation. After winning a battle, Marqués and Paco (Banquo) encounter the three brujas (witches), who prophesy about Marqués's future at the head of the cartel. When David Ibarra (Duncan) rewards Marqués for his bravery and names him Señor de los Cabos, the latter believes the prophecy to be true. He and Doña Marqués kill Ibarra, and Marqués accedes to his place, quickly launching a wave of bloodshed as he attempts to cement his

power. Comandante Mendez (Macduff) learns that his wife and children
have been killed, and he joins forces with Ibarra's son Manuel (Malcolm) to
kill Marqués. Doña Marqués takes her own life, and Marqués gets killed. The
story ends with Marqués beheaded and Manuel belatedly taking his father's
place. The bloody and violent tale remains bloody and violent, despite the
many changes to characters and play. Set in contemporary Mexico, the play
includes Latinx signifiers throughout, from the brujas with skull-painted Day
of the Dead faces, to references to Don Julio tequila, Pacifico beer and a home
altar. Marqués is a physically smaller man than his Shakespearean predecessor
– an architect, not a warrior, who gets involved with violence only due to
happenstance when he offers his friend Paco some help. He is humanised and
given motivations not found in Shakespeare's script.

  Marqués foregrounds Mexico and brings the audience into the world of
Latinx subjectivity. Latinx Shakespeares are part of American theatre, and
the American theatre writ large has a disproportionately small number of
plays and productions that centre Mexico.[7] The action takes place mostly
in Baja California Sur, shifting from Cabo San Lucas at the southern tip of
Baja California by the Sea of Cortez, to Todos Santos and the La Paz ferry
station to the north, and Ánimas Bajas to the east. The 'merciless Guaymas'
whom Marqués and Paco best in battle at the beginning of the play (the battle
that results in the wounded man's story in the second scene and in Ibarra's
rewarding of Marqués) are from Sonora.[8] They are outsiders, northerners and
mainlanders – but they are Mexican. By not placing Mexico in opposition
to the United States, or Latinxs in opposition to whiteness, the play's authors
make Latinx subjectivity the story rather than a point of division that forces
the audience to identify or objectify opposing sides.

  The premiere production of *Marqués* used set design to immerse the audience in the world of the play. The production was staged in the Experimental
Theater, a black box theatre at UC Santa Cruz. The stage consisted of two
intersecting thrusts so that the audience sat in four segmented quadrants
looking up at the actors on stage. As leader, Marqués (like Ibarra before him)
spoke directly to the audience, looking and motioning downward to them,
exuding an intimate confidence, and never needing to project to distant,
elevated spectators. Numerous asides in the text allowed the audience to gain
insight into Marqués and empathise with his struggles.

  Several devices in the play and the performance fostered audience engagement in the action. In a number of scenes, two female actors wearing pink
sweaters and bullet belts stood on the sides of the stage, against the wall.
Modern iterations of Shakespeare's First and Second Murderers, they killed
Don Julio (the man who betrays David Ibarra and is shot in the stomach in
the second scene) and later Banquo, but otherwise their role was largely a
detached witnessing of the events onstage. These henchwomen functioned

similarly to a Greek chorus, modelling a moral passivity for the audience and thereby making the audience complicit in the action. Video projections on the two walls of the intersecting thrusts denoted locations and permitted a quick change in setting. *Macbeth* is noted for its fast pace, especially in the first half of the play, and *Marqués* followed suit with rapid scene changes aided by a lack of set pieces.

Both on the page and in performance, *Marqués* made use of several conventions that are common to the theatrical construction of Latinidad: it involved a mostly Latinx cast, all of the characters were bilingual or semi-bilingual, and several signifiers of Latinx culture were invoked. All of these elements worked together to suggest a more holistic – and therefore realistic – subjectivity among the depicted Mexicans. *Marqués* included contemporary English, Shakespearean English, contemporary Spanish, variations of 'Spanglish' and a variety of accents spoken by the characters. In addition to spoken language, the soundscape included diverse musical genres with vocals in both English and Spanish, including songs by Shakira, Louis Armstrong, the Eagles, Vicente Fernandez and the Colombian band Groupo Niche, as well as music by French pianist Erik Satie and traditional chamber music.

Along with the aural soundscape that was developed in performance, *Marqués* relies on another primary theatrical signifier of Latinidad: religion. The play uses multiple religious figures to challenge the notion of a singular religion associated with Mexican culture and, in so doing, theatricalises both indigeneity and Catholicism. The home altar of Doña Marqués has an image of the Virgen de Guadalupe, but that is the extent of positive Catholic imagery in the play. Rather, this play focuses on a society that keeps company with the devil. Seyton (Macbeth's porter) becomes Satán, played in the original production by a female actor in little make-up, khaki pants, a white collared shirt and later a black blazer. Satán has a much larger role in the play than does Seyton in *Macbeth*. Leaning 'against the guard shack, rolling a joint', he takes the place of Shakespeare's Old Man, who talks to Ross (Macbeth's cousin) outside the castle after the regicide.[9] Satán is porter at the Gates of Hell, and he is both attaché to Marqués and mirror of what Marqués will become, doing drugs and providing them for others. After Marqués views video tapes of Paco and others doing deals behind his back – proof of their disloyalty to him – Satán gives him a vial of concentrated crystal meth that he snorts before hiring the killers to go after Paco and Felipe (Fleance).[10] In the battle at the end, when Marqués knows he will fight to the death, Satán remains with him. They both don bulletproof vests, and they 'look at one another and smile'.[11] They are in this together. Satán accompanies Marqués as, 'with a calm finality', they watch the men coming to attack them.[12]

Macbeth's three witches are the prophets referred to as the 'weird sisters' and 'hags'.[13] They are largely indistinguishable in Shakespeare's play, although the

First Witch has more lines. In their place, Richter and Andrade offer three witches/brujas. These women chant in Spanish to perform their incantations, but they also speak English. In performance, they were dressed in black with Indigenous Aztec Calavera Catrina-painted faces. Each woman wore black clothes and a black hat rimmed with brightly coloured flowers. Bruja 1 exemplified sexuality, Bruja 2 was blonde, graceful and had animal horns coming out of her hat, and Bruja 3 embodied masculinity, wearing pants and unembellished painted make-up.[14] They were individualised, each with their own style.

By making the three brujas Indigenous and individuated, *Marqués* offers more stage time and diverse representation of Aztec religiosity than Catholicism. In Shakespeare's play, the three witches call on Hecate, the Greek goddess of witchcraft. Here they call on Tonantzin, the Aztec mother goddess, who appears as a 'beautiful woman with bare feet and long hair [that] rises from beneath the sand [. . .] [in] a white flowing linen dress', and they address her as 'mother'.[15] The shift in female authority from a Western goddess of witchcraft to an Indigenous goddess of the earth reinstates the power of Tonantzin, whose temple was destroyed in the Spanish conquest and replaced with a chapel to the Virgen de Guadalupe. In this sense, *Marqués* recovers the importance of indigeneity to Mexican identity.

Another way that *Marqués* complicates the stereotypical representation of Mexican culture for an American audience is its handling of violence. This twenty-first-century adaptation involves less staged violence than does Shakespeare's play, and it displaces and remediates much of the remaining violence. In Shakespeare's play, we see the wife and children of Macduff as their murderers approach, and the scene conveys their fear and knowledge that they will be killed. In *Marqués*, in contrast, Major Burns succinctly states that Mendez's family was 'savagely murdered'.[16] Further, the torture of Ramón and the killing of Don Julio are seen by the audience through prerecorded video. This device displaces the violence from the 'live action' and removes it from the physical stage. Patricia A. Ybarra examines the economic violence of neoliberal policies and concludes that 'Latinx artists' concerns with these conditions in the Americas have encouraged them to develop innovative theatrical modes of representation to address this violence'.[17] The use of video to theatricalise violence in the live theatre, in an adaptation of a violent play, establishes a necessary distance from this representation of Mexican culture. Bruja 3 smears red blood on the forehead of a character to signal death, and Brujas 1 and 2 walk the actor offstage. Although the warring feudal lords are transposed to drug cartels, the adaptation does not devolve into 'gangsploitation'. The drug trade serves as background, not foreground, to the story, and both the violence and the drug trade itself are largely relegated to offstage.

Mexico has always been subordinate in the American conceptualisation of the world, emblematic of what Walter Mignolo describes as a 'Third World [that] was economically and technologically underdeveloped, with the traditional mentality obscuring the possibility of utilitarian and scientific thinking'.[18] Much of the language and politics around immigration, border detention and anti-Latinx racism in the United States derive from the desire to limit Mexico to an abject Third World position. The Mexico of *Marqués* reveals advanced technology, money, guns and expensive name brands. In its focus on the wealthy elite, *Marqués* counters the perception of Mexico as belonging to the Third World. The story revolves around successful business-men; Ibarra and his men are dressed with high technology and material signs of wealth, 'in cowboy chic: dark sunglasses, jeans, boots, bluetooth earpieces, black blazers, Rolex watches, and cowboy hats'.[19] Marqués is an architect with a seaside palace outfitted with 'White couches, divans, [and] marble tables'.[20] Luxury hotels figure prominently, in both Coronado and Cabo San Lucas, and characters at the Marquis Los Cabos Resort and Spa are described as wearing 'white linen, raw silk, and Tommy Bahama'.[21] Everyone in the play wears expensive clothing, and money is not a concern or even a point of discussion.

Mexican subjectivity dominates, and only towards the end does the play offer an outside vantage point, something with which the audience could identify: the action shifts to San Diego, California. In Shakespeare's play, Macduff and Malcom escape from Scotland to England and there join forces against Macbeth. In *Marqués*, Comandante Mendez escapes to Coronado Island in San Diego, the site of a US military base. The marines chant and run, and Mendez sees Manuel and talks with him of Mexico's beauty. Here, Macduff's 'Bleed, bleed, poor country!'[22] refers not to Scotland but to Mexico. He regrets what has come of it: 'México lindo y querido . . . when will you ever see your wholesome days again?'[23] Just then, a female marine, Major Burns, approaches and speaks to Mendez, mistaking him for a waiter:

MAJOR BURNS: Excuse me . . . señor?
COMANDANTE MENDEZ: Yes?
MAJOR BURNS: A vodka martini, neat.
          (Mendez flags down a waiter.)
COMANDANTE MENDEZ: Un vodka martini sin hielo para esta vieja y una Heineken para mi por favor. Keep the change.[24]

In the production, Major Burns was a white American, with a thick southern accent. The waiter that Mendez flagged down was also white, in khakis and a traditional white Havana waiter shirt. Mendez is unfazed by the racism that governs Burns's error, and Burns does not apologise for the mistake. Instead, she tries to recruit Manuel and Mendez to fight against Marqués. When

Manuel says that he is not fit to lead, Major Burns replies, 'Well, hell, son we don't need no Benito Juarez. We just need someone to play ball. This ain't about right and wrong. It's about restoring order, the natural order of things.'[25]

This issue of natural order is at the heart of *Marqués*, just as it is in *Macbeth*. In Shakespeare's play, natural order is subverted through the non-normative gendered appearance of the witches. The witches play a similar role in *Marqués*, where the natural order is also disrupted by the apparitions who are powerful, beautiful and connected to the earth mother yet live in the municipal dump. Although Marqués immediately greets the sisters as 'Señoritas', only after one of them caresses Marqués's hair does he say, 'So, you're women . . . But I don't care how pretty you are.' They dance circles around Marqués, upsetting him, and he calls them 'Malditas güeras mugrosas'.[26] – wicked, fair-headed and filthy. Marqués cannot place them within any traditional standards of femininity, morality or status.

The black magic that Shakespeare's witches conjure with 'Double, double, toil and trouble; / Fire burn, and cauldron bubble'[27] is transformed into a segment with erotic male dancers. The action takes place at Club Heat (whose sign would read 'Heath' but for a burnt-out final H). Seeking the three witches in order to reaffirm their prophecy, Marqués asks for 'the three fatal güeras'. The voice behind the door asks, 'Men or women?' and Marqués names the latter only to have the door shut in his face. He knocks again and says, 'I meant . . . men', and the bouncer permits him to enter.[28] As Marqués enters the club, the song 'I Can't Get No Sleep (Insomnia)' by Faithless plays, alluding to Shakespeare's theme of 'Sleep no more!'[29] Inside the swanky nightclub, the güeras – the brujas – stuff large bills into male dancers' thongs. The bartender brings a bottle of liquor, which the brujas mix with 'peyote, mescal, y hongos, fermented nine months in the Jalisco sun',[30] and Marqués drinks the liquid.

Marqués gags, his eyes dilate and he falls into 'a mescaline-induced stupor'.[31] The apparitions begin to appear: first, a male dancer in a G-string and a Trojan helmet, then another who breakdances, and then another who moonwalks; the brujas tip them well. One apparition does a Pina Bausch-inspired dance.[32] Shakespeare's Eight Kings become here the Cabo Kings, male dancers in thongs, each wearing a crown on his head. The last king holds a mirror in his hand and is revealed to be Paco, with his still-bloody head.[33] The almost-nude dancers form a male conga line.

The showcase of male exotic dancers disrupts gender expectations. Marqués's enjoyment of a lap dance from one of them disrupts expectations of sexuality categories, as well as Latinx masculinity. Conversely, the normalising of genderqueer identity amplifies all other instances of gender play and gender subversion in the play. Donalbino, for example, is referenced variously with both male and female pronouns – as David's daughter, as Doña Marqués's 'favorite godson' and as 'Manuel's Little sister'.[34] Comandante Mendez refers to Donalbino as los Marqués' 'new daughter, el niño Donalbino'.[35] Donalbino's gender fluidity is a priori to the story.[36]

In *Marqués*, the confrontations with things most unnatural – weird sisters, gender play, video truths and violent economic models – all converge when Mendez asks Burns what she means by 'natural order'. She responds, 'The way things were before this Marqués stepped in and screwed everything up. He must be stopped gentlemen. People start getting the wrong ideas, next thing you know we got bodies hangin' over the 405. You understand where this sort of thing leads to.' The United States, via Major Burns, cares only about the status quo. In a faux extension of empowerment, Burns offers to 'help' Mendez and frames the murder of Marqués as obligatory, saying, 'It is your responsibility to lead your people, son, and we're gonna help you do it!'[37]

In *Macbeth*, Macduff – who kills Macbeth to avenge his family – possesses the quality that the witches state is necessary to defeat the tyrant: 'The power of man, for none of woman born / Shall harm Macbeth.'[38] But Mendez does not have a special quality that will save him. And Marqués is more representative of the average man than is Macbeth: the twenty-first-century character ultimately fails because he trusts the system, trusts the United States, and believes in the natural order when he perceives it to be convenient for him. He – like the audience of this play – had thought that Mexico was central, when in fact it is locked into an inferior position vis-à-vis its northern neighbour. This becomes evident in the killing of Marqués. Marqués wounds Mendez in the arm. Mendez kills Satán, and Marqués puts down his gun so that he and Mendez can grapple. The witches enter. Mendez handcuffs Marqués, and Major Burns exclaims, 'What the hell are you doing, Mendez?' He responds that he will bring Marqués to justice. She cautions Mendez to step away, then 'unloads her entire magazine into Mendez'. Marqués awakens and says, 'I thought the United States was supposed to help the Mexican people.' Burns replies, 'We are helping the Mexican people',[39] and then she shoots Marqués dead. Mendez (Macduff) does not survive the story, and he does not kill Marqués (Macbeth). Burns (the United States) kills them both.

Abjectification and Indigeneity

The United States and Mexico have different customs and primary languages, but the mechanisms of retaining order are the same: violence and manipulation. When coercing Mendez and Manuel to aid in killing Marqués, Major Burns says, 'Hell, everybody has a choice. [. . .] It's either gonna be bad or worse. It's up to you.'[40] There is no way out for them. But this attitude has already been absorbed by the narco traffickers. Los Marqués repeat the refrain:

LATINX IDENTITY AND MEXICAN SUBJECTIVITY

one must 'do a great wrong for the sake of a much greater right'.[41] Doña Marqués says it to him first, about killing Ibarra, and he repeats this phrase to her when referring to his order to execute Paco and Felipe. It even imbues his friendships. For example, Paco and Marqués are close friends (Paco is the only one who addresses Marqués by his nickname, Lalo),[42] yet Marqués still orders his murder. Likewise, los Marqués love and care for Donalbino, yet they do not hesitate to kill her father.

As the audience begins to realise that Mexico is not the subject position within this theatrical tale of economic, political and physical violence, the American abjection of Mexico becomes clear. Indigeneity – most notably represented in the three brujas – is displaced, from a respected position within Mexican culture to an abject position at the hand of American (white) order. The weird sisters are first seen in the municipal dump, where they are described as 'beautiful skull-faced women with wild hair'[43] who play with plastic grocery bags among the manufactured waste.

The brujas come from human-made trash yet worship their Indigenous mother earth; they represent how people have treated the earth, and they are the trash of economic exploitation. Despite the fact that they (like everyone else in the play) are bilingual, those in power question their ability to communicate. Paco speaks to them in English and then, when they don't respond, he says, 'Me entienden?'[44] No one else in the play is queried in such a manner. They have a questionable language, gender and relationship to the earth. They live outside of the city, interact with no one but Marqués and Paco, and remove the dead bodies from the stage.

Yet, later in the play, in the dance club and apparition scene, the brujas integrate into society. Marqués sees both the brujas and the male apparitions in this public place while on the drugs that the brujas give him. The strobe lights intensify and the music blares. Satán appears as the drugs wear off, and when Marqués asks Satán about the güeras, who have exited the stage as the music and drugs began to fade, Satán doesn't understand who he is referring to. But the audience has just seen them, and they are as real as the male apparitions. Their presence in the club, just like the male lap dancers, disrupts the natural order: the integration of precolonial indigeneity into society proves horrific to Marqués and imperceptible to Satán.

Once Americans and the geographic space of the United States are introduced into the play, the brujas lose their power and presence. They speak only one more word, 'No', to protect Marqués from being killed by Major Burns. And they fail.

MAJOR BURNS: This country don't need another revolution, it needs order.
    (She walks toward Marqués. The brujas watch her.)

MARQUÉS: Who's [*sic*] order? Yours?
> (Burns looks at the brujas and smiles. She looks back at Marqués.)
MAJOR BURNS: Naturally. This thing of darkness I acknowledge mine.
[Points pistol]
MARQUÉS: Güeras malditas . . .
LAS BRUJAS: No!
> (The brujas run towards Marqués. HEAR a gunshot.)[45]

Burns uses Prospero's racist slur about Caliban against Marqués, reinforcing legacies of coloniality and violence against people of colour.[46] Even as the white American marine points a gun to his head, Marqués blames the (abject) Indigenous women for his plight.

The brujas, though seen in this moment by white American culture, are powerless to help one of their own community. Although Tonantzin called for peace and to 'Remove this thorn [Marqués]. Restore the state',[47] the brujas scream to protect Marqués from the hands of the Americans who remove him for their own reasons and in their desired manner.

The US government positions Latin America in the same space as the Indigenous brujas, and the movement towards the recognition of Mexican subjecthood threatens gender, economic, political and societal structures. Although Marqués is Mexican, his disgust for and derision towards the brujas stem from his failed interpretation of their prophecy, which he understood as an alternative version of the American Dream. He complies with violent business and subjugation to sustain his well-being. The play exemplifies what Mignolo identifies as phagocytosis: 'precisely that moment in which the reason of the master is absorbed by the slave'.[48] In *Marqués*, the transition of power is disrupted and later restored; the natural order in *Marqués* is not hereditary governance, but regulated neoliberalism that must include both economic and social violence. The characters in *Marqués* cannot escape from this ideology.

Mediatised Equivocation

Setting the stage for the play that follows is an opening video of Donald Trump on the campaign trail in 2015, announcing his presidential platform by demonising Mexico:

> And now they are beating us economically. They are not our friend. [. . .] When Mexico sends its people, they're not sending their best. They're not sending you. They're not sending you. [. . .] They're bringing drugs. They're bringing crime. They're rapists. And some, I assume, are good people.[49]

The segment cuts out and is followed by a black-and-white television clip, in English but with Spanish subtitles, of a woman reading a famous line from *Twelfth Night*: 'Some are born great, some achieve greatness, and some have greatness thrust upon 'em.'[50] The title slide cuts her off, and the live production begins. The video projections not only establish the setting and maintain a quick pace, they also represent mediatised equivocation, a rhetorical device and theme that marks Shakespeare's *Macbeth*. Here, equivocation – 'The use of words or expressions that are susceptible of a double signification, with a view to mislead; *esp.* the expression of a virtual falsehood in the form of a proposition which (in order to satisfy the speaker's conscience) is verbally true'[51] – transposes to the language of the media.

For example, during the party at los Marqués, 'Lilia [Ibarra's wife] and Manuel glance across the room at each other, mischievously, then return to their texting.'[52] After everyone wakes to find Ibarra and Lilia murdered, Comandante Mendez's men discover text messages on Lilia's phone from Manuel. Manuel flees because he had been having an affair with his stepmother, and he is seemingly implicated in the deaths of his father and her. Technology reveals a truth (the affair) and a lie (the murderer) at the same time.

Further, Marqués learns of Paco's suspicion of him by watching security camera recordings. He sees Paco give a suitcase of money to Comandante Mendez, and he sees 'business partners and "friends" making deals and doing business behind his back'. Watching this footage, he feels 'exhausted and heartbroken'.[53] The surveillance videos become the ocular proof that Marqués needs to authorise the killing of Paco and Felipe, even though Marqués had no actual proof of a threat, and the consequences of Marqués's command to kill Paco harm him greatly and lead to his own death.

In this way, media serves as a seeming truth-teller, a double-sided news delivery system. Similar to the show opening, with the back-to-back Trump and Shakespeare clips, the opening of the second act juxtaposes video footage of the drug war in Mexico with mariachi-style music. When these lights go out, the videos switch abruptly to a 'Noticias: Special Report' news show on the 'Azteca station'. The three news anchors, one Latina and two white men, show brutal images of hanged people and decapitated heads, all resulting from Marqués's drug wars. There are two sides to all of these situations, two versions of Mexico projected to the outside public. The Shakespearean rhetorical tool that caused confusion and mistrust becomes the media today, and we clearly see the repercussions of trusting this outlet.

But nobody in *Marqués* can be trusted, which proves the violence necessary to retain the status quo or, rather, the violence *of* the status quo. After Marqués's death, the audience learns that Lupita, Doña Marqués's maid, is a member of the CIA. This revelation changes the meaning of an earlier moment, in which Lupita leaves pills behind for Doña Marqués to kill herself. No longer an act of kindness by a trustworthy companion to relieve her from pain, the gift of the pills is revealed to be a betrayal. Likewise, Ibarra describes Don Julio as 'a man in whom I built an absolute trust',[54] yet Ibarra has slept with multiple women in the latter's family (from his daughter to his grand-mother) and then kills him.

The 'natural order' that Major Burns desires and achieves includes the resto-ration of primogeniture, but only because it is economically better for every-one. The 'natural order' has nothing to do with moral order: Manuel, who ultimately takes Ibarra's place in the cartel, is a sexual predator. He tells Burns:

> there is no bottom to my voluptuousness, major, none. There is absolutely no end to my . . . to my sexual desires, me explico? Neither you, your sisters, your daughters, your old women, and your young maids together could not satisfy my lust. My desire would overpower anyone who stood in my way. It would be better for Marqués to rule than someone like me.[55]

But Manuel has exactly the qualifications that the United States seeks in a cartel leader. He is incompetent, more interested in sex than business. Moral corruption is not a disqualifier; indeed, it may even be a prerequisite for the job. Further, in performance, he was played by a white, blond actor with a higher-pitched voice and dressed in a white blazer and bright turquoise shirt. His ethnic outsiderness (whiteness) to the majority Latinx cast, coupled with his sexual predator behaviour, conveyed another equivocation of norms, embodied in the actor-character of Manuel. Ybarra discusses how being gay 'is conflated to perform narco-masculinity',[56] and Marqués offers a heterosexual, blond, white predator as the inheritor of the narco business. Manuel, and the genderfluid Donalbino, are the future of the narcotics trade.

Mignolo writes, 'Neoliberalism, with its emphasis on the market and con-sumption, is not just a question of economy but a new form of civilization.'[57] Drugs are both the product and the means for survival, Marqués's business is the drug trade, and he loses his wife to a prescription pill overdose, while he, Manuel and Satán take illegal drugs that do not appear to permanently harm them. The 'natural order' includes a fraught capitalist consumer system, where violence permeates business transactions, and where consumer culture is anti-subaltern violence.

This new form of civilisation is impossible to escape; one cannot live out-side of it. Marqués is an architect who got involved with the cartel 'because I had to be a decent person and pull over to see if you [Paco] were in trouble'.[58] Once he becomes Señor de los Cabos, he realises that he is trapped. He says, 'I must decline and tell David [Ibarra] I cannot accept this. I'm an architect, not a criminal. But if I offend him I am dead. Everyone I care about will be dead.'[59] These fears are exacerbated by a suggestion from Doña Marqués that Ibarra had her father killed. But it is not just the fear of death that motivates him to kill Ibarra; he is also driven by jealousy, after he sees Ibarra give Doña Marqués a piece of diamond jewellery and try to fondle her.

As an architect, Marqués does not have (or know how to wield) the weapons of a warrior. He looks at a block of knives on the bar at the party and says, 'Is this a dagger I see before me, the handle toward my hand?'[60] In the scenes with his wife, he is humanised, portrayed as a good and decent husband. We see his pain in the opening scene when his wife is in labour and then loses the baby; and when los Marqués greet each other, they always do so with love. When Marqués plots to kill Paco and Felipe, he doesn't tell Doña Marqués his plans: 'Be innocent of the knowledge, mi amor.'[61] He attempts to protect his wife, not just from violence but also from knowledge of the violence he must commit in order to maintain their lives.

There are no heroes in *Macbeth*. And despite the humanising of Marqués, this adaptation takes soullessness one step further through the character of Doña Marqués. When she kneels to pray at her home altar before the arrival of Ibarra and her husband, 'she turns the statue of the virgin [of Guadalupe] away and instead addresses the photo of her father, "Papá . . . ayúdame, por favor. . . . Give me the strength to be like you tonight, to do a great wrong for the sake of a much greater right."'[62] According to Ybarra, in Latinx plays about narcotraficantes, women typically function as the moral centre of the play.[63] Major Burns is racist and a killer, Lupita is a double agent and killer, and Doña Marqués, also a killer, does not embody nor look to a moral or spiritual guide. She does not pray to the Virgen or interact with the brujas or Satán. She has no relationship to the earth or religion, and she is never seen outside of her home. She prays to her father, who was killed as part of the same violent system. The deaths in *Marqués* serve to maintain an economic system that dehumanises people south of the American border, an economic system that depends on that subjugation to maintain a dominant subject position. This superiority is (white) supremacy and cousin to the economic superiority that results (and requires) compliance and death of people of colour.

Just like the feudalistic *Macbeth*, *Marqués* – with its violent hyper-capitalism as natural order – offers no redemption in the end. Advancements in technology do not further knowledge or public happiness if they are not rooted in ethics, morals or humanity. What *Marqués* showcases is that everything crosses borders and languages, from Shakespeare to violence to coloniality to culture. The first time David greets Marqués, he says, 'Welcome to the Hotel California, compadre.' Marqués responds, 'It's a lovely place', and David 'roars with laughter' and continues the verse.[64] The song, by the American band The Eagles, reflects the high life of Los Angeles in the 1960s and 1970s. But the characters sing it at the hotel of the same name in Todos Santos,

Mexico, founded in 1947 by a Chinese immigrant. Mignolo argues that 'coloniality is the logic of domination in the modern/colonial world', and that this logic persists beyond the context at hand, whether the 'imperial/colonial country' is England or Spain or (now) the United States.[65] Just as Mr Wong, the Chinese immigrant who founded the Hotel California, changed his name to Don Antonio Tabasco to fit into the Mexican culture around him,[66] culture adapts and crosses borders when capitalism and profit can find a home.

According to Patricia A. Ybarra,

Latinx writers' most recent foray into intellectual transnationalism has sometimes come with what for some critics and readers is a more difficult intervention into U.S. dramaturgy: the choice to interrogate, deemphasise and/or dispense with U.S. liberal subject formation as the primary mode with which to narrate Latinx experience and identity.[67]

We see these processes at play in *Marqués*, which ends with Major Burns pulling in everyone alive (and Marqués's decapitated head) for a selfie:

(Major Burns attaches her iPhone to a selfie stick then squeezes in with the group.) Come on, closer . . . One . . . two . . . (The camera clicks. Projection of the picture overhead. Shakira's 'La Despedida' plays.) LIGHTS FADE.[68]

Here, the displaced media image conveys a positive outcome, despite the decapitation, multiple killings, and an incompetent leader put into power. As Latinx theatre, *Marqués* critiques the political and economic systems of oppression and of the points of positionality, including both the United States' and Mexico's active roles and complicity in it. Ybarra argues, 'we are evinced to act as neoliberal subjects not only in our actions in response to the employment conditions and shifts in social welfare policy, but in all aspects of our lives, including through our quotidian utterances and practices'.[69] The last spoken words we hear are those of Major Burns, the dominant, English-speaking, southern-inflected marine. The last sounds we hear are the click of the camera, distancing the audience from the violence we just witnessed. The last music is by the Colombian singer Shakira, a song she composed for the 2007 film adaptation of Gabriel García Márquez's *Love in the Time of Cholera*. The song and the story it lyricises are about loss. The final words are these in Spanish, 'No hay más vida, no hay . . .'[70]

Notes

1. Stephen Richter and Mónica Andrade, *Marqués: A Narco Macbeth* (CreateSpace, 2016), 14. All citations of *Marqués* are from this script,

and references to the production are from the filmed version of the stage production directed by Erik Pearson at the University of California, Santa Cruz, in 2016.

2. Richter and Andrade, *Marqués*, 16.

3. Richter and Andrade also adapted *Oedipus at Colonus* as *Dos(e): A Neo Noir for the Stage* (2015), and Richter adapted *Medea* as *Maria, a Telenovela for the Stage* (2015). Richter's *Moore: A Pacific Island Othello* (written under the name Kepano Luna Kanawai Richter) is forthcoming in 2020. Andrade is an award-winning film-maker.

4. William Shakespeare, *Macbeth*, in *The Norton Shakespeare*, 3rd edn, ed. Stephen Greenblatt, Walter Cohen, Suzanne Gossett, Jean E. Howard, Katharine Eisaman Maus and Gordon McMullan (New York: W. W. Norton, 2016), IV.iii.52–3.

5. Ayanna Thompson, 'What Is a "Weyward" *Macbeth*?' in *Weyward Macbeth: Intersections of Race and Performance*, ed. Scott L. Newstok and Ayanna Thompson (New York: Palgrave Macmillan, 2010), 4.

6. See Newstok and Thompson's *Weyward Macbeth* for a thorough discussion of this topic.

7. *The Bad Man* (1920) by Porter Emerson Browne, *The Night of the Iguana* (1961) by Tennessee Williams and *La Turista* (1967) by Sam Shephard all feature American characters in a Mexican setting. More recently, a few Latinx playwrights have featured Mexican characters and set the action in Mexico. These include *Nowhere on the Border* (Carlos Lacamara, 2005), *El Nogalar* (Tanya Saracho, 2017) and *Into the Beautiful North* (Karen Zacarías, 2017).

8. Richter and Andrade, *Marqués*, 11.

9. Ibid. 51.

10. Ibid. 62.

11. Ibid. 99.

12. Ibid. 100.

13. In the First Folio, 'weird sisters' is instead 'wayward sisters' (Shakespeare, *Macbeth*, I.iii.33).

14. Elysia Summer Mandolin Ellis, 'The Eternal *Macbeth*: A Tale of Wicked Transformation', MA thesis, University of California, Santa Cruz, 2016, 29–37.

15. Richter and Andrade, *Marqués*, 77, 78.

16. Ibid. 90.

17. Patricia A. Ybarra, *Latinx Theater in the Times of Neoliberalism* (Evanston, IL: Northwestern University Press, 2018), x.

18. Walter Mignolo, *Local Histories / Global Designs: Coloniality, Subaltern Knowledges, and Border Thinking* (Princeton, NJ: Princeton University Press, 2000), 113.

19. Richter and Andrade, *Marqués*, 10.
20. Ibid. 57.
21. Ibid. 58.
22. Shakespeare, *Macbeth*, IV.iii.31.
23. Richter and Andrade, *Marqués*, 87.
24. Ibid. 87–8. 'A vodka martini without ice for this old lady and a Heineken for me please' (All translations my own).
25. Ibid. 88.
26. Ibid. 19, 20, 21.
27. Shakespeare, *Macbeth*, IV.i.10–11.
28. Richter and Andrade, *Marqués*, 79, 80.
29. Shakespeare, *Macbeth*, II.ii.38, 44, 47.
30. Richter and Andrade, *Marqués*, 81.
31. Ibid. 82.
32. Ibid. 83.
33. Ibid. 85.
34. Ibid. 31, 33, 34, 94.
35. Ibid. 52.
36. In performance, the role was played by Emiliano Montoya, an actor with shoulder-length hair.
37. Richter and Andrade, *Marqués*, 88, 89.
38. Shakespeare, *Macbeth*, IV.i.79–80.
39. Richter and Andrade, *Marqués*, 102.
40. Ibid. 89.
41. Ibid. 31, 67.
42. Ibid. 14, 39.
43. Ibid. 17.
44. Ibid. 19. 'Do you understand me?'
45. Ibid. 103.
46. 'this thing of darkness I / Acknowledge mine', *The Tempest*, V.i.278–9.
47. Richter and Andrade, *Marqués*, 79.
48. Mignolo, *Local Histories*, 157.
49. Donald Trump, presidential announcement speech, 16 June 2015, Trump Tower, New York.
50. Shakespeare, *Twelfth Night*, in *The Norton Shakespeare*, 3rd edn, II.v.126–8.
51. *OED*, s.v. 'equivocation', 2a (accessed 11 May 2020).
52. Richter and Andrade, *Marqués*, 34.
53. Ibid. 61.
54. Ibid. 26.
55. Ibid. 89.
56. Ybarra, *Latinx Theater*, 158.
57. Mignolo, *Local Histories*, 22.

58. Richter and Andrade, *Marqués*, 16.
59. Ibid. 24.
60. Ibid. 42.
61. Ibid. 66.
62. Ibid. 31. 'ayúdame, por favor': 'help me, please'.
63. Ybarra, *Latinx Theater*, 149.
64. Richter and Andrade, *Marqués*, 26.
65. Mignolo, *Local Histories*, 7.
66. 'History', Hotel California Baja, www.hotelcaliforniabaja.com (last accessed 11 November 2020). Since 2001, the Hotel California has been owned by a Canadian couple.
67. Ybarra, *Latinx Theater*, 11.
68. Richter and Andrade, *Marqués*, 104.
69. Ybarra, *Latinx Theater*, 5.
70. Shakira and Pedro Aznar, 'La Despedida' (Epic Records, 2007). 'There is no more life, there is . . .'

2

¡O Romeo!
Shakespeare on the Altar of Día de los Muertos

Olga Sanchez Saltveit

TITANIA: *Amigos, bienvenidos a nuestro cuento*
             A trifle of a work about reunion
             One household, *ubicada en Inglaterra*
             Set within this humble wooden M[1]
             Un escritor famoso, William Shakespeare
             Himself lives here but near the gates of death
             He is not well, *él tiene un catarro*
             We'll catch his spirit at his dying breath.

¡O Romeo! is a bilingual musical play based on the life, work and death of William Shakespeare. The cross-cultural show, which I conceived and directed for Milagro Theatre's annual Día de Muertos celebration in 2014, used Shakespeare's penchant for writing from extant sources to illustrate the history of colonialisation that cultivated modern-day Día de Muertos traditions. Spain's cultural intrusion in the Americas syncretised Catholic and Indigenous ceremonies honouring the dead. These traditions were made popular in the late nineteenth century through the engravings of José Guadalupe Posada. Día de Muertos recognises that death is a great equaliser; no matter how wealthy or powerful a person may be in life, everyone is reduced to bones in death. Accordingly, the revered Bard is levelled in *¡O Romeo!* by mortality, remorse and cultural ineptitude.

Milagro is the Pacific Northwest's premiere Latinx culture and arts organisation. It is located in Portland, Oregon, and was founded in 1989. Every year since 1995, when the company established its home at El Centro Milagro, it has created an original Día de Muertos production. *¡O Romeo!* premiered on 16 October 2014 and ran to 9 November 2014; it received the 2015 Drammy Award for Outstanding Achievement in Devised Work.[2] This chapter describes the production, its dramaturgical questions, and its humourous critique, in traditional Día de Muertos fashion, of Shakespeare's practice of creative appropriation.

Shakespeare and Día de Muertos: the Motivation

¡O Romeo! was created in alliance with the Complete Works Project (2014–16),[3] a two-year Portland-wide celebration of the 450th anniversary of Shakespeare's birth and the 400th anniversary of his death. Milagro, of which I was then artistic director, was invited to join in, but the project was outside of our mission as a company dedicated to producing Latinx playwrights. Nevertheless, we decided to participate by engaging Milagro's most meaningful staging: the altar of Día de Muertos.

¡O Romeo! is an *ofrenda* to Shakespeare's big-hearted legacy and his human frailty. Día de Muertos *ofrendas* are altars and ritual displays constructed in honour of departed loved ones, embracing the joyful and complicated nature of life. In the spirit of the holiday, we crafted a play that imagined Shakespeare's appropriation of Mexica (Aztec) culture, as well as his deathbed regrets. This imagining of the final days of his life and his journey to *el otro lado* wove Shakespearean tropes into a traditional Day of the Dead story of longing and reunion, with love, laughter and song.

Many of Milagro's Día de Muertos productions are devised; that is, rehearsals begin without a script. Devised work can take many approaches, but in this case, as the director, I arrived at the rehearsal process with an outline, some development strategies, and thoughts about which actor might play which role. The show featured an intentionally diverse cast, both in acknowledgement of the global resonance of Shakespeare's works and in keeping with Milagro's other productions. Portland has a relatively small Latinx population. This situation has always complicated casting for Milagro's shows, but it also multiplies non-Latinx actors' encounters with Latinx theatre-making, deepening their understanding of our history and cultures. The process of creating ¡O Romeo! encouraged the actors to bring their expertise with Shakespeare's work into conversation with pre-Columbian beliefs. This respectful encounter, unlike the colonial project of supremacy that sought to quash Indigenous traditions, proved challenging and fruitful.

Reviewing his canon, I determined that our play would feature Shakespearean archetypes such as villains, a clown, a pair of young lovers, a wise counsellor and a supernatural being. These personalities, together with Shakespeare, his son Hamnet and a fictional housekeeper named Rifke, would people the new play. In rehearsal, I asked the actors to explore the nuances of performing different characters within the same archetype. For example, one actor explored the differences between the archetypal ingenues Ophelia and Juliet, while another explored the archetypal villains Richard III and Claudius, to determine which role they would take on. Once selected, the characters' unique backgrounds and motivations informed the actors' improvisations, fleshing out the scenarios that structured the script.

With the traditions of Día de Muertos in mind, we questioned what it meant for a fictional character to die – that is, to be erased. If a work of art and all its records were destroyed, would that mean it never existed? Could a deleted character be restored, in the way that spirits return to the land of the living to enjoy the sweetness of life again? We decided that fictional characters did have life, could die and – by the traditions of Día de Muertos – could return to commune with the living, provided that an altar were built for them. The logic of the premise was grounded in Latin American spirituality.

Finally, we worked with Shakespeare's text directly. While Milagro has produced several Spanish Golden Age plays by Lope de Vega and Calderón, its Día de Muertos productions have been set in more contemporary times. When work began on ¡O Romeo!, the closest the company had come to crafting a Día de Muertos production based on a classical text was with ¡Viva Don Juan!, which I devised and directed in 2011. ¡Viva Don Juan! wove portions of Tirso de Molina's classic script into a plot that imagined the notorious Don Juan making a deal with the devil in order to perform in the play that bears his name. ¡O Romeo! was the first time that a Milagro Día de Muertos production would work with a non-Spanish- or non-Latinx-heritage source for inspiration. Shakespeare's text found its way into lines of dialogue and lyrics for songs such as 'Now Is the Winter of Our Discontent', a duet sung by Richard III and Lady M. Thanks to the multilingual cast, Shakespearean lines were occasionally delivered in Spanish, Korean, German and Russian. This practice was unusual for Milagro, where multilingualism generally involves English, Spanish and Indigenous languages such as Nahuatl or Quechua.

In the spirit of Día de Muertos, ¡O Romeo! was a comedy about reunion, upholding the belief that death cannot separate us, only change our relationships with the once-living. Love transcends death. The most meaningful reunion of the play was between Shakespeare and his long-lost son, Hamnet. Even as ¡O Romeo! honoured Shakespeare's artistic contributions and poked fun at his colonising appropriation, it ultimately humanised him as a father still grieving over the death of his young son. The widespread notion of a universality in Shakespeare's work found a mirror in the universality of mortal concerns raised by Día de Muertos.

¡O Romeo! in Performance: Plot and Critique

The show revolves around the creation and performance of Shakespeare's 'final work', an imagined trilingual (English, Spanish and Nahuatl) play informed by received Mexica culture and the history of Mexico's colonisation by the Spanish. Shakespeare (performed by Tony Green) is writing the first literary dramatisation of Día de Muertos, in a play titled *The Mystical Story of Love and Reunion of Xochiquetzal, the Aztec Maiden, and the Spanish Conquistador Don Armando.*

Rifke (Sofía May Cuxím) is Shakespeare's housekeeper, a Jewish woman from Spain who has fled the Inquisition to find work in Stratford caring for Shakespeare and his family. Her brother, who also fled for his life, has made his way to Mexico City, in New Spain.[4] Shakespeare is rapt as he listens to Rifke read her brother's letters aloud; they are filled with details about the wonders of the New World. Together, Rifke and Shakespeare learn of the customs of the Aztecs, such as a marvellously potent beverage called *xocolatl* that cures all ills, and a month-long celebration in honour of the dead during the time of year when the veil between the living and the dead is thinnest. Inspired by these accounts, Shakespeare has begun writing the play he believes will be his final and greatest work. In a nod to the theories questioning Shakespeare's authorship, we see that Rifke is his co-writer.

Rifke is especially taken by the idea of creating an *ofrenda*, wondering whether such a ceremony might enable them to be reunited with Hamnet, whom she misses dearly. Rifke produces a jacket that belonged to the boy, but Shakespeare immediately rejects her idea, so she leaves the jacket by the windowsill and exits. On his way to bed, Shakespeare stops by the window, puts down his candle, picks up the jacket and holds it close. Clearly, he too misses his son. Returning the jacket to the windowsill near the candle, he unwittingly creates a simple *ofrenda*. By tradition, the *ofrenda* bears a candle for the honoured departed and a belonging of significance to that person, such as clothing, tools or mementos, meant to make the spirit feel welcome. The jacket and candle are enough to draw Hamnet to Shakespeare's room.

Sensing that his father is near death, Hamnet (Otniel Henig) summons Titania (Tara Hershberger), who in turn beckons Hamlet (Heath Hyun), Ophelia (Rebecca Ridenour), Polonius (Arlena Barnes), Lady M (Danielle Chaves), Richard III (Enrique Andrade) and Yorick in the flesh (Jacob Wiest). Shakespeare identifies each by name until he reaches Hamnet. Perhaps he can't believe his eyes, perhaps his heart won't let him, but for whatever reason Shakespeare mistakenly greets his son by saying, 'O, Romeo!' and Hamnet won't permit the others to correct his father. The gathering is happy, except for Lady M and Richard III, who are bitter about their portrayals as villains. They despise these bad reputations and, after singing their duet, conspire to convince the Bard to destroy all his works before he dies.

Playing on Shakespeare's lingering grief, Lady M and Richard III persuade Shakespeare that his work, which kept him in London while Hamnet fell ill, caused him to neglect his son, leading to Hamnet's death. Despondent over the thought, Shakespeare orders Rifke to burn all his manuscripts. The other spirits are dismayed and, stalling for time, tell him that such a destructive act demands that they prepare a ceremony. Lady M and Richard III suggest they perform Shakespeare's newest work, arguing insincerely that it will convince him of the worthiness of his endeavours, when they intend the opposite. His new play is filled with Shakespearean tropes such as forbidden young love, villains in disguise, a sword fight, a dumb show, speeches by a goddess and bewitchment. However, the two villains secretly plot to sabotage the performance of this unfinished play so that he goes ahead with the destruction of all his works. Richard III becomes a petulant actor, uncooperatively complaining about everything, and Lady M recites her lines in the most stilted iambic pentameter imaginable.

To round out the cast, Titania places Rifke under a spell that allows her to see and act with the spirits, whereupon she performs the role of Citlali, the Aztec priestess and mother of Xochiquetzal. Shakespeare, in an effort to be authentic, has written dialogue for Citlali in Nahuatl, the language of the Mexica. Of course, Shakespeare does not speak Nahuatl; he merely cobbles together bits of vocabulary sent by Rifke's brother:

CITLALI: *(mistrustful)* Huitzilopochtli, papalotl, elote, tecolote.
ARMANDO: Excellency, on this site must I build,
                     A grand cathedral honoring our king
                     Though on the grounds of your sacred retreat
                     And temple to the Goddess Coatlicue.
CITLALI: *(offended)* Coyote, ocelote, aguacate, tácate, nopal!
ARMANDO: I will simply have to take that chance.
CITLALI: *(demanding)* Guatemala, Yucatan, Jalisco, Mazatlan.
ARMANDO: One more sacrifice? That cannot be!

We can only infer what Citlali means from context, inflection and Don Armando's responses. Milagro's audiences are familiar with this approach to bilingual work; rather than hearing a translation for every line, which is tedious, the audience is trusted to grasp meaning beyond a literal interpretation. Here, however, the use of Nahuatl words that over time have been absorbed into Mexican Spanish and even English, causes the audience to understand that what Shakespeare has written is an absurdly ignorant version of the 'native language'. Shakespeare knows that his Elizabethan audience will find these unfamiliar words to be a raw, exotic experience, as unintelligible as the Indigenous were to the Conquistadores. However, since those words are familiar to many in Milagro's audience, the comedy works on two levels: the Nahuatl words strung together are absurd, and Shakespeare's supremacy as a master poet (and representative of the coloniser class) is humbled in a light-hearted protest against offensive misrepresentation.

At the play's climax – a sword fight between the young lover Don Armando and Gertrudis, the Conquistador's jealous daughter in disguise as the Bishop – the young lover is slain. The play stops, partly because the rest of it has not yet been written, but also because it is shocking. Shakespeare is beside himself: this death is not at all what he intended. 'This is the New World,' he cries, 'a place of better human nature, of infinite potential. A place where we might have learned from our mistakes before it's too late.' At this, Hamnet jumps in and improvises an ending that reinforces the fundamental theme of this Día de Muertos play, that death is but a beginning, and that love continues on:

HAMNET: Think death has won, but you are mistaken.
              Death will not kill their love. Although they met
              But briefly while on earth, they now possess
              Eternity's embrace. They laugh at death.

Shakespeare is astonished by 'Romeo's' ability to craft the right ending for his play, and in this moment, he finally recognises his son. The playwright dies happy and is escorted away by his fellow spirits, who sing 'Full Fathom Five' (from *The Tempest*) in a harmoniously haunting arrangement by musical director and composer Amir Shirazi. Rifke, waking from what she has perceived as a dream, realises that her master has died, and she goes about collecting all the items strewn about by the performance – swords, a crown, flowers – placing them on the *ofrenda* of the play. Her act unintentionally beckons the spirits back, including Shakespeare and her beloved Hamnet, and the play ends in reunion and dance.

The interplay between Shakespeare and Latinx and Indigenous cultures prompted a creativity in devised theatre that Portland audiences lauded and that the cast welcomed as means to integrate canonical Western theatre with the cultural traditions they embody and practise. ¡O Romeo! honoured Shakespeare's dramaturgical concerns while staying true to Día de Muertos traditions of spirituality, irreverence, transcendent love and reunion between realms of existence. By poking fun at Shakespeare's cultural insensitivity, the play made a broader comment against colonising forces that sought (and seek) to eradicate Indigenous traditions. Those traditions have prevailed, albeit altered, for centuries, and they found a way to speak back to a hero of European culture in the voice of ¡O Romeo!

Notes

1. 'M' here refers to the symbol/monogram for Milagro Theatre, where this production was staged.
2. 'Since 1979, the Drammy Committee has striven to promote live theatre in

Portland by recognizing and rewarding the outstanding work of Portland-area actors, directors and designers. An all-volunteer group of critics and theatre artists, we attend over 100 local productions each year, culminating in an awards ceremony in June.' 'About', Drammy Awards, 4 December 2019, https://drammyawards.org/about/ (last accessed 11 November 2020).

3. Geneva Chin, 'First Time Nationwide: Portland Presents All of Shakespeare's Works in Two Years', Oregon Public Broadcasting, 28 March 2014, www.opb.org.

4. The Alhambra Decree, which expelled Jews from Spain, took effect just four days before Christopher Columbus first set sail west for the Indies in 1492.

3

Passion's Slave: Reminiscences on Latinx Shakespeares in Performance

Frankie J. Alvarez

Give me that man
That is not passion's slave, and I will wear him
In my heart's core, ay, in my heart of heart,
As I do you.

Hamlet, Prince of Denmark, confiding in his close friend Horatio
William Shakespeare, Hamlet

Muéstrame un hombre que no sea exclavo de sus pasiones, y lo alojaré en mi corazón; sí, en el corazón del corazón como lo hago contigo.

Hamlet, Príncipe de Cuba, confiando en su buen amigo Horacio
Nilo Cruz, Hamlet, Príncipe de Cuba

It seems impossible to discuss Latinidad and Shakespeare without discussing the word so often used to describe Latinx people: *passionate*. It can feel like a rather reductive term, a generality carelessly applied to a vast and complex cultural identity that refuses to be defined and confined by one mere word. Nevertheless, passion was the key that would unlock my work in two Latinx Shakespearean productions between January 2011 and May 2012. At the time, I found myself in a most enviable position for any young actor fresh out of drama school: performing in three Shakespeare plays in two of the most respected regional theatres in America. In 2011, I was a company member at the Oregon Shakespeare Festival (OSF), performing as Claudio in *Measure for Measure*, and as Lucius/Metellus Cimber in *Julius Caesar*. While performing those two productions in repertory, I was cast and began preparations for one of the most challenging and rewarding roles of my life: the titular role in the 2012 bilingual repertory production of *Hamlet, Prince of Cuba* at the Asolo Repertory Theatre in Sarasota, Florida. Both *Measure for Measure* and *Hamlet, Prince of Cuba* engaged in the bilingual nature of these characters, but the productions dealt with these complexities in language in radically differing ways.

'Passion's slave' is an appropriate way to describe both Claudio and Hamlet. In one play, Claudio gets arrested and is condemned to die for fornication (sex before marriage), a crime of passion that could put one in prison back in the 1600s; in the other, Hamlet is charged with avenging the death of his father, who was murdered by Hamlet's uncle Claudius in an effort to usurp the Danish throne and legitimise his passionate affair with Hamlet's mother, Gertrude. Both young men set forth on a painful journey of self-reflection in an attempt to free themselves from the various passions that threaten their personal and professional lives.

Measure for Measure

OSF's 2011 production of *Measure for Measure*, directed by Bill Rauch, was set in an unspecified urban American metropolis in the 1970s, a radical era that reacted to the sexual freedom of the 1960s and forecast the moral clampdown of the conservative, Reagan-led 1980s. For Rauch, the multi-ethnoracial cast was not only illustrative of the increasing diversity of OSF's acting company, emblematic of his time as artistic director, but also reflective of the demographics of the United States and the very American way that race and class are so inextricably linked here. Claudio, Isabella and Angelo were all played by Latinx members of the company, while the duke who has left Angelo ruling the city was played by a white actor. Thus, we have an upwardly mobile Latino in Angelo who makes a clear example of a young Latino offender of the law in Claudio in order to show the greater community that he means to rule by the letter of the law regardless of any race-based sympathies. When the young novitiate Isabella pleads for her brother's life to Angelo, he propositions her: make love to me, and I'll free Claudio. This exchange sets the scene for the emotional rollercoaster of Act III, scene i.

This was my favourite scene to perform every night; we did it 120 times. It begins with the duke, in disguise as a friar, preparing Claudio's soul for his impending death. Claudio has two lines in this portion of the scene, which sandwich the friar's larger rumination on death. Though I didn't have much dialogue, I had the given circumstances of the scene and those layered within our setting to guide me along. At the top of the scene, I am escorted in handcuffs into the visitation room. As I sit, I slouch in my seat and look far off to the distance, actively disengaging from this priest, played by acclaimed actor and friend Anthony Heald; his whiteness is symbolic of a race that has actively oppressed my people for generations, while his friar garb is symbolic of a religion that provides me comfort while simultaneously oppressing me for the sole crime of loving my sole partner. A Latino youth in the 1970s – all swagger and sideburns – finds no solace in the presence of this friar, and my body language conveys that: he slides a Bible towards me, and I push it right back towards him. As his monologue begins, I dialogue with him physically. The friar proclaims, 'Be absolute for death; either death or life / Shall thereby be the sweeter';[1] I roll my eyes and look away from him, rejecting his thesis. But as the friar proceeds, it becomes clear that his advanced age has taught him a few things about our daily wrestling match with mortality. Not only that, but the friar is the first person I engage with in the play who actually treats me like a grown man; that show of respect is not lost on me, and he begins to win my attention. The friar continues: 'Thy best of rest is sleep, / And that thou oft provok'st, yet grossly fear'st / Thy death, which is no more.'[2] I smile at his rhetoric, so very empathetic to my current state: the only rest I could possibly find these days is in sleep, but I'm so scared of dying that I am sleepless, hence I get no rest. I begin to lean in as the friar concludes his speech, 'Yet in this life / Lie hid more thousand deaths, yet death we fear, / That makes these odds all even.'[3] We share a laugh at this, and in the span of thirty lines, the friar has taken me on a journey from resistant to his final blessing to grateful for his help and willing to die.

Once Isabella arrives, the chemistry in the air is irrevocably changed. The cultural connection of Latinidad helped amplify the storytelling and create real fireworks onstage. I rush to my only sister, eager for her consoling embrace, and am restrained by a guard and forced to my seat. She takes the friar's old seat, eyeing the Bible that the friar has left behind for me. I take in the new circumstance: I haven't seen my sister since she left home to become a novitiate, and this is the first time I see her in her nun's garbs. In this production, we replaced a few of Shakespeare's words with some Spanish phrases and colloquialisms; the ease with which we switch between languages is a sign not only of our familial comfort with each other but of the high stakes of the scene drawing out the primal language of our mother tongue. After obfuscating for forty-five lines or so, Isabella finally admits that there is one thing that will save me: 'Dost thou think, Claudio, / If I would yield him my virginity / Thou mightst be freed?'[4] I complete the pentameter of her line with utmost shock in my native language: 'Dios mio, no puede ser.'[5] She admits she must do it tonight, or I will die. I quickly reassure her, 'Thou shalt not do't.' She adds, 'Oh, were it but my life, / I'd throw it down for your deliverance / As frankly as a pin'; I respond again in Spanish, 'Gracias, querida Isabel.'[6] At this point, we hold hands, place them atop the Bible and begin to recite the Apostle's Creed in Spanish.

This creed is familiar to many Latinx audiences of the Catholic faith and is usually recited in Spanish by the entire congregation. But in the middle of our recitation in *this* morbid context, I interrupt her and attempt to bargain with her: from my estimation, if Angelo is condemning me to death for a crime that he willingly wants to commit with Isabella, then maybe it isn't too big a crime – or sin – at all. At this point, I stand and launch into Claudio's famous meditation on death: he fears the afterlife and is steadfast in his view that even the most abhorrent parts of life – 'age, ache, penury, imprisonment' – are a 'paradise' compared to 'what we fear of death'.[7] As I throw the Bible to the ground, I plead to her on my knees: 'Hermanita, let me live. / Oye, what sin you do to save a brother's life, / Nature dispenses with the deed so far / That it becomes a virtue.'[8] Isabella, in outright disgust and disappointment, insults me: 'O you beast!' Then she kicks it up a notch and chides me in Spanish, almost as if she were my mother: 'O cobarde sin fe! O desgraciado!'[9] She condemns me to die, and I'm dragged away by the guard, crying out, 'O, escuchame, Isabela!'[10] Even though Claudio only speaks in just four scenes of the play, there is a vast array of story that can be told non-verbally. It was always an incredible ride with Stephanie Beatriz, who played Isabella. Both of us are first-generation Latinx Americans, and the shared cultural knowledge of these two siblings and their passion for their respective causes always drove this scene to exciting heights. There were always new nuances to respond to and listen for, and Stephanie and I continued to challenge each other throughout our nine-month run. The bilingual nature of the scene helped deepen the familial relationship between Claudio and Isabella. We inherently accessed the distinct tone and musicality of a bilingual sibling relationship, and that specificity – the vast love, the bitter disappointment, the real passion – is what made the language choices really pop for audiences in a universal way.

While that scene functioned as the centrepiece of Bill's bilingual production, he also used bilingualism to startling effect in other scenes. When Angelo propositions Isabella, he uses Spanish as a tool to shrink the disconnect between them in an attempt to get her into bed with him. Later, when the unstable Mariana is introduced, she sees Angelo in a vision; Bill staged it so that Angelo would actually appear in the scene and sing a Mexican ballad to her. One of the most successful elements of this production, though, was the stunning music by mariachi band Las Colibrí. The production began with three Latina cleaning ladies cleaning the duke's boardroom. These women, the audience quickly learns, are the unseen – and unappreciated – force in the city keeping everything in order. They then transform into a beautiful mariachi band, and their presence functions as a Greek chorus throughout the show. Mariachi bands are traditionally present at Mexican celebrations and rites of passage: baptisms, funerals, birthdays and weddings. Las Colibrí's songs, all in Spanish, bookended scenes and introduced others, and they helped carry the emotional arc of the play up to and including the final breath that abruptly ended the show.

Hamlet, Prince of Cuba

A tragic violin theme escalates as the growing reverb of an electric guitar overtakes it, culminating in the percussive slamming of a chamber door. From the silence, we hear the unmistakable sound of a male Cuban voice singing a cappella, 'Que sé con su mirada, desde los pies hasta el pecho',[11] as our eyes focus in on a young man lying at the front of a dark and empty stage, dead. As the music continues, he rises, looks at us, and begins to change into a beautiful turn-of-the-century black suit. This was the opening beat for our bilingual repertory production of *Hamlet: Prince of Cuba*, a production that exists as Hamlet's dying fever dream, as he tries in earnest to retrace the steps that led him to this precise moment and discover whether he was indeed successful in fulfilling the ghost's charge.

The music of the show, designed by Fabian Obispo (with whom I had already worked on a few productions at Juilliard), helped transport the audience to an 1898 Havana ravaged by the Spanish–American War. More importantly, it also tuned the audience's modern ear towards the vast array of human experience contained in Shakespeare's famous language and introduced the audience to this distinctly Cuban royal family. Similar to *Measure for Measure*, *Hamlet* exists at the busy intersection between politics, religion and family dynamics; it is as much about the political as it is about the personal.

When I auditioned for the role, I sent in a self-tape with two soliloquies: 'To be or not to be' in English into my bathroom mirror, and 'O, what a rogue and peasant slave am I' in Spanish on the Bowmer stage, where I had been performing *Measure for Measure*. A few weeks later, I got a call from my agent alerting me that I was in the final running for the role, and that the production's director, Asolo Rep's artistic director Michael Donald Edwards, was going to fly to Ashland to see me perform in *Measure for Measure*, and to watch both monologues in person. He arrived on a Wednesday, watched our *Measure* matinee, and conducted my in-person callback for an hour. By Thursday morning, I had the role.

From July 2011 to January 2012, I ate, slept and breathed *Hamlet*. I read every critical response I could get my hands on, looked up the meaning of each and every word I would say, and watched at least a dozen different interpretations of the role on film and at the New York Public Library for the Performing Arts. I didn't take any notes from the other interpretations I examined; my prevailing thought was that if an idea were useful in my own interpretation, it would ultimately burrow its way into my subconscious and sneak its way into my performance.

Andhy Mendez (our Laertes, and a fellow first-generation Cuban American from Miami) and I were called down to Sarasota a week earlier than the rest of the cast in order to spend some time learning the complex rapier fight that functions as the climax of the play. Though the play sets up Hamlet and Laertes as foils, it was important to us that they felt like brothers cleft in twain, that perhaps under different circumstances they would be close friends. The extra time on the fight proved to be extremely valuable for two reasons. By the time opening night rolled around, we had been refining the fight choreography for seven weeks, and the moves had become second nature. In fact, our fight choreographer Bruce Lecure became concerned during previews, when, adrenaline pumping through our veins, the fight ended up happening three times faster than intended! But, even more importantly, the extra week gave us some time on our own to bond; I truly believe that our budding friendship made its way into the dynamic between Hamlet and Laertes. The time that we spent together off stage – not only commiserating about our common upbringing by Cuban refugees in Miami but also revelling in the joy of two Cubans playing Cubans in a Shakespeare play – was crucial to our interpretation of their relationship.

My preparatory text work unlocked two key words: *obey* and *passion*. In the opening scene, Claudius announces to the court that Hamlet must not return to grad school in Wittenberg: 'it is most retrograde to our desire'. Gertrude – my mother and my uncle's new wife – agrees and pleads, 'I beg you, stay with us.' Hamlet responds: 'I shall in all my best *obey* you, madam.' This is where Hamlet lives for the first few scenes of the play, in a state of 'unmanly grief' and in full obedience of his elders, without any agency of his own.[12] As a Cuban man beloved by his people who was presumably next in line for the throne (it was no accident that my thick moustache and slicked-back hair were in absolute homage to the great Cuban poet-warrior José Martí), Hamlet is clearly not behaving as he normally would. The death of his father is a traumatic event that strips him of his lifeblood and prevents him from being his true self. He is sleepwalking through life – until the afterlife breathes new life into him!

In our production, after hearing from Horatio that he saw the ghost of the king, Hamlet visits a Santero priest. Amid a cleaning ritual involving cigar smoke and the blood of a chicken, the ghost appears and takes over Hamlet's body. The ghost reveals that his death was not of a natural cause; he was *murdered* by his usurping brother. I had a mic on me specifically for this scene that allowed the sound engineer to amplify and modify my voice in the moment when the ghost assumes control over my faculties and issues his challenge:

If you have nature in you, bear it not.
But howsoever you pursue this act,
Taint not your mind nor let your soul contrive
Against your mother aught.
Leave her to heaven.[13]

Michael's insight proved immensely useful here: the ghost's demand is to 'Revenge his foul and most unnatural murder',[14] but his challenge is to do it without corrupting Hamlet's mind, and without acting as judge, jury and executioner towards Hamlet's mother. This would be my guide every night and with every moment that Hamlet is paralysed by inaction or seduced by insanity: he cross-checks his plans and his impulses with the ghost's challenge.

From this point, my performance awakens, as Hamlet's life has a renewed purpose: 'The time is out of joint: O cursed spite, / That ever I was born to set it right!'[15] It was important to me that my Hamlet use every ounce of energy, every muscle in his body and every synapse in his brain in service of 'setting it right' for his father. The next time I appear onstage, my hair is unkempt, my shirt is untucked, my suspenders are cross-gartered, and I pace about barefoot, consciously acting out my 'antic disposition'. Michael gave me absolute freedom in my blocking; the thought was that these characters truly have no idea what Hamlet is going to do next, so why not arrange it so we have no idea what Frankie is going to do next? Sometimes I did a full-on impression of Polonius; other times I collapsed on the ground and chewed on my toenails. In one special performance, I managed to flick Polonius off with my middle toe! It was an absolute privilege to be given that kind of freedom, and it was important to me not to abuse it; that freedom of impulse was always about enacting my objective at any given moment.

'O that this too too sullied flesh would melt' and 'To be or not to be' were both performed seated, the former on a chair and the latter on the ground. By contrast, 'O, what a rogue and peasant slave am I!' and 'How all occasions do inform against me' were on my feet, kinetic, alive and inclusive of the audience. My Hamlet was an intense lover of clowning and theatre; he is overwhelmed with joy at the sight of the 'tragedians of the city' and moved to tears by the Player King's speech from *Dido, Queen of Carthage*. In fact, it is during 'O, what a rogue and peasant slave am I!' that the word *passion* emerges again. Hamlet is baffled by the fact that the Player King could 'in a dream of passion / [. . .] force his soul so to his own conceit [. . .] / And all for nothing!'[16] He is in absolute awe of the passion stirred within this actor over an imaginary circumstance, while also chiding himself for not being able to act on the very real circumstance of the ghost's charge.

It was my favourite soliloquy to perform. There are several twists and turns in it, and much like the rest of the show, the speech demands that the actor make discoveries on the lines and truly stay in the present moment. I'll never forget one performance where there was an older gentleman in the front row with a copy of *Hamlet*, faithfully following along with the text. He would hem and haw every time he noticed a text change or disagreed with the pronunciation of a word. By the end of the speech, I was at my wit's end with him. He had the audacity to say the words of the final couplet before I had spoken them! I slid over to the lip of the stage right above his seat, snatched the play from his hands, and (as I leafed through it) delivered my final couplet with a knowing look to the audience: 'the play's the thing / Wherein I'll catch the conscience of the king'.[17] The audience let out a riotous laugh, and I was happy to see that same gentlemen at another performance, this time sans script, ready to enjoy the live performance happening in front of him. It can be a dangerous thing for an audience to worship at the altar of Shakespeare: his words were not meant to be read but rather were meant to come to life through the active use of the actors' bodies. Those that cut off their performances at the neck are missing out on the exceptional physical opportunities presented by Shakespeare's language. My physical training under the legendary Moni Yakim proved essential for me throughout our rehearsal period because it emphasises using the entire capacity of one's body and impulses.

Once Claudius's guilt is revealed in direct response to *The Mousetrap*, the play-within-the-play, Hamlet engages in a deliberate lazzi (a series of physical gags and bits in the commedia dell'arte tradition) in order to expose the king's minions (Polonius, Rosencrantz and Guildenstern) as the puppets they truly are. I rampage through the tragedian's prop box and lampoon them all, managing to use a wig, the famous pipe, a red clown nose and even my impression of the boisterous Mexican comedian Cantinflas[18] (though not time period appropriate, it proved to be a fun Easter egg for Latinx audiences). Hamlet continues to wield his morbid wit through his confrontations with Gertrude and Claudius, before being exiled to England. But once Hamlet sees a deliberate and commanding Fortinbras raise a powerful army all for a small plot of land, he begins to see how he can claim revenge without corrupting himself, and he returns to Cuba from his brief deportation as a deliberate and emboldened grown man. The moment when the gravedigger digs up Yorick's skull becomes an opportunity for Hamlet to recall his more innocent and jovial upbringing with his beloved court jester and meditate on how death inevitably comes for us all. Holding Yorick's skull up to my face, I would reminisce with him: '¿Qué se hizo de tus burlas, tus saltos, tus cantares, de aquellos chistes que hacían reventar de risa a todos en la mesa?'[19] As I put one hand in my pocket, I'd discover something that had been hidden there throughout my entire exile: the tragedian's red clown nose, a symbol of my inner child. I'd place the nose around Yorick's skull and then commune with him again. When I hand him back to the gravedigger, he is no longer just another nameless skull, but a specific man buried in his signature nose. At this point, I learn that Ophelia is dead, and the burial of my personal clown nose is significant: it is now time to put away childish things and embrace my fate.

The idea of a Shakespeare repertory in both English and Spanish was inspirational, but in some ways Asolo Rep's production left me hungry for an even more sustained and comprehensive immersion into the world of bilingual Shakespeare. The plan was to have a total of twenty-six performances in English, with ten additional performances in Spanish that would run concurrently with the English version for the final few weeks of the run. Things did not go as smoothly as planned, however. The first issue was one of time. We had six weeks to rehearse and stage the text in English, but only ten days allotted for the Spanish. I had seven months to prep the English text; due to other writing commitments, we did not receive the final version of Nilo Cruz's translation of the text until fourteen days prior to opening night of the Spanish production. I could never have been able to memorise and execute the Spanish-language *Hamlet* without the help of two exceptional men: my dad, Frank Alvarez, who came up to visit for a weekend and helped me drill lines relentlessly; and our bilingual vocal coach Antonio Ocampo-Guzman, whose astonishing skill and insight proved integral to my entire rehearsal process. The second issue was one of language and casting. When I had been originally cast in July, I was told that we would have a fully bilingual cast performing in both the English and Spanish productions. However, when I arrived at Asolo in February of the next year, I learned that the ensemble actors playing Polonius, the gravedigger and the Player King were all Caucasian actors with no Spanish-speaking experience. On top of that, the production cast some of the third-year actors from Asolo Rep's graduate acting programme, and only one of the six was bilingual. As a result, Michael went down to Miami and cast two older actors to play the above ensemble roles for the Spanish production, while the grad student actors were to remain in both productions. The enlistment of a Player Queen, Marcellus, Osric and others who were obviously not Spanish speakers proved to be a detriment to the audience's ability to fully suspend disbelief. All told, the production felt less Cuban than it could have been. If there had been a deeper understanding of these issues by the artistic staff, if every effort had been made to have a truly bilingual cast, and if the Spanish translation (and by proxy the Spanish production) had been given the same amount of rehearsal time as the English (to all intents and purposes, it was a *new play* and should have been treated as such), the repertory would have been a much more satisfying experiment for all audiences. Which is not to say that this experiment was not exciting and fruitful: just that it also points to the greater potential for future bilingual repertory shows, provided that these issues of time and casting are tackled.

Nevertheless, every problem presents opportunities. For example, Rosencrantz and Guildenstern are Hamlet's grad school buds from Wittenberg, and their broken Spanish was both a charming circumstance to play with and further evidence of the growing gulf of understanding between Hamlet and his school chums. In fact, playing several scenes with two different actors as Polonius, the Player King and the gravedigger was another circumstance that forced me to stay in the present moment. I could not play

the Spanish scene in the same way as the English: not only was I playing
the scene with a different scene partner, but Nilo's gorgeous translation was
distinctly Cuban in tone and in word choice. My blocking varied for each
scene, and each language forced me to use different tactics to get what I
wanted. As we began to perform both productions in rep, I found that my
performances were in constant conversation, and I would learn something
from the Spanish version that would prove useful to me in the English
version, and vice versa. Those last few weeks were an absolute whirlwind,
and the Herculean task of getting to do both shows proved to be an exciting
circumstance for audiences.

The word *passion* and its cognates are used in Shakespeare's *Hamlet* fourteen
times in the First Folio edition.[20] The importance of the word took on a
greater significance when we finally began sharing the production with Latinx
audiences in Sarasota and Miami, Florida. I was floored by the conversations
I was able to have at the stage door. Some memorable responses included: 'I
feel so lucky that this was the first Shakespeare I've ever seen', 'I never knew
Hamlet could be this *funny!*' and 'It was so powerful to see actors up there
that looked and sounded like me'. But if an argument is to be made for the
relevance of Latinx Shakespeares in performance, then it came from a young
Cuban mom who brought her thirteen-year-old to see our final Spanish performance in Miami, on the eve of Mother's Day. As I signed her son's playbill,
she shared, 'I want to see more Shakespeare in Spanish. I finally understood
it – it felt like I was watching a telenovela.'

Two epic scripts somehow lodged in my brain, months of tireless preparation, and my entire self poured into this role: it all culminated in her beautiful
and cathartic response. Under Michael's bold and inspired leadership, we
managed to build a bridge from Shakespeare's dated language to the present-day arena where heightened and passionate Latinx stories are told, where
the modern Latinx family's greatest provider of drama lies: the telenovela. We
brought the past directly into the present.

Latinx Interventions in the Canon

In OSF's production of *Measure for Measure* and the Asolo Rep's *Hamlet,
Prince of Cuba*, both artistic directors staged shows that helped illuminate
Shakespeare's text by casting Latinx actors in lead roles and using their cultural background and language in exciting and relevant ways. The bilingual
exercise of both productions revealed the passion and density of emotion
found in Shakespeare's text, and helped connect two centuries-old texts to
the complexity of the modern Latinx family in a way that felt fresh, familiar
and familial.

OSF's *Measure for Measure* shed light on the true circumstances of racism and sexism within the distinctly white patriarchy in the United States, and the use of Spanish in particular highlighted the bifurcated nature of life in the distinctly American version of Bill Rauch's Vienna. In contrast, *Hamlet, Prince of Cuba* was a story about a Latino man who is not a rapist, not a gangster, but a sweet prince, trying his absolute best to honour his father. It was a necessary statement, one that is more relevant than ever in these political times. It was an exceptional privilege to play Shakespeare's Hamlet as a Latino,[21] in all his three-dimensional beauty and complexity. I sincerely hope that the future of Latinx Shakespeares – and all Latinx theatre – continues to grow and find its place in the American canon, free from the generalities and stereotypes that threaten to bury it.

Notes

1. William Shakespeare, *Measure for Measure*, in *The Norton Shakespeare*, 3rd edn, ed. Stephen Greenblatt, Walter Cohen, Suzanne Gossett, Jean E. Howard, Katharine Eisaman Maus and Gordon McMullan (New York: W. W. Norton, 2016), III.i.5–6.
2. Shakespeare, *Measure for Measure*, III.i.17–19.
3. Ibid. III.i.39–42.
4. Ibid. III.i.96–8.
5. Ibid. III.i.98. 'O heavens, it cannot be.' All translations in this production were my own.
6. Ibid. III.i.102–5. 'Thanks, dear Isabel.'
7. Ibid. III.i.130–2.
8. Ibid. III.i.133–6. 'Sweet sister.'
9. Ibid. III.i.136–7. 'O faithless coward, O dishonest wretch!'
10. Ibid. III.i.148. 'Listen to me.'
11. Fabian Obispo, original music for *Hamlet, Prince of Cuba* (2012). 'What do I know with his gaze, from feet to chest.'
12. Michael Donald Edwards, *Hamlet, Prince of Cuba*, adapted from William Shakespeare's *Hamlet* (unpublished script, 12 March 2012), 2.
13. This is the line the author spoke on stage. In the final script, it reads, 'Fare you well at once.'
14. Edwards, *Hamlet, Prince of Cuba*, 8.
15. Ibid. 10.
16. Ibid. 23.
17. Ibid. 24.
18. Cantinflas (1911–93) was a Mexican film actor and comedian known for language play.
19. Nilo Cruz, *Hamlet, Príncipe de Cuba*, adapted from William Shakespeare's *Hamlet* (unpublished script, 3 January 2012), 61. 'Where be your gibes

now? your gambols? your songs? your flashes of merriment, that were wont to set the table on a roar?'

20. Pervez Rizvi, *Shakespeare's Text*, last updated 4 June 2019. Available at www.shakespearestext.com (last accessed 11 November 2020).

21. Although Hamlet has been played by (relatively few) other Latino actors, this was the first time the character of Hamlet was portrayed as a Latino or Latin American in any major regional, repertory or equity theatre in the United States.

4

The Power of Borderlands Shakespeare: Seres Jaime Magaña's *The Tragic Corrido of Romeo and Lupe*

Katherine Gillen and Adrianna M. Santos ·

In contrast to treatments of Latinx Shakespeares that focus on cosmopolitan cultural hubs such as New York City and Los Angeles, this essay turns toward more regional, community-based theatre in the Texas–Mexico borderlands to examine how theatre-makers engage with Shakespeare as they grapple with the colonial legacies shaping life en la frontera. The border is a site of ongoing humanitarian crisis. While the most recent anti-immigrant policies have intensified this crisis, the social inequities of the border have been shaped by centuries of colonialism, both Spanish and US, in which the land, labour and culture of Indigenous Americans and their descendants have been expropriated and exploited. Borderlands Shakespeare, we suggest, is a subset of Latinx Shakespeares that engages with these colonial forces and draws on Chicanx theatrical, cultural and linguistic traditions to disrupt them.[1] Arturo J. Aldama, Chela Sandoval and Peter J. García argue that instances of borderlands performance 'work as de-colonizing, interventionary deployments that become systematically linked and raised to the level of method through practitioners' shared understanding of performance as an effective means of individual and collective liberation'.[2] As such, Borderlands Shakespeare acknowledges Shakespeare's role as an agent of colonisation and questions his universal applicability, but it also appropriates Shakespeare to empower local communities and, at least momentarily, 'generate[s] a pause in the activity of coloniality'.[3]

As a case study in Borderlands Shakespeare, this chapter examines Seres Jaime Magaña's *The Tragic Corrido of Romeo and Lupe* (2018), a bilingual appropriation of *Romeo and Juliet* performed by the Pharr Community Theater in Pharr, Texas, and commissioned by artistic director Pedro Garcia.[4] Nearly all the characters in *The Tragic Corrido* are Mexican American, and some are undocumented immigrants. Romeo's mixed-race Anglo and Latinx family runs the Campbell Irrigation Company, while the majority of Lupe's family members are more recent Mexican immigrants who work in the fields. Like many appropriations of *Romeo and Juliet*, the play uses Shakespeare's story to explore broad questions of love, identity and justice. *The Tragic Corrido*, however, grounds these explorations in the hybrid context of the Rio Grande Valley (RGV), Texas, and it foregrounds colonialism, environmental destruction and labour rights. As it does so, *The Tragic Corrido* engages critically with its Shakespearean source text, with its conclusion revealing that Shakespeare's story of family reconciliation may not adequately contain – and certainly cannot resolve – the complex colonial conflicts shaping the valley. Nonetheless, throughout the majority of the play, Magaña provocatively appropriates *Romeo and Juliet* for a border context, using it not as an oppressive mould in which to fit life on the frontier, but as a malleable frame that can be transformed by the region's hybrid cultures, languages and genres.

Borderlands Shakespeare, as we are defining it, is influenced by the Chicanx theatre tradition. Reflecting a complex lineage, Chicanx theatre, or teatro, addresses matters of social import and emphasises dynamics of colonisation, indigeneity, and cultural and linguistic hybridity. Activist objectives are central to Chicanx theatre, which primarily arose with El Teatro Campesino, the theatrical wing of the United Farm Workers (UFW). David Román notes how El Teatro Campesino helped Chicanxs 'reformulate[] their sense of identity from one of oppression and victimization to one of resistance and survival'.[5] More broadly, teatro is influenced by decolonial politics and methodologies, in particular the work of Gloria E. Anzaldúa, who theorised the US–Mexico border as 'una herida abierta [an open wound] where the Third World grates against the first and bleeds, with lifeblood of two worlds merging to form a third country – a border culture'.[6] It therefore presents border residents less as migrants than as hybrid colonial subjects, inhabiting a land to which they have Indigenous ancestral ties but in which their culture has been both influenced and suppressed by Spanish and Anglo imperialist violence. Cognisant of Shakespeare's colonial potential, borderlands Shakespeares mixes Anglo, Spanish and Indigenous traditions and interrogates the place of Shakespeare within the hybrid context of the US–Mexico borderlands. It also engages with Shakespeare to critique the neoliberal and imperialist policies that have resulted in high levels of labour exploitation and poverty throughout the region, and that have both criminalised migration and created the conditions in Mexico and Central America that have forced migration to the United States.[7]

As perhaps may be expected, not all Shakespeare performed near the border qualifies as Borderlands Shakespeare in this decolonial sense, and some relatively high-profile productions have adapted Shakespeare in ways that reproduce colonial epistemologies. Shakespeare on the Rocks' bilingual *Romeo and Julieta*, directed by Hector Serrano in 2015 and performed in the binational Chamizal National Park, which straddles El Paso, Texas, and Ciudad Juárez, Chihuahua, provides a salient example of the fraught politics of Borderlands Shakespeare performance. Spanish colonial history is evoked by the play's setting in a nineteenth-century hacienda, as haciendas were landed estates that employed both free and enslaved Indigenous labour. This colonial dynamic is reinforced by the play's use of early modern Spanish. With a script compiled by actor Jesse Snyder using an early modern Spanish translation, *Romeo and Julieta* uses linguistic difference to mark the division between the English-speaking Montagues and the Spanish-speaking Capulets. Though intended to appeal to Spanish-speaking audiences, this approach has the limitation of asking border residents to identify with one of two colonial powers, and it presents the border as a space of stark separation rather than of hybridity. As Estefanía Seyffert writes in a review in *Borderzine: Reporting across Fronteras*:

> Originally inspired by the Broadway revival of West Side Story [. . .] Snyder's bilingual script allows El Pasoans and Juarenses to identify themselves with the monolingual characters from different families who don't understand each other. Unlike the common usage of Spanglish that happens in the border, the Shakespearean characters speak in strictly Renaissance Spanish and English.[8]

Here *Romeo and Julieta* adheres to what Alfredo Michel Modenessi calls 'the unwritten and widely applied rule that rendering Shakespeare in Spanish "naturally" demands the use of European Spanish norms and forms with a somewhat archaic colour', thus keeping Shakespeare removed in a distant past.[9] Although the play features Mexican American actors and attempts to draw on the region's rich linguistic heritage, *Romeo and Julieta* uncritically employs the language and settings of Spanish colonialism. The appropriation accepts Eurocentric interpretations of *Romeo and Juliet* as universally applicable to any political or cultural division, when in fact the play might ultimately misrepresent border conflicts as stemming from an unfortunate misunderstanding.

Decolonial Borderlands Shakespeare, we argue, is more likely to be found in community theatres that cater to local residents than in larger regional theatres, those geared towards largely white patrons and donors. These community theatres maintain the tradition of the teatros, which, Yvonne Yarbro-Bejarano contends, 'played largely to "community" audiences in non-traditional venues: working-class Chicano communities in cultural centres in the barrios (Chicano/Latino neighborhoods), picket lines, political rallies, prisons, and schools'.[10] In addition to interrogating the supremacy of Anglo theatre, the activist-oriented teatro disrupts narratives of Shakespeare's cosmopolitan universality. As Elizabeth Klein and Michael Shapiro argue, local productions can unsettle dominant narratives about 'what "Shakespeare" is or what "Shakespeare" should sound like', opening up new interpretations and raising new possibilities about who can rightfully claim Shakespeare's texts.[11] Attending to these new interpretations is essential for Shakespearean scholars. Ruben Espinosa contends that 'there is little need for others to tell a marginalised individual *how* to connect with Shakespeare, but there is a pressing need to listen when that individual explains *what* makes him or her connect and why this happens'.[12] Borderlands community productions, in particular, offer crucial insight into Shakespeare's cultural significance, as their decolonial approach reveals what Espinosa calls 'a stranger Shakespeare not yet filtered through a critical apparatus that often privileges and takes for granted his universality'.[13]

Magaña's *The Tragic Corrido* brings this local, community-oriented interpretive lens to *Romeo and Juliet* in ways that unsettle Shakespeare's perceived dominance and foreground Tejano culture, land, language and art forms. It interpolates *Romeo and Juliet* into the Mexican genre of the corrido (or dramatic ballad), employs the multiple and mixed languages used on the border, and makes concrete references to life in the Rio Grande Valley. Rather than the universalised, cosmopolitan Shakespeare often imposed on marginalised communities, this is a Shakespeare of and for la frontera. As such, it rejects the assumption that producing Shakespeare is a mark of Anglocentric assimilation and instead uses *Romeo and Juliet* as a vehicle through which to negotiate related questions of colonisation, labour exploitation, and linguistic and cultural hybridity. In its appropriation of Shakespeare, the Pharr Community Theater centres the voices, histories and ways of knowing of border dwellers, fashioning the theatre as a space in which the community can forge collective responses to common challenges. And yet, there are limitations to Shakespearean appropriation, as Magaña's (extremely generative) engagement with Shakespeare makes clear. The ending of Magaña's play suggests that *Romeo and Juliet*'s tragic yet conciliatory plot arc hinders a depiction of Chicanx resistance and ultimately proves inadequate for conceptualising conflicts engendered by centuries of colonialist practices.

A Place-based Critique of Colonial Agribusiness

The Tragic Corrido of Romeo and Lupe is set during the early twentieth century in Pharr, which is connected by bridge to its sister city of Reynosa in Tamaulipas, Mexico. This geographic specificity is highlighted from the beginning of the play, which the bilingual corrido singer opens by welcoming the audience to 'Cage Boulevard here in the city of Pharr'.[14] When Romeo searches for Lupe after their initial, mysterious meeting, he asks the corrido singer where Lupe lives; the singer responds, 'On the corner of Cage and

Polk', a location about a mile from the theatre.[15] The sense that the play is situated within the community is augmented by its intense focus on the broader
region of the Rio Grande Valley, which for the most part constitutes the
world of the play. For example, Lupe's father, Don Díaz, mentions that 'Mi
Lupita nunca ha salido del valle. No conoce el mundo',[16] reminding audience
members of the intensely local culture of the valley – a place that is perhaps in
some ways analogous to Romeo and Juliet's walled city of Verona – in which
many people's mobility is limited by immigration checkpoints, poverty and
familial ties. Romeo pledges to 'search through the valley, whether it be cold
and raining, regardless of what others might say', revealing an assumption that
Lupe would not venture outside of the region.[17] The Rio Grande River itself
plays a central role in the play, whose conflict in part revolves around who has
rights to the water that sustains the valley's land and culture. In this way, *The
Tragic Corrido* fits with the Pharr Community Theater's 2018 season theme of
water politics, a subject that reflects the importance of the river to the region
and its inhabitants.

While the location is specific, the play's temporal setting is somewhat
unstable. Though presumably set in the 1940s, against the backdrop of the
Second World War, *The Tragic Corrido* relies on contemporary contexts in its
fashioning of Chicanx identity, engaging deeply with the tradition of labour
protest and the return to Indigenous symbolism that arose out of the UFW
and Chicano Movements of the 1960s and 1970s. This shifting temporality
permits the play to engage with legacies of colonisation that include histories of racism, labour exploitation and environmental destruction, as well as
the militarisation of the border and forced deportations. This transhistorical
approach, moreover, makes apparent the mutating but always present systems
of oppression that have affected the lives of valley residents, implicitly linking,
for example, the Bracero Program of the 1940s, in which Mexican agricultural workers were invited to the United States to ameliorate labour shortages,
with today's forced deportations of undocumented people, including those
whose labour has been exploited in the interests of US capitalism. This expansive historical vista connects to, and in a sense justifies, Magaña's choice to
appropriate a late sixteenth-century European play: the colonialism that began
in the region in the sixteenth century continues to affect it today.

In part because of this palimpsestic sense of overlapping and mutually
informing histories, the valley is presented as a contested space, referred to by
multiple names that reflect conflicting political and cultural orientations. In
the twentieth century, the region was shaped by agribusiness, which exploded
after the introduction of irrigation technologies and the railroad at the turn
of the century. The Campbells, Romeo's family, own the Campbell Irrigation
Company and are in the process of buying up land so that they can expand
their irrigation pipelines. As such, they promote a vision of the region as the

'Magic Valley', which, as María Herrera-Sobek explains, is 'the nickname its chamber of commerce seductively imagined for it'.[18] Christian Brannstrom and Matthew Neuman note that,

> in the first decade of the twentieth century, land developers and boosters promoted the Lower Rio Grande of Texas as the 'Magic Valley,' a place for Anglo farmers to obtain water for irrigating vegetable and citrus crops and to exploit Hispanic labor. [. . .] The Magic Valley idea [. . .] attracted thousands of Anglo settlers to practice irrigated agriculture in a place that quickly developed into a major horticultural and citrus-producing region sustained by impoverished and segregated Hispanic workers.[19]

In addition, the term 'Magic Valley' Anglicises the Spanglish name Rio Grande Valley and interpolates the region into an American and white Texan imaginary. This move is echoed in the play: Padre Lauro (the friar) reminds Romeo that 'Romeo Campbell is the Republic of Texas, and the Republic of Texas is Romeo Campbell'.[20] The surname evokes the Campbell's soup brand, a highly recognisable symbol of processed food and American consumerism, as made famous by pop culture artist and icon Andy Warhol.[21]

The Campbells' celebratory use of the name Magic Valley reflects their economic interests as key players in the region's agricultural economy. Driven by the desire to extract wealth from the land and its people, they exploit the region's human and natural resources. The corrido singer (and narrator) explains: 'nothing can stop their visions, as they build their dreams through refugees, as they build their dreams through people's homes'. For this reason, Mr Campbell is 'respected by most and most detested by some'.[22] As the Campbells see it, however, they deserve their profits:

> This land is ours. We earn it fair and square, through all the hard work we put into our vision. All we are doing is in fact serving the valley. It's true! We have brought technology unlike this place has seen. You wait a couple of years and just watch how much this place grows.[23]

Mr. Campbell's role is complicated by his marriage to a Mexican American woman, from whose father he inherited his land. His wife supports his vision, arguing that he has enriched the valley, and she sees him as helping build an authentically Tejano prosperity. As she explains to a skeptical Romeo,

> Comenzó a vender terreno, a construir un pueblo, y enriqueció. Hizo de la tierra algo suyo. Trajo a su gente del norte, trajo palmas, trajo maquinas, y se volvió parte de un sueño que de pronto emergió, ese de construir un valle mágico, que no sea de aquí ni de allá, pero auténticamente tejano.[24]

In this narrative, the resources of the North that Mr Campbell transports to the valley are productive rather than colonising, contributing to the creation of 'un valle mágico' that is characterised by hybridity ('que no sea de aquí ni de allá') and by a strong sense of place.

But this sympathetic vision of the Campbells' Magic Valley is not universally shared. Mr Campbell's personal history reflects the expropriation of Mexican lands, albeit through familial attachments, and, as Romeo replies to his mother, 'Toda paciencia tiene su límite. La gente de esta tierra se agota de lo que mi papa está haciendo.'[25] Further, Lupe's father explains that the Campbells' coercive purchases of land for irrigation ditches have had devastating consequences: 'Tan solo la semana pasada esos Campbells sacaron al Pepe y su familia de su casa, que para escavar un canal.'[26] The complex dynamics surrounding the influx of Anglo settlers to the region are a key source of conflict in the play, especially as it pertains to agricultural practices that exploit workers, affect the environment and displace the community. This tension, moreover, is also evident in Mrs Campbell's use of the phrase 'ni de aqui, ni de alla' (neither here, nor there), which is commonly used to describe the bicultural identity of people who have ties to both sides of the geographic border and who often grow up speaking two languages. Mrs Campbell frames this identity as a positive, uniquely Tejano state of being, even though the phrase – in its wider use – often reflects a sense of displacement, of belonging neither to US nor to Mexican society. Gloria E. Anzaldúa describes this tension as a state of *nepantla*, a Nahuatl word meaning 'torn between ways', and expounds on this split:

> Because I, a *mestiza*,
> continually walk out of one culture
> and into another,
> because I am in all cultures at the same time,
> *alma entre dos mundos, tres, cuatro,*
> *me zumba la cabeza con lo contradictorio.*
> *Estoy norteada por todas las voces que me hablan simultáneamente.*[27]

Reflecting *The Tragic Corrido*'s emphasis on community issues, Romeo and Lupe meet not at a party but at a protest against the Campbells' colonialist vision and practices. The protest is organised by Lupe's cousin Placido (analogous to Shakespeare's Tybalt and, like him, decidedly not placid) and is staged at the Birthday of the Magic Valley, an event intended to celebrate the region's rich agricultural abundance. The protesters, many of them farm workers like Placido, emphasise the exploitative labour conditions, environmental destruction and colonisation inflicted by white agribusiness. Ramón, another cousin of Lupe, raps, 'what is buried is the conflict in the food we pick / breathing in chemical vapors it make us sick / like two sides to a coin, I'm calling you to join in breaking every chain'.[28] His 'tejano lament' draws on the Indigenous heritage of Chicanxs to cast the Campbells as colonisers. His use of a musical form with Black American roots highlights the importance of African influence to the cultural mestizaje of the borderlands and nods to the solidarity of distinct but interconnected social justice movements of the civil rights era. Ramón claims: 'we worked this earth first you returned it to us cursed / your handshake agreement is but double cross coerce / your logic is rehearsed and your compassion is even worse'.[29] The rap indicates that the locals know that the duplicity of white landowners has led to poverty and oppression. Moreover, the protestors reject the implication of the birthday celebration that white settlers are responsible for the valley's plenty. Instead, as Herrera-Sobek writes,

> Without Mexican and Mexican American labor tending the endless agricultural fields of onions, lettuce, tomatoes, cabbage, cotton, carrots, peppers, green beans, and so forth, the verdant Magic Valley would have perished; it would have been a sterile place and not the fertile vegetable and fruit cornucopia nourishing the world.[30]

From this position of workers' power, and fuelled by the 'Aztec tejano' blood that flows through their veins, the activists seek to redress their oppression by taking back the land and driving 'the gringos out'.[31] Channelling a popular protest slogan, Ramón raps, 'they tried to tear us down like weeds / didn't know that we was seeds'.[32] The land and its people reject colonial oppression.

Adding a spectacular dimension to this musical protest, the activists disrupt a fashion show designed to highlight the bounty of the valley. The first model wears a dress meant to represent grapefruits. Rather than conforming to the expected tone of the event, she references Anzaldúa's description of the border as 'una herida abierta' in her angry lament: 'This valley here is a grapefruit, anywhere you make a cut the nectar from the land spills out like an open wound. You cut deep into it. And you drain it of its soul.'[33] The second model, in a dress representing grapes, adds, 'I was hungry and wandering, I saw a woman eating grapes, I told her, "Please, give me one for my child." She said, go away, your feet are muddy and I despise your stare.'[34] With her costume recalling the famous Delano grape strike and boycott, led by César Chávez and Dolores Huerta of the UFW (1965–70), the activist calls attention to the inequality of labour relations, which permits a worker to produce food that she herself cannot afford to buy. As Ramón asks, 'what is a man's labor that can't feed his fam?'[35] The activist continues with an indictment of the system of enslavement that shaped the Republic of Texas, saying that she sees a man 'sucking on sugar cane like a thumb, all the time he cries "I want more"', unable to sate his lust for the fruits of exploited labour.[36]

This protest draws on a tradition of border residents subverting dominant American ideologies, one that Norma Cantú has outlined in her discussion of ostensibly patriotic events such as George Washington's birthday, an event similar to the Magic Valley's Birthday Party.[37] Placido and his fellow activists transform the Campbells' celebration into a decolonial spectacle, demonstrating that the wealth created here was built through occupation and corruption. They refuse to accept or promote this nostalgic and whitewashed image of the region and call attention to their own lived experience as Chicanx youth. When interrupted by the Campbells' security guards, the activists chant 'We do not want your segregation, your discrimination, your dreams. Esta tierra no te quiere aqui. This is not your magic valley, this is the RGV. This is not your magic valley, this is the RGV.'[38] The RGV, in contrast to the Magic Valley, is fashioned as a space that centres the lives and labour of border residents and that acknowledges the material realities and racial and class-based inequalities that shape the region. Romeo and Lupe's love arises from these fraught contexts, emphasising that the feud between their families is far from senseless: it is rooted in centuries of oppression and therefore has extremely high stakes. As the corrido singer states, 'On these fertile lands / Of opportunity / Covered in blood and strife, / Blooms a forbidden love.'[39]

Embracing Mestizaje: Hybrid Genres, Languages, Spaces and Cultures

The Tragic Corrido's response to these colonial conflicts is to celebrate hybridity or mestizaje, which Rafael Pérez-Torres defines as 'an affirmative recognition of the mixed racial, social, linguistic, national, cultural and ethnic legacies inherent to Latino/a cultures and identities'.[40] The play itself is a collective, intertextual project in which aspects of *Romeo and Juliet*, translated and adapted by Magaña into a mixture of Spanish, English and Spanglish, are integrated into the tradition of the Mexican corrido, or dramatic ballad. A genre with deep roots in the US-Mexico borderlands, the corrido is known both for its malleability and for its frequent themes of border crossing and immigration.[41] The genre is known both for its malleability and for its frequent themes of border crossing and immigration. According to Herrera-Sobek, 'Corridos have been the voice of the Mexican and Mexican American people narrating their history, love stories and tragedies; the exploits of famous bandits, deeds of revolutionary heroes and heroines, and any other newsworthy event.'[42] It is a music for the people that reflects the lived realities of the border residents who both create and consume the corridos. Magaña uses the form throughout the play, both in the actual songs of the corrido singer and in the broader depiction of Romeo and Lupe's love story as one that would be told in a corrido. His fusion of the form with a Shakespearean story reflects the plasticity and resilience of border culture and enacts decolonial performatics as it critiques Anglocentric constructs of the Rio Grande Valley.

Driven by their love, Romeo and Lupe attempt – through an emphasis on intercultural and interlinguistic exchange – to transcend the conflicts that shape their lives. They are both disguised when they first meet at the protest, Lupe because her protective family does not want her to attend, and Romeo because he is the son of Mr Campbell and thus cannot be seen at the protest. This initial encounter reflects Romeo and Lupe's tendency to privilege hybridity over the divisions that consume their family members. They code-switch throughout the scene, seamlessly moving between Spanish and English. Romeo approaches Lupe first in English, commenting on her beauty hidden under a veil. Lupe then responds with 'Buen peregrino, you do wrong your hand too much. Qué clase de devoción es esta?' with the word *peregrino* (a direct translation of *pilgrim*) acquiring added resonance in a border context characterised by migration and attempts to impede it.[43] Romeo, ironically, is a peregrino not because he has crossed any national borders but because he has abandoned his familial allegiance in order to learn more about the protestors' cause. Romeo and Lupe's mixture of Spanish and English is complemented by a sense of religious hybridity, captured in Lupe's name, which invokes la Virgen de Guadalupe, Mexico's most famous symbol of the interweaving of Christian and Indigenous traditions. Lupe not only reveres la Virgen, whose likeness is framed above her bed, but also prays to an Aztec god. Similarly, the lovers' initial exchange integrates Indigenous myth and geography with the Christian references of Shakespeare's text. Romeo expounds, 'Before me stands the essence of life itself, your fingers are the petals of the Dahlia, your words are a hummingbird's flight, your eyes a volcano that awakens, like Iztaccíhuatl melting down her snow.'[44] Here the hummingbird evokes Huitzilopochtli, the Aztec god of sun and war, while Iztaccíhuatl is a dormant volcanic mountain whose name means 'white woman' and references a mythological princess of Mexican folklore. The scene thus speaks to the need to revise Shakespeare for a border audience whose cultural and religious backgrounds envelop the complicated histories of the Rio Grande Valley and its residents.

Indigenous spirituality, furthermore, informs Romeo and Lupe's depiction of the valley itself. In contrast to the other characters, who rely on political constructs – the Magic Valley, the RGV, the Republic of Texas, Aztlán, the United States, or Mexico – to describe the region, Romeo and Lupe emphasise the richness and hybridity of the valley's natural environment. Magaña replaces Shakespeare's references to plants and animals with species found in the valley, whether indigenous or introduced. Like Friar Laurence, Padre Lauro grounds his apothecary work in the land; he alludes to Indigenous practices of curanderismo, and he draws his treatments from local plants such as sabila, or aloe. Like Juliet, Lupe references animals to prolong her night with Romeo, saying 'Ese no fue el gallo el que perforo tu tímpano. Listen, la chicharra still sings, cada noche canta mientras reposa sobre el mezquite. While it sings, time is ours.' Romeo responds, 'That is not the chicharra. That is the green jay, and the great kiskadee, and the crow that waits for our final consequence. I must go.'[45]

The spirit of the Valley's resilient land infuses the love of Romeo and Lupe, who repeatedly use agricultural images to describe their feelings for each other. Referring to Lupe as the sun, Romeo commands, 'Cast off the night, the seeds in the fields won't spur their roots without your touch. Burn away this veil of dreams, it is like unripe fruit, incomplete, and unfulfilled.'[46] Lupe, like Juliet, is the sun, but she is a sun that fuels the agricultural life of the valley. Using this same line of metaphor, Lupe talks about their love as a harvest, projecting that 'Estas raíces que aquí nacen, quizás crecerán a una cosecha cuando nos volvamos a ver.'[47] Their love, like the labour in the fields, cultivates roots that will produce a great harvest.

The play's emphasis on the sacredness of the earth and its connection to love is also linked to histories of resistance in the borderlands. By emphasising the lovers' rootedness in the land, Magaña's production allows us to consider a 'decolonial imaginary' that disrupts the colonial constructs imposed on the region. Emma Pérez describes this imaginary as 'a rupturing space, the alternative to that which is written in history [. . .] that time lag between the colonial and postcolonial, that interstitial space where differential politics and social dilemmas are negotiated'.[48] The land becomes the contested space that makes possible an interrogation of the historiographies of the region. Chicanx labor, love and land work in conjunction to rewrite Shakespeare's classic within a colonised setting, placing resistance to oppression at the centre of the narrative. As Anzaldúa states, 'This land has survived possession and ill-use by five countries: Spain, Mexico, the Republic of Texas, the U.S., the Confederacy, and the U.S. again. It has survived Anglo-Mexican blood feuds, lynchings, burnings, rapes, pillage.'[49] In *The Tragic Corrido*, the land itself is depicted as resisting this colonial violence. As the protesters assert to the Campbells, 'Esta tierra no te quiere aqui', a sentiment that Romeo echoes when he says that 'la tierra aun lo sigue rechazando'.[50] Grounding their love in this resistant land, Lupe and Romeo embrace a vision of the hybrid space of la frontera that rejects colonialist political constructs of the region and leaves behind the nationalism that has separated their families. Romeo, although once aligned with the republic of Texas, comes to regard the republic as his enemy when his father seeks to separate him from Lupe. Lupe asserts, instead, their place in the borderlands: 'Somos de ambos lados, y de ninguno', and 'the future of our love is here. En la frontera'.[51] Or, as Anzaldúa concludes, 'This land was Mexican once / was Indian always / and is / And will be again.'[52]

The Boundaries of Borderlands Shakespeare

Driven by the logic of Shakespeare's love story, Lupe and Romeo's dismissal of political constructs can seem naïve, as they seem to dismiss the political divisions that consume their families and the colonial histories that shape their environment. For example, in her rendition of Juliet's 'A rose / By any other name would smell as sweet', Lupe references 'poinsettias or noche buenas', proclaiming that by either name, 'they would still be as red'.[53] Even as Lupe asserts the equal validity of Spanish and English terms and ostensibly elides power dynamics informing these names, her comment calls attention to the fraught colonial history of the poinsettia/noche buena. The flower is indigenous to Mexico and was used by the Aztecs for dye and medicine. It acquired its Mexican name, noche buena, in the sixteenth century when it became associated with Christmas Eve. The English term is derived from the name of Joel Roberts Poinsett, the first US minister to Mexico, who introduced the flower to the United States. The US poinsettia industry grew largely through exploitation of Latin American labour. The difference in a name – poinsettia or noche buena, or the unstated Nahuatl name cuitlaxochitl – is therefore not immaterial as it points to the colonial histories that have shaped the region. But perhaps Lupe's range of expression is limited by the logic of Juliet's line. Perhaps she, like Juliet, suspects that names do matter – as they ultimately do in both plays, even as she wishes otherwise.

Deep conflicts, caused by centuries of colonisation, cannot ultimately be reconciled through Romeo and Lupe's love. Their idealism and desire for peace are not shared by those around them. During the fight in which Mercutio is nearly killed, Placido offers a cynical perspective on their relationship when he accuses Romeo of being 'like [his] father', desiring to 'get with a Mexicana just so you can get what you want out of her, her land, the land of her parents'.[54] The results of the fight, which Romeo hopes to disrupt, are catastrophic: both Placido and Mercutio are deported; Romeo is sent to the military; and Lupe's family resolves to send her to Mexico. Magaña's replacement of the literal death of Shakespeare's characters with the social death of deportation hints at the high stakes and potentially deadly consequences of exile, particularly for those who choose to come back across the border. The time period of the 1940s also conjures the mass repatriation of both US- and foreign-born ethnic Mexicans beginning in the 1930s, and the anti-immigrant sentiment that had been mounting since the great wave of migration after the Mexican Revolution.[55]

Given these circumstances, Lupe and Romeo's love cannot be sustained in the real world of the Rio Grande Valley. Even Padre Lauro admits, 'My thought that your marriage could bring peace to this conflict in our valle was infantile.'[56] Rather than leaving for the military, Romeo escapes to see Padre

Lauro, who will help him reunite with Lupe in Aztlán, the ancestral homeland of the Aztec people and spiritual homeland of Chicanxs. Thought to be located in Northern Mexico or the US Southwest, Aztlán was a source of artistic inspiration and a symbol of belonging during and after the Chicano movement, part of a resistance to discrimination and erasure by mainstream society. It continues to hold a semi-mythical status for Chicanxs, and in the context of the play it signifies an almost utopian space apart from the sociopolitical realities of the region. That this is the only place Lupe and Romeo could live happily suggests the impossibility of their love – and perhaps of their vision of hybrid culture and language. In the absence of a mythical homeland, such love is possible only in death, a space that, drawing on Indigenous traditions, is depicted as part of the endless cycle of life, death, rebirth and immortality, a hybrid or third space, a 'new world where we love one another por toda la eternidad'.[57] For this reason, Lupe regards the lovers' mortal miscommunication, which mirrors that of Shakespeare's play, not as tragic but as 'perfect'. When she awakens to find Romeo dead, she says, 'This is just as planned. I woke, and you are here, to take me to a world where our love can be free.'[58]

Despite the magnitude of the conflicts facing the two families, Shakespeare's plot arc – in which the death 'bur[ies] their parents' strife' – ultimately prevails, compelling a reconciliation that rings somewhat hollow after Magaña's searing critique of the colonialism, racism, labour exploitation and environmental destruction undergirding the Campbells' success.[59] The once resistant Díaz family ultimately embraces some aspects of the Magic Valley propaganda that the Campbells promote. Romeo's cousin, Nelson Campbell, opportunistically noting that Romeo's death has made him heir to the Campbell Irrigation Company, promises, 'Our cousins did marry, after all, and now we are family. From now on I will persuade our parents to negotiate, if need be find other routes for our irrigation systems. We will continue to grow, yet grow as neighbours and brothers.' And Ramón, speaking for the Díaz family, agrees to work as 'carnales' (brothers) to foster love and prosperity in the Magic Valley: 'Estoy de acuerdo. This Rio Grande Valley is in fact un valle magico, "Magic Valley" like you call it. Because only in a place magical can love like this happen.'[60] The play thus ends with a somewhat tentative sense of promise, albeit one dependent on the sacrifice of Romeo and Lupe, with Padre Lauro hoping that 'This flame that was born between them, if it is born amongst us again, may it glow across the Rio Grande Valley.'[61] But the 'if' is important here. Despite the newfound amity between the Díaz and Campbell families, Romeo and Lupe's love seems unlikely to heal the colonial wounds of the borderlands. The union of the Díaz and Campbell families, moreover, relies on patriarchal power constructions similar to those inherent in the colonial land politics critiqued throughout the play, as no women are involved in this reconciliation.

This conciliatory ending may suggest that even community theatres in the Texas–Mexico borderlands must appeal to broad audiences that include Anglos, especially when they produce and adapt Shakespeare. We overheard an interesting conversation between two actors before a performance of the show at the Pharr Community Theater. One of them casually inquired, 'How's the audience, mostly bolillos? The other replied, 'Nah, mostly raza.' The term *bolillo* (lit., white roll or white bread) is slang for a white person, while *raza* (lit., race) signifies a deep connection to the Mexican American community and its resistance to socioeconomic and racial oppression. With its casual Spanglish, the exchange reflects the translingual and transcultural nature of the city and the theatre. But it also reflects the whiteness of Shakespeare. As Ayanna Thompson observes, 'Shakespeare represents the epitome of Western culture because he represents the exclusivity of white culture.'[62] This presumed whiteness may thus restrict the potential of Borderlands Shakespeare performances to truly formulate coherent Chicanx responses to the political and cultural dynamics shaping the Rio Grande Valley.

Furthermore, the conclusion to *The Tragic Corrido* exposes the limitations of the *Romeo and Juliet* framework for representing any given social or cultural division. Many Latinx adaptations of *Romeo and Juliet*, including *The Tragic Corrido*, employ what Carla Della Gatta calls 'the *West Side Story* effect', referencing the 1957 musical. This effect 'involves the reinscribing of Shakespearean representations of difference of various kinds – class, locale, familial – as a cultural/linguistic difference'.[63] The premise of *Romeo and Juliet*, of course, is that the Montague and Capulet households are 'both alike in dignity' and that the feud between them is senseless.[64] This story, therefore, cannot fully accommodate the complex histories and power imbalances that inform relationships between Chicanxs and Anglos, between farm owners and fieldworkers, or between irrigation companies and those forced off their land to clear space for pipelines. These conflicts might be negotiated, but they cannot be easily reconciled. And to reconcile them simply through the romantic love and death of the protagonists short changes the trenchant critiques of the protesters at the fashion show as well as the history of Chicanx activism on which they draw. *The Tragic Corrido*'s ending thus points to the challenge of using Shakespeare to tell Chicanx stories, as it exposes the boundaries of *Romeo and Juliet*'s purportedly universal applicability. Nevertheless, *The Tragic Corrido of Romeo and Lupe* reflects how Borderlands Shakespeare resides in the in-between, tethering Indigenous roots with colonial influences and harnessing the power of the hybrid spaces from which it arises.

Notes

1. The term 'Chicanx' arises from the Chicano movement for the political liberation of Mexican Americans, and it emphasises Indigenous heritage, with the more recent addition of the 'x' connoting an openness to a spectrum of gender expressions. We use 'Chicanx' when we are referring to this political tradition, the artistic movement associated with it, and people who identify with it. When we refer to people of Mexican and/ or Indigenous descent living in the United States who may or may not identify as Chicanx, we use the term 'Mexican American'.
2. Arturo J. Aldama, Chela Sandoval and Peter J. Garcia, 'Toward a De-Colonial Performatics of the US Latina and Latino Borderlands', in *Performing the US Latina and Latino Borderlands*, ed. Arturo J. Aldama, Chela Sandoval and Peter J. Garcia (Bloomington: Indiana University Press, 2012), 1–27, esp. 2.
3. Aldama, Sandoval and Garcia, *Performing*, 3.
4. Magaña, a poet and playwright originally from Guadalajara, Jalisco, Mexico, was educated and currently resides in the Rio Grande Valley, where the play is set. The production referenced was directed by Pedro Garcia, Pharr Community Theater, Pharr, TX, 16–29 April 2018. We attended the performance on 22 April 2018.
5. David Román, 'Latino Performance and Identity', *Aztlán*, 22.2 (1997): 151–67, esp. 153.
6. Gloria E. Anzaldúa, *Borderlands/La Frontera: The New Mestiza*, 3rd edn (San Francisco: Aunt Lute Press, 2007), 25.
7. For more on Latinx theatre's engagement with neoliberal policies and their consequences, see Patricia A. Ybarra, *Latinx Theater in the Times of Neoliberalism* (Evanston, IL: Northwestern University Press, 2017).
8. Estefanía Seyffert, '"Romeo and Julieta" Opens Door to Future Bilingual Productions in the Borderlands', *Borderzine: Reporting across Fronteras*, 10 December 2015.
9. Alfredo Michel Modenessi, 'Of Shadows and Stones: Revering and Translating "the Word" – Shakespeare in Mexico', *Shakespeare Survey*, 54 (2001): 152–64, esp. 154–5.
10. Yvonne Yarbro-Bejarano, 'The Female Subject in Chicano Theatre: Sexuality, "Race," and Class', *Theatre Journal*, 38.4 (1986): 389–407, esp. 390.
11. Elizabeth Klein and Michael Shapiro, 'Shylock as Crypto-Jew: A New Mexican Adaptation of *The Merchant of Venice*', in *World-Wide Shakespeares: Local Appropriations in Film and Performance*, ed. Sonia Massai (New York: Routledge, 2005), 31–9, esp. 33.

12. Ruben Espinosa, 'Stranger Shakespeare', *Shakespeare Quarterly*, 67.1 (2016): 51–67, esp. 56.
13. Espinosa, 'Stranger Shakespeare', 61.
14. Seres Jaime Magaña, *The Tragic Corrido of Romeo and Lupe* (unpublished script), 3.
15. Magaña, *The Tragic Corrido*, 22.
16. Ibid. 8. 'My Lupita has never left the valley. She does not know the world.' All translations are our own.
17. Magaña, *The Tragic Corrido*, 22.
18. María Herrera-Sobek, 'Gloria Anzaldúa: Place, Race, Language, and Sexuality in the Magic Valley', *PMLA*, 121.1 (2006): 266–71, esp. 266.
19. Christian Brannstrom and Matthew Neuman, 'Inventing the "Magic Valley" of South Texas, 1905–1941', *Geographical Review*, 99.2 (2009): 123–45, esp. 123.
20. Magaña, *The Tragic Corrido*, 38.
21. In an interesting reversal of the typical mispronunciation of Latinx names by Anglos, Campbell was pronounced Camp-bell throughout the Pharr Theater's production.
22. Magaña, *The Tragic Corrido*, 3.
23. Ibid. 28.
24. Ibid. 21. 'He started to sell land, to build a town, and enriched it. He made the land his own. He brought his people from the north, brought palm trees, brought machines, and became part of a dream that suddenly emerged, that of constructing a magic valley, that was neither from here nor from over there, but authentically Tejano.'
25. Ibid. 21. 'All patience has its limit. The people of this land are exhausted from what my dad is doing.'
26. Ibid. 8. 'Just last week those Cambells removed Pepe and his family from their home to dig a canal.'
27. Anzaldúa, *Borderlands/La Frontera*, 99–100.
28. Magaña, *The Tragic Corrido*, 4.
29. Ibid. 33.
30. Herrera-Sobek, 'Gloria Anzaldúa', 267.
31. Magaña, *The Tragic Corrido*, 3, 20.
32. Ibid. 3.
33. Ibid. 17; Anzaldúa, *Borderlands/La Frontera*, 24.
34. Magaña, *The Tragic Corrido*, 17.
35. Ibid. 33.
36. Ibid. 17.
37. Norma E. Cantú, 'Sitio y Lengua: Chicana Third Space Feminist Theory', *Landscapes of Writing in Chicano Literature* (2013): 173–87.
38. Magaña, *The Tragic Corrido*, 17.

39. Ibid. 2.

40. Rafael Pérez-Torres, 'Mestizaje', in *The Routledge Companion to Latino/a Literature*, ed. Suzanne Bost and Francis R. Aparicio (New York: Routledge, 2013), 25.

41. Américo Paredes, *"With a Pistol in His Hand": A Border Ballad and Its Hero* (Austin: University of Texas Press, 1958), 149.

42. María Herrera-Sobek, 'The Border Patrol and Their Migra Corridos: Propaganda, Genre Adaptation, and Mexican Immigration', *American Studies Journal*, 57 (2012): 2.

43. Magaña, *The Tragic Corrido*, 17. 'What type of devotion is this?'

44. Ibid. 18.

45. Ibid. 40. 'This was not the rooster who pierced your eardrum. Listen, the cicada still sings, each night it sings while it rests on the mesquite tree.'

46. Ibid. 22.

47. Ibid. 24. 'Those roots that are born here, perhaps they will grow to a harvest when we meet again.'

48. Emma Pérez, *The Decolonial Imaginary: Writing Chicanas into History* (Bloomington: Indiana University Press, 1999), 6.

49. Anzaldúa, *Borderlands/La Frontera*, 112.

50. Magaña, *The Tragic Corrido*, 17, 21. 'This land does not want you here. [. . .] the earth still rejects it.'

51. Ibid. 42, 43. 'We are of both sides and of none', and 'the future of our love is here. In the borderlands'.

52. Anzaldúa, *Borderlands/La Frontera*, 113.

53. William Shakespeare, *Romeo and Juliet*, in *The Norton Shakespeare*, 3rd edn, ed. Stephen Greenblatt, Walter Cohen, Suzanne Gossett, Jean E. Howard, Katharine Eisaman Maus and Gordon McMullan (New York: W. W. Norton, 2016), II.i.85–6; Magaña, *The Tragic Corrido*, 23.

54. Magaña, *The Tragic Corrido*, 34.

55. See Fernando Saúl Alanís Enciso, *They Should Stay There: The Story of Mexican Migration and Repatriation during the Great Depression* (Chapel Hill: University of North Carolina Press, 2017), 136.

56. Magaña, *The Tragic Corrido*, 43.

57. Ibid. 43. 'for all of eternity'.

58. Ibid. 47.

59. Shakespeare, *Romeo and Juliet*, in *The Norton Shakespeare*, 3rd edn, prologue, i.8.

60. Magaña, *The Tragic Corrido*, 48. 'I agree. This Rio Grande Valley is in fact a magical valley, "Magic Valley" like you like to call it.'

61. Ibid. 48.

62. Ayanna Thompson, *Passing Strange: Shakespeare, Race, and Contemporary America* (Oxford: Oxford University Press, 2011), 41–2.

63. Carla Della Gatta, 'From *West Side Story* to *Hamlet, Prince of Cuba*: Shakespeare and Latinidad in the United States', *Shakespeare Studies*, 44 (2016): 151–6, esp. 152.
64. Shakespeare, *Romeo and Juliet*, prologue, i.1.

Part II: Making Shakespeare Latinx

In a Shakespearean Key

Caridad Svich

I was living in Hialeah, Florida, when I was in the fourth grade. Nestled somewhat uncomfortably in a Cuban American and immigrant Cuban neighbourhood while studying at a Catholic elementary school, I reached for a copy of *A Midsummer Night's Dream* on my school library's shelf because both the title and the cover looked inviting and seemed like an 'escape' from the everyday concerns of being a multicultural, bilingual (English–Spanish) Northeasterner transplanted to the American South.

It may seem odd to signify the Cuban American enclave of Hialeah in the 1970s as part of the American South. In the collective consciousness of the United States, the South usually evokes complex, necessarily troubled images of the American Civil War, the history of slave trade and labour, dust bowl era displacement, civil rights era protests, signifiers of 'redneck' country's deep poverty and racism, and Black communities steeped in the legacy and sound of the diasporic Delta blues. But the South is also Indigenous, Spanish, Creole, Cajun, Asian, Mexican, Haitian, Dominican, Puerto Rican and Cuban, among many other ethnic markers. It's interesting how convenient it is for the Spanish colonial, immigrant and native Latinx cultures of the South, especially, to be 'erased' in discussions of its history. But the suburb of Miami named Hialeah is most definitely in the South, and in the 1970s, it was predominantly a working-class city populated by immigrant Cubans and first-generation Cuban Americans.

I landed there, direct from living in both Philadelphia, Pennsylvania, and Paterson, New Jersey, when my Cuban Spanish and Argentine Croatian parents moved to pursue a new job opportunity. In the neighbourhoods in which I had lived before, we were usually the only Latinx family on the block. Spanish was spoken at home, and English 'outside'. I grew up, thus, with a clear separation between the language of home and the language of the 'world'. But in Hialeah at that time, there was no separation. Spanish was everywhere: on storefront window signs, on the street, in the music that blared from radios, and in the *chisme* heard at school, where about 80 per cent of my classmates were first-generation Latinx-ers.

To say that landing in Hialeah was a culture shock for me is to put it mildly. As a young person starting to shape their identity, I felt almost betrayed by the sudden lack of separation between home and world, as I had previously perceived it, especially from a linguistic perspective. If there was no separation, then how could I navigate the boundaries of my existence? If what had felt 'private' before was no longer so, where could I find a semblance of privacy?

A Midsummer Night's Dream held the key. With its ornate cover, the Folger Library edition of the play sat on a shelf in the school library alongside single editions of *Hamlet* and *Othello*, and larger volumes that grouped Shakespeare's history plays, comedies and tragedies. Somehow the romances were relegated to the much bigger collected works tome, which seemed far too heavy to carry in my plaid bookbag. Opening the pages of *Midsummer*, I fell into a very strange world indeed. And it is important to consider how strange this play that we take for granted these days truly is. Here we have a fairy king and queen, a set of restless and reckless young mortals caught in the wild entanglements of mimetic desire, a shape-shifting sprite hell-bent on making mischief, a company of travelling community actors that are rehearsing a play for the mortal king and queen (not to be confused with the fairy king and queen), a band of fairies and creatures, a man who turns into an ass and makes love to the fairy queen, and more. If the plot of this play were to be synopsised to a theatre these days, I am sure they would think it made little sense and demand it be made accessible at once! But thankfully, this strange play exists in all its queer charm and dark magic. My initiation into Shakespeare could not have been more prescient: its spell is all over my own playwriting to this day, even in the plays that have very little visible marking of Shakespeare's influence.

In *Midsummer*, I found not only intoxicating poetry and images meant to be performed but also, for the first time (though I was already a voracious reader), a door into another world. If I was wrestling indeed with being a Yankee in the South, then Elizabethan England – or should I say, Shakespeare's rendering of a British 'Attica' where an Amazonian Greek Queen (Hippolyta) and a Greek king (Theseus) preside and where a figure from medieval English literature like Oberon meets a newly coined fairy queen Titania – was a deliriously exciting portal through which to allow my imaginary to enter.

Soon I was reading more Shakespeare on my own, not quite understanding it, but nonetheless struck by the beauty and wildness of the language and the dramatic situations. Part of my day I was eating rice and beans and listening to boleros, rumbas and salsa, and in the other part of my day I was spirited headlong into writing that felt neither Yankee nor Latinx, but maybe, perhaps, an odd fusion of both.

I joke with some of my colleagues that I consider Shakespeare as Latinx as Euripides, Tennessee Williams, Sam Shepard and Ntozake Shange (all significant, early influences). Although they come from disparate theatre traditions, ethnicities and upbringings, the radical positioning of these writers' works as they contemplate human existence feels like kin to me. I mean here to challenge what may already be essentialised identity-based readings of Latinx writing. Julio Cortázar, Jorge Luis Borges, Roberto Bolaño and Clarice Lispector, for example, all drew from writing influences outside their countries of birth. Cortázar was enamored of Jules Verne and Edgar Allan Poe's works. Bolaño loved the Beat generation writers. Borges was inspired by Schopenhauer, Marinetti, Apollinaire and Oscar Wilde. Lispector contested Kafka.

In Shakespeare, before he was a writer on my syllabus in high school and, therefore, part of the colonial violence of the canon that I was told I must rebel against, I started to find a sense of home. In this othered language – poetic, daring and inventive, mixing in what we may call a syncretic manner high and low registers, philosophical thought, and fearless commitment to the possibilities of the stage – I began to connect the different ways I experienced and used Spanish and English daily, and to understand how this so-called Yankee, whose early identity was forged in the industrial landscape of the Northeast, was a Southern writer.

In Florida, and later in North Carolina, where I spent my formative years in high school and college, I began to think about theatre and specifically writing for the theatre. Although the Northeast has always been in my blood, Attica (England), Hialeah and Charlotte are my touchstones when I make plays, and no more so than in a play like *12 Ophelias*, which cracks open Shakespeare's *Hamlet* to create a new identity for one of literature's most troubled women.

Set in a neo-Elizabethan, Appalachian landscape, *12 Ophelias* (2008) began as a bluegrass play. Drawing from the sounds and musical traditions of bluegrass, deeply influenced by the folk archives of murder ballads and mountain songs of this part of the South, the play is structured like a negative mirror of *Hamlet*. In it, Ophelia rises from the water to find herself in a new world that is populated by ghosts from her literary past. These ghosts are not the same as when she last saw them in Shakespeare's play. Gertrude now runs a brothel, Rosencrantz and Guildenstern are androgynous gossips that do the emotional and physical labour of cleaning and tending to the town, Hamlet is now called Rude Boy, Horatio is simply called H, and someone not from her past at all, a young woman named Mina, a sex worker in Gertrude's house, becomes her spirit guide. A chorus is also living in this terrain, and this chorus is made of other Ophelias: young, neglected women driven mad and abused by patriarchal systems that never listened to them or that negated their voices and beings.

The play-poem is composed in a series of short scenes, some of which remix, distort and fracture language from Shakespeare's *Hamlet*, alongside non-verbal scenes, dances and songs that illuminate what I like to call the 'soul terrain' of the play. Instead of advancing the 'plot', the songs in *12 Ophelias* are windows into consciousness, and, specific to this play, ones affected by trauma. A conventional Latinx reading of the play would locate Ophelia's trauma of entry into a new world after having committed suicide as an analogy for the trauma of exile and repatriation, of a border crossing in which one leaves behind and yet cannot leave behind the 'ghosts' of the old country, and of a colonised being remaking herself as the postcolonial author of her own narrative – subjugated no more!

Such a reading would be fair to consider, though I would like to problem-atise it just a bit. In my contestation, response and reclaiming of Shakespeare from a feminist, queer and phenome-logical perspective influenced by Hélène Cixous, Judith Butler and Sara Ahmed, I am also reconnecting with Shakespeare in the way I did back when I picked up *Midsummer* from the library shelf – allowing myself to be transported to another world and an/other language, but also acknowledging that this language is mine too. In the same way that I ask audiences to contemplate the fact that a Latinx writer finds herself at home in bluegrass, I am doing the same with Shakespeare.

Yes, the canon exists, and yes, Shakespeare is part of it. But he has been placed there not by his own doing, but rather by the academy and the field. This point may seem small, but it is still crucial. Great writing knows no bor-ders. In and out of translation, if it is awake, alert and filled with the spirit of deep play, it transcends nation, state, locality and referentiality by being itself: the sheer dare of the inky signs and soul map on the page. The larger question here is why some works have been asked by governing systems to do a duty outside themselves, to serve as colonising forces of the imagination on other nations and peoples.

Shakespeare intervened in, challenged and contested existing narratives. He plundered, stole and remade stories to craft a new image. In a slightly left-of-centre way, one could argue that he intervened in the existing canonical works of his time before a canon ever came into being. Questioning and repurposing received texts are among our jobs as writers. Queering Shakespeare in *12 Ophelias* seems to me a very Shakespeare thing to do. But one could also say that it's a very post-*nueva trova* thing to do. In Cuban popular music, for instance, the *nueva trova* movement was characterised by a return to folk-based songs of protest and reflections of contemporary life. Post-*nueva trova*, then, in my reading of it, is music and work that recognises what *nueva trova* stood for and moves past it to explode and reanimate the musical landscape through a postmodern, postcolonial lens.

In my journeys thus far with reconfiguring Shakespeare's works – *12 Ophelias, The Booth Variations* (2002, also after *Hamlet*), *Perdita Gracia* (2002, after *The Winter's Tale*), *The Breath of Stars* (2016, after *The Tempest*) and *Holler River* (2018, after *King Henry IV, Part I*) – I have used Shakespeare's material as a kind of avatar for my own writing in the way that poets wink at, allude to and call on other poets' works, or the way composers and musicians riff on and nod at what has become the stream of history. The fact that I am a female writer is not lost on me because it does mean, still, that the intervention and reconfiguration is coming from a place of asserting power where once no power was allowed. Making and inscribing a space that had been reserved for men for hundreds of years is a different position from which to write, and for a hybrid Latinx writer this position is made even more acute. So, when I say that this language is mine, I am not only speaking of English, which is my first and primary language although I learned Spanish at the same time, but also staking a claim (as a historically unheard voice) to the stage and page, and saying with quite an independent streak in regard to conventional modes of dramatic production and (historically gendered) expectations of how narrative functions in the theatre, 'I am here.' Just like Ophelia does in my play.

But let me take this a step further. Back when I picked up *Midsummer* from my library shelf, I also stumbled on Virginia Woolf's work. (I was quite a heady fourth grader!) And one of the first lightning-bolt moments that I had while reading Woolf was an encounter with her own profound wrestling with what it means to be female and be a writer. In my understanding of writing as androgynous, I feel a strong connection to Woolf. We might call this now a genderqueer position, but I would like to stay with the word *androgynous* for a bit longer because it cuts to the heart of the being-ness of writing, and perhaps to the way that one approaches another writer's work (in the case of this essay, Shakespeare's). In writing, one is everything. One can be everything, which is to say, writing is a free act and therein lies its most radical otherness. It is not limited to or by (except by outside forces and systems of thought, law and governance) where a writer is from, or what their cultural make-up may be. If the imagination is free, then it can go anywhere, and the danger and vitality of this acceptance of potentiality – ever changing, never fixed, resistant of categorical and essentialised identities – is what gives writing its power against authority.

My androgynous 'I'/eye faces the page with the full knowledge of being female and Latinx but also with the fact that when this 'I'/eye looks at the blank canvas, they are also thinking about form and shape, line and composition, the complex sounds and etymologies of words, and the way that the Southern-ness of their voice – located in *el sur* of the North American, Eurocentric imaginary – is also the South of the blues, gospel, *el son*, *cante jondo* and its *duende* (tracing the nomadic trail of song), and secular hymns sung in many languages across at least one ocean or two. So, that when I/they inscribe the holler cries of the traumatised soldiers in *Holler River*, for instance, as a reflection of Falstaff and Hal in *King Henry, IV Part I*, it is coming from a 'third' place of seeing. This third space – or maybe by now it is fifth or seventh, depending on one's sense of history – allows for the multiplicity of the 'I' to render worlds outside themselves and thus simultaneously within.

Reading Shakespeare as a precocious youth was a first step in my journey towards understanding the complexities of being a multicultural human, ironically enough. Stumbling across Woolf led me towards a deeper comprehension of the beautiful instability of identity. Growing up partly in the American South awakened me to the complex, violent and difficult histories of the United States, especially in its acts of erasure, but also allowed me to recognise and find kinship with cadences desirous of freedom at all costs.

6

Caliban's Island: Gender, Queerness and Latinidad in Theatre for Young Audiences

Diana Burbano

I am an immigrant. I was born in Colombia, and my family emigrated to Cleveland, Ohio, in the mid-1970s. My family was the only Spanish-speaking family in the area. I was forced to learn English as quickly as possible. My mother struggled, but because I was younger, I had an easier time of it. I sat in front of the TV and absorbed English from Alaina Reed on *Sesame Street* and Morgan Freeman and Rita Moreno on *The Electric Company*. I loved language, the odd, hard, tongue-twisting English consonants. The crunch of them, the howl of the diphthongs. Unfortunately, I also had a severe lisp, and I could barely make myself understood in either language. I got plopped into theatre classes to help with my English, my shyness and my speech.

I was introduced to Shakespeare as a freshman in high school. We worked on *Romeo and Juliet*, which felt like a slog. To my dyslexic eyes, the play was as impossible to read as it was to understand. It didn't click until our teacher, Mrs Mack, wheeled in the old AV unit and popped in a videotape. Some man came onstage, and I rolled my eyes in anticipated boredom. Then he started a riff, playing Romeo *and* Juliet, making those words sing in a way I didn't know was possible. It was Ian McKellen's *Acting Shakespeare*.[1] I was riveted.

McKellen flew through characters with nothing more than a change of posture and his resonant voice. Unfortunately, we only got to watch forty-five minutes of the tape, and then the bell rang. This same thing happened four years in a row. I only saw the end of the show when, several years later, McKellen performed in San Francisco and I was lucky enough to be one of his onstage corpses. Listening to that gorgeous baritone sing 'Once more unto the breech' cemented my love both for McKellen and for the Bard.

Much to my immigrant parents' disappointment, I decided to study acting. The truth was, due to my learning disabilities, I was considered a terrible student. I had fantastic language skills, however, and I loved to be on stage.

I had an affinity for 'speaking the speech'. Shakespeare became my passion. I was lucky enough to have instructors who believed in me, and who gave me wonderful, challenging roles. I played La Pucelle, Lady Anne and Macbeth's First Witch. I adored the language. The power of the word. The power of his words in my mouth. I became a professional actor, and I studied Shakespeare at the Royal Shakespeare Company and the National Theatre of Great Britain.

However, opportunities to work in classical theatre were few and far between for a young Latinx woman. Despite my classical training, I got my Equity card doing Theatre for Young Audiences (TYA). I worked in TYA for most in my career as a stage actor as it offered some of the only opportunities to work professionally as a performer of colour. In contrast to the work being done on the main stages, TYA was the place where stories for and about people of colour flourished. When BIPOC (Black, Indigenous, and people of color) kids found a strong connection to the story being told, it was clear from their enthusiastic reaction how important and magical it was. In this essay, and through a focus on my 2017 play *Caliban's Island*, I detail my trajectory as a performer and playwright to attend to the ways in which classical training and Latinx identity can intersect in children's storytelling.

Creating Theatre for Young People

I started in TYA at the Bilingual Foundation for the Arts, a Latinx theatre company in Los Angeles that was founded by Carmen Zapata, Margarita Galban and Estela Scarlata in 1973. This company produces Latinx plays and often does the same play in English and Spanish, alternating the language weekly. At the Bilingual Foundation I performed for young children (up through the fourth grade), mostly English-language learners and children of colour, and often from impoverished backgrounds. Theatre was not a part of their lives. I lived for the change in the children's eyes as they started to buy into a story. The way the atmosphere in the room shifted and grew with a good performance was magical. The tired teachers would thank us, and tell us over and over again, 'They've never seen a play before; sorry if they were noisy.' They *were* noisy – they were engaged, worried about the characters, yelling at the bad guy, rolling their eyes at the sappy stuff.

I found this work exhausting, frustrating and educational. The kids told us right away if they thought something was stupid or dishonest. The late 1990s was a time when every TYA had a badly written 'rap' shoehorned into the show. The writers didn't seem to respect or understand rap as a form. A well-done rap is as thrilling as a well-spoken Shakespeare monologue and often even scans into iambic pentameter. The raps in these plays were not well done. They were a half-hearted effort to reach the primarily Latinx and African

American audience theatrically and they often failed spectacularly. I learned that you cannot pander to children; they won't let you get away with it.

Kids appreciate a good story. They don't behave like jaded subscribers, and the kids in our audience needed us. I loved being able to entertain them. Yet I learned early in my career that TYA tends to abandon kids after age ten or eleven. The plays I performed were always geared towards younger children. Perhaps that is what the grants that paid for the performances specified. I always felt that we did a major disservice to both the kids and the theatre by not trying to connect with the (admittedly more cynical, more difficult) middle school-aged kid.

The first play that I wrote, *Caliban's Island*, was for a TYA audience. I wanted to work on a piece for older kids that touched on themes of gender identity, 'Othering' and self-acceptance. I chose to adapt characters from Shakespeare mostly because I love the plays and never had a chance to perform them myself. I also figured that I could pitch the play to non-Latinx artistic teams. A female Latinx writer has a lot of strikes against her as far as the majority theatre is concerned, and, frankly, I wanted them to know I could speak their language.

Caliban's Island is a mash-up of *Twelfth Night* and *The Tempest*, with assorted Shakespearean characters and tropes. There are twins, a terrible storm, an island with magical beings. It begins with a storm that shipwrecks a young girl named Vi on a deserted island. A peculiar creature of indeterminate species named Cal is watching her as she awakens from her ordeal. He claims to have rescued Vi from certain death at sea. Vi is grateful to him, but her twin brother, Bast, is still missing, and she cannot rest until he is found.[2]

Shakespeare wrote wonderful roles for women, and that certainly appealed to me as a young person. Viola is brilliant and able, and also vulnerable and funny. Vi is the hero of the story; she is fighting against sexism and gender norms. She is on a difficult quest, and there is no romance at the end of it. She has to save her beloved brother, who is in distress and who needs her to rescue him. Shakespeare's Viola does find love at the end of *Twelfth Night*, but my Vi doesn't. I wanted my heroine's journey be an adventure and my play to show that women can be friends with men and not have it become sexualised. I wanted to explore a journey between people who have more on their minds than their hearts. These characters are all fighting to be allowed to live authentic lives and not be shoehorned into the roles society expects them to play. Vi and Cal become good friends, but there is no hint of a romance to mar the honest bond that happens between them.

I wanted to work on relationships between girls. In popular media, young girls are encouraged to be catty to one another, in a way that reinforces patriarchal dominance. Young women can't be allies because they can't be friends with one another. I created Mira, a character based on *The*

Tempest's Miranda, to represent the opposite of Vi. Mira is feminine and impulsive. She is a lonely girl who holds terrible power and doesn't know how to control it. I felt that it was important to show a young woman wrestling with her natural gifts and wishing to hide them. When we meet Mira, she is a lonely, vain, arrogant and bossy young girl who herself was shipwrecked on the island as a baby. The fairy Fluffy has been her primary companion ever since. Mira thinks Vi would make an amusing playmate, so she casts a spell and takes her prisoner. Vi and Mira seem to have nothing in common, but they learn to work together and to respect each other. Both have unique talents; Vi uses hers with ease, but Mira's gifts are too powerful, frightening, for a young girl. She feels embarrassed at her abilities because she cannot control them. With Vi's encouragement, Mira starts to own her power.

I teach students in the fifth and sixth grade. The change that happens to girls as they turn into tweens and teens is marked. They often go from being strong, bossy and outspoken to being shy, afraid to speak out, afraid to seem smarter than the boys. They start to get looks and comments about their bodies and faces, and they lose the freedom they had in childhood. Their bodies mature much faster than their minds, and confusion, anger and anxiety begin to play a bigger role in their lives. Mira embodies their confusion and their quicksilver personality changes. Vi is the fearless girl, who hasn't hidden her true personality. Vi and Mira, working together, learn that what makes them different also makes them an unbeatable team. The incorporation of magic adds an element of fun and style true to the original Shakespeare.

I chose to mash up *Twelfth Night* and *The Tempest* because I have always loved Viola's wit and felt great sympathy for Caliban; I wanted to see how they would behave with each other. With Caliban, my purpose was to reverse the tropes associated with him. Caliban, a person who does not fit into societal norms, is described as a monster. He is othered, outside, different and thus dangerous. I certainly related to that. I came to the United States as a child, unable to speak English. I worked hard, but I always felt different, uncomfortable. I failed miserably at school because of my learning disabilities, which made concentration difficult. I brought home one bad report card after another. I also got into trouble because, having been a victim of molestation at a young age, I was acting out my sexuality in 'inappropriate' ways. I became an outcast, both at school and in my family. The way Caliban is treated in *The Tempest*, as if he were stupid, as if he had no right to education or sexuality, seemed to me unfair and short-sighted. And it made me, perhaps unfairly, dislike Prospero, the adult who interferes, controlling and thus taking the joy out of magic.

As our society slowly opens up to non-binary sex roles, I wanted to give children a character that reflects that fluidity. Fluffy is a kid's version of Ariel, and they are a gender-fluid fairy. The other characters don't quite know what to make of Fluffy: what they are, whether they are servile, feral or sentient. Mira has trapped Fluffy. She commands them to do her bidding. Fluffy is misnamed, misgendered and enslaved. They also need to be seen as whole so they can live freely as their true self.

Along with creating two female protagonists and a gender-fluid fairy, I wanted to address the challenges of a patriarchal version of masculinity. Bast is Vi's twin brother, a Shakespearean trope that I use to emphasise both characters' discomfort with their gender norms. Where Vi is fierce, feisty and adventurous (read: masculine), Bast is gentle, shy and scholarly, a boy who is happier reading in his study than practising swordplay with his sister. I imagine the fights with his father, and the guilt that Bast must feel for not living up to his role in a patriarchal society.

The 'monster' in my play for children is a society that cannot accept differences. The journey is how they come to accept each other. There isn't a 'happy' ending. Vi and Bast, with Cal's help, devise a way to escape the island, to return to the world of 'normal' human society. Mira wants to come with them, but Cal knows how dangerous that world would be for her: human beings would not treat kindly her astonishing magical powers. Only when she has learned to suppress and control them could she hope to survive in that world. Mira sees the truth in Cal's words and awakens to the fact that he loves her and wants only to protect her. She is nevertheless disappointed, so, to mitigate her sadness and loneliness, she takes a forgetting potion. Vi and Bast sail away towards home.

I felt that tying things up in a neat bow would be a disservice to middle school-aged children. They have a deeper understanding of the vicissitudes of life. *Caliban's Island* was written as a way for middle schoolers to engage with Shakespearean language and tropes, while centring the issues that most affect them. The play was chosen for Creede Repertory's Headwaters Festival and is published by YouthPLAYS. It was described as 'part *Peter and the Starcatcher*, part Shakespeare, [the work of an author who] writes with a unique voice all her own'.[3] I believe the work is successful as well as accessible, and I am proud of it.

Making a Latinx Play

Caliban's Island isn't explicitly Latinx in its conception or characterisation. TYA may be the only theatrical form in America where 'diverse' casting is the norm. I had a development reading of the piece with Breath of Fire Latina Theater Ensemble in Santa Ana, California. The cast comprised, entirely, Latinx performers with classical training. I emphasise in the notes that the actors should be people of colour, but will they be? As someone who was often frozen out of opportunities because of my ethnicity, I fear that casting may default to the majority.

I am a Latinx playwright, so anything I write would and should be considered a Latinx play. My love of language and Shakespeare brought forth this play. I am bilingual, proficient and fluid in both languages. I like large, complicated words. Tom Stoppard is an immigrant playwright for whom English is a gleefully acquired language, and the way he examines and manipulates English delights me. I sometimes use words 'wrong' because I like the placement, the feel of them. Like Stoppard, I am an autodidact, and hence I never learned 'the rules'. I paint in words with abandon.

I ask my actors to really use their mouths and their lips. I want a heightened sense of language. I feel that Latinx actors have not been encouraged to use their voices in big, theatrical ways. They have been asked to flatten their accents, in order to be understood. Ian McKellen, in contrast, uses his own natural dialect, a beautiful Mancunian lilt that he employs to great effect. I love to hear the musical Latinx dialects really bite into the English language and reclaim it with their own music intact – no flattening to be understood, but a glorious dive into the different vowel sounds, the lisps and trills. The natural dialect enhances elevated language, conveying truthfulness, and it is my hope that actors who perform in my work feel able to use their natural voices in big, compelling ways.

Despite the fact that *Caliban's Island* is not explicitly marked as a 'Latinx play', it is permeated by Latinidad because I am Latinx. I would be honoured to hear, in ten to fifteen years, that a production of this piece has set another young immigrant on a path to becoming a writer. TYA is where I learned and honed my craft as a storyteller. For a long time, it was the only place I saw actors of colour performing diverse and virtuosic roles, and it was one of the only places where stories for Latinx people were actively solicited and presented. As things begin to shift in the American theatre – and as Latinx practitioners nudge their way into theatre spaces where previously they were not welcome – it is important to value TYA as an important piece of the narrative, and to not neglect the very important young audiences that deserve to see themselves reflected on stage. I will always return to TYA with joy for the gifts that it has given to me in my life and career.

Notes

1. First performed in 1980, the one-man show was broadcast in 1982. McKellen plays multiple Shakespearean roles.
2. The play text can be found online: Diana Burbano, *Caliban's Island* (Los Angeles: YouthPLAYS, 2017). Available at https://www.youthplays.com/

play/calibans-island-by-diana-burbano-418 (last accessed 12 November 2020).
3. 'Headwaters New Play Festival', Creede Repertory Theatre, updated August 2017. Available at http://www.creederep.org/headwaters-festi val-2017/ (last accessed 12 November 2020).

7

La Voz de Shakespeare: Empowering Latinx Communities to Speak, Own and Embody the Text

Cynthia Santos DeCure

Voice, speech and language are an act of rebellion. Deep-seated misconceptions that Shakespeare's words should primarily be spoken by the elite, with lofty voices, have contributed to our Latinx community's reluctance to speak Shakespeare aloud. These misgivings have suppressed our voices and have sown doubts that our voices may not be 'good enough' to tackle classical texts. As a result, Latinx acting students in learning institutions and in community theatres often apologise or communicate embarrassment when asked to work on Shakespeare's texts. However, the journey of learning, exploring and voicing Shakespeare can be a productive way to declare our vocal rights. In this chapter, I chronicle my experience vocal coaching and directing Shakespeare's *The Tempest*, and teaching predominantly Latinx students. I discuss the voice and speech methodologies with which I teach our community to manifest their vocal power, urging them to employ their unique voices to develop freedom, focus and presence. Ultimately, I argue that through the power of language and command of Shakespeare's text, Latinx actors can change our perceptions of voice and speech.

Shakespeare Is for All; *Shakespeare es para todos*

Shakespeare wrote for the masses, and to maintain his livelihood. Yet for some young Latinx actors, Shakespeare's utility and broad accessibility is not immediately evident. As an acting, voice, speech/dialects teacher and director, I have found numerous students and fellow Latinx actors to be reluctant, and even fearful, of working with Shakespeare's text. Their objections are laden with self-doubt – 'I don't understand it'; 'my English is not that good'; 'it's just not for me'; 'I have an accent'. These and other apprehensive rationales have created a shared perception within much of our community that Shakespeare's language belongs to the 'elite' – to those who seemingly naturally understand Elizabethan verse and have command of it. For many in our Latinx community, the result is exclusion from exploring and working with classical language.

From 2009 to 2011, I worked with Long Beach Shakespeare Company as a director and heading the education department. During that time, I co-created a Shakespeare Camp with the company's then co-artistic director. The camp served children of grades K–12. Students spent two weeks delving into all aspects of a Shakespeare play, including plot, characters, text, scenic design, costume and sound. In that short time span the campers learned their lines, created costumes and helped build the sets. The experience culminated with a showcase presentation of an adaptation of the chosen play. Our first-year camp worked on *The Tempest*. The text was abridged, but none of the language was altered, modernised or paraphrased.

One of the most remarkable discoveries I made working with younger camp students was the substantial degree of fearlessness they possessed when speaking and seeking to understand Shakespeare's language. The text was considered precious and they investigated it, then claimed ownership without reserve. And why not? No one had told them Shakespeare was inaccessible to children; no one had decreed them to be too young, or not possessed of the 'correct' voice or dialect to speak this text. These kids simply knew this was rich, abundant language packed with exciting discoveries.

At the end of the summer, as a finale of sorts, I directed a production of *The Tempest* for the Long Beach Sea Festival, at an outdoor pavilion in a lovely park beside the ocean. The production incorporated a combination of professional actors and recent college theatre graduates. A few high school students that had attended the camp also played minor roles. There were five Latinx actors in total out of sixteen in the cast. As I began to work through rehearsal, I discovered that the Latinx actor playing Ferdinand, a recent college theatre graduate, was having difficulty with text. When asked go through the text, his voice would crack with nervousness and he would stop and start, often not finishing the thought with breath. He would apologise about his voice, and for not receiving enough Shakespeare instruction in college. He revealed that despite his undergraduate programme's affiliation with a Shakespeare festival on campus, Latinxs were not frequently asked to work on Shakespeare. Although he had earned his degree, he felt sad and ashamed of his lack of command of the language. He found himself hesitant to work freely, physically and vocally, especially in the presence of the more experienced actors in the cast.

Unfortunately, I have encountered multiple Latinx actors in the classroom that shared similar sentiments. They recounted receiving disparaging critiques from a teacher, or an outspoken classmate, leading them to believe Shakespeare was not for them; furthermore, such criticism fostered the corrosive notion that unless their voices had a prescribed sound and they could easily decode Elizabethan language, they had no business speaking Shakespeare aloud.

Attitudes about language and the hierarchy of speech sounds have subjected actors to injurious comments in academia and the profession. Our education system has propagated the 'othering' of non-native English speakers and those with idiolects outside of the perceived standard American English pronunciation. For our Latinx community, which includes many dual language speakers, this bias against perceived outsiders can lead to feelings of linguistic persecution and linguistic insecurity. In their book *Latinos Facing Racism*, sociology professors Joe R. Faegin and José A. Cobas note the diminishment Latinx communities have faced due to speech alone:

> Language devaluing entails whites ignoring speakers of Spanish even when they have a good command of the-middle-class version of English. In various social settings Latinos are oftentimes ignored by whites as people not worth listening to, as if their mother tongue renders their message meaningless and underserving of white attention.[1]

They further document how Latinx racial characteristics, even outside of language pronunciation, can elicit discriminatory behaviour. These institutional perspectives, and prejudicial treatment, may well contribute to the fear and trepidation Latinx actors feel when attempting to perform Shakespeare.

Yet the sounds on Shakespeare's original stages did not follow any prescriptive or homogeneous speech pattern. In fact, the performers of his works in Elizabethan and Jacobean times represented many regions of what is now a unified United Kingdom. There was no 'standard accent' in that era; the pronunciation encompassed a diverse blend of accents coming from various parts of the country. The British linguist David Crystal has extensively researched and documented Original Pronunciation (OP).[2] Original Pronunciation, as Crystal describes it, is the reconstructed sound system (the accent) as it would have been heard in the period of Early Modern English, during Shakespeare's time. This historical phonology offers a new way to pronounce Shakespeare in contrast to the modern Queen's English or Received Pronunciation that is most widely utilised in England. I was fortunate to participate in a Shakespeare OP workshop that David and his son, actor and director Ben Crystal, taught at the Royal Central Speech and Drama. The workshop demonstrated the myriad of accents and pronunciation variances that were employed in Shakespeare's plays in Elizabethan times. We looked at the phonetic transcription of the text in OP and learned which sounds influenced pronunciation. One of the most memorable impressions I had was that the OP – in particular, the expressiveness of the prosody, the musicality, and the tone and rhythm – sounded much like the blended accents of my

Latinx students in East Los Angeles. Yet English teachers and authors such as John Barton, Cicely Berry and Patsy Rodenburg, among others, have written analyses of the 'classical' techniques of speaking and performing Shakespeare. These approaches have influenced not just actor training in the United States but the manner in which Shakespeare's work is examined and produced.

Working on Shakespeare demands deep investment in the words, not just as we speak them with our voices, but with a physical, emotional connection to the text. My mentor, Catherine Fitzmaurice, creator of Fitzmaurice Voicework,[3] stresses that 'voice is action', meaning it affects both the speaker and the listener. In working with Latinx actors, I urge them to experience the text with their whole bodies, to personalise the words and embody the emotional weight of each vowel and the power of each consonant. It is a far freer and more intuitive process to listen to the text with its marvellous variety of sounds, rather than to merely follow uniform, conventional speaking patterns.

The late voice teacher Kristin Linklater promoted engaging one's imagination as a way to go beyond mere fixed speech patterns and actually connect with words; she explained, 'By indulging sensory, sensual, emotional and physical responses to vowels and consonants – the component parts of words – we begin to resurrect the life of the language.'[4] My training in the voice and speech techniques of Rodenburg, Linklater, Fitzmaurice Voicework and Knight-Thompson Speechwork has provided me with multiple ways to help actors achieve a sense of vocal freedom, including the activation of imagination.

Linguistic Rebellion – Claiming and Embodying Shakespeare as Our Own

My task is to guide the Latinx actor to embody the language, but also to empower her to unapologetically claim it as her own. I like to think Shakespeare would approve, as he understood how colonisers forced their subjects to adopt the oppressor's language. When Caliban rebels against his coloniser, Prospero, he declares:

You taught me language, and my profit on 't
Is I know how to curse. The red plague rid you
For learning me your language![5]

In the summer production of *The Tempest*, I worked one-on-one with the struggling Latinx actor playing Ferdinand to first expand his connection to breath. We began with Fitzmaurice Voicework's 'destructuring' process, which employs yoga-like, tremor positions to activate the transversus abdominis and encourage more expansive breath capacity.[6] These positions also help wake up the nervous system and the imagination. We followed by using words from the text, in particular the nouns and verbs in Ferdinand's log speech:

> There be some sports are painful, and their labor
> Delight in them sets off. Some kinds of baseness
> Are nobly undergone, and most poor matters
> Point to rich ends. This my mean task
> Would be as heavy to me as odious, but
> The mistress which I serve quickens what's dead
> And makes my labours pleasures.[7]

I encouraged the actor to spend time with the images, 'on breath', one image at a time. For example, with the word '*sports*', we worked on Fitzmaurice Voicework's tremoring (inducing involuntary shaking to free the body), and breathing the image; for '*painful*', breathing in a new image; for '*labour*', locating a new image, and so on. The actor was able to connect in a sensory way. The stronger the image, the stronger the communication. His breath expanded and his volume and tone increased. I did not prompt him to become louder; his connection to images guided the breath. The dynamic effort of the tremorwork mirrored the image of '*my mean task*' in the text and continued to work through the piece connecting the body and the images.

This mode of working was the jumping-off point for the actor to access the text. The connection to words and images also allowed him to find more vocal variety, pitch, stress and rhythm. When actors make a connection to the emotional and vocal truth of Shakespeare's text – and when they experience it with their whole body – they can begin to embody the language as their own. This has been my primary approach in the classroom with Latinx students. Orientation with the English language varies from student to student; I'm sensitive to that fact based on personal experience. English is not my first language; although I was taught English in primary school in Puerto Rico, my primary language is Spanish. We all have a personal history with language, and I adjust my approach to meet each student's individual experience and needs. For the actor playing Ferdinand, I was able to relate to him more easily by speaking to him in both Spanish and English.

I recall the late Puerto Rican actor Raúl Juliá, and the vibrant and unabashed command of Shakespeare's text he displayed in several productions in Joseph Papp's Public Theater in New York. His performances were my most early influences as an actor. The *New York Times* critic Brock Brower wrote of Juliá's textual command in August 1978, noting his originality:

> [. . .] his rhythm is not that of Elizabethan rhetoric. He has a Latin cadence that may say something about why they call English blank verse . . . blank.

When he pulls it all together, making the words fit the reggae, what audiences get from Raul Julia – at 37, commonly acknowledged one of the best actors in Joseph Papp's stable – is an upended, zealous, but oddly classical reinterpretation.[8]

Juliá himself was vocal about bringing his own culture and rhythm to his approach to Shakespeare, stating that 'Shakespeare is too big to be put into one little way of doing it'.[9] It is towards that freedom and experimentation that I coach actors.

The path to learning and having command of the language has been a long one for me, but in studying acting and specialising in voice and speech, I have gained a unique perspective of the actions of speech from the point of view of both a Spanish and an English speaker. I understand the challenges my students, Latinx or non-Latinx, encounter when approaching Shakespeare or other classical texts. Most recently, I worked with a young actress from Puerto Rico on one of Emilia's monologues from *Othello*'s Act IV, scene iii. Her first pass at the monologue lacked clarity and a full understanding of what she was saying. We talked about what Emilia was saying, about husbands and wives, why Emilia's statements were important at this time in the play, and how the text still related to marriages today. I then asked the actress to simply speak the text as if she were gossiping with a friend in Puerto Rico. I asked her to use her whole body as she spoke the text. What emerged vocally was a passionate Emilia full of unforced vocal variety and rhythm – a voice authentic to this actress, expressive and true to the text. Even in the short time we spent working through this monologue, she was able to find and navigate a physical and emotional path to the text. For the both of us, teacher and student, it was a unique experience as Latinas – *Puertoriqueñas* – to culturally connect through the unparalleled words of Shakespeare.

As Latinx actors we need to be bold and rebellious like Caliban, to take on the language of the coloniser and make it our own, to use our bodies and the full extent of our imaginations, to find the cadence – the music – in our authentic rhythms of speech. Voice and speech work is for everyone. *Shakespeare es para todos.*

Notes

1. Joe R. Faegin and José A. Cobas, *Latinos Facing Racism: Discrimination, Resistance, and Endurance* (New York: Paradigm Publishers, 2014).
2. David Crystal, *The Oxford Dictionary of Original Shakespearean Pronunciation* (Oxford: Oxford University Press, 2016).
3. Fitzmaurice Voicework is a voice system that combines adaptations of classical voice training techniques with modifications of yoga, shiatsu,

bioenergetics, energy work and many other disciplines. This integration serves to integrate the voluntary and involuntary aspects of nervous system and the voice.

4. Kristin Linklater, *Freeing Shakespeare's Voice* (New York: Theatre Communications Group, 1992).

5. William Shakespeare, *The Tempest*, in *The Norton Shakespeare*, 3rd edn, ed. Stephen Greenblatt, Walter Cohen, Suzanne Gossett, Jean E. Howard, Katharine Eisaman Maus and Gordon McMullan (New York: W. W. Norton, 2016), I.ii.362–4.

6. Destructuring is the initial stage of Fitzmaurice Voicework which promotes awareness and liveliness in the body, spontaneous and free breathing, and wide-ranging vocal expressivity – using Tremorwork® and a variety of other dynamic exercises and hands-on work.

7. Shakespeare, *The Tempest*, III.i.1–7.

8. Brock Brower, 'Shakespeare's *Shrew* with No Apologies', *New York Times*, 6 August 1978. Available at https://www.nytimes.com/1978/08/06/archives/shakespeares-shrew-with-no-apologies-shakespeares-shrew-with-no.html (last accessed 6 July 2020).

9. *Kiss Me, Petruchio*, dir. Christopher Dixon, perf. Meryl Streep and Raúl Juliá, USA, 1981.

8

Shakespeare's Ghosts: Staging Colonial Histories in New Mexico

Marissa Greenberg

A keyword search for 'Shakespeare' in historical newspapers published in New Mexico turns up a striking range of results.[1] In English- and Spanish-language publications from the mid-nineteenth century onward, we routinely find quotations from Shakespeare's plays and allusions to popular characters, reviews of world-renowned performances and advertisements for local productions, debate pieces on the authorship question and literary discussions by enthusiasts and scholars alike. While scholars have shown how Shakespeare haunts US history, culture and identity, the American Southwest has received relatively scant attention and New Mexico virtually none. Yet New Mexican historical newspapers, written in the languages of foreign and domestic imperialism, register Shakespeare's impact in a region shaped by legacies of colonialism.

This chapter explores the role of Shakespeare, both as a body of work and as a cultural icon, in New Mexico's 'double colonial history'.[2] Colonised first by Spain and then by the United States, New Mexico, like much of the American Southwest, is haunted by peoples speaking diverse languages but unified by shared experiences of systemic subjugation and homogenisation. This essay examines some appropriations of Shakespeare's plays and iconic status to tell this double colonial history. In New Mexico, I argue, Shakespeare makes audible the ghosts of empire building, if at times also contributing to the suppression of spectral voices.

As a critical trope, ghosts offer both challenges and opportunities. Alice Rayner warns: 'On the one hand, [ghosts] remain imaginary figures and can thus be dismissed as imaginary. [. . .] On the other, these figures represent realities so horrifyingly real either personally or historically that the trope may trivialize those realities.'[3] With these limits in mind, Rayner claims ghosts and ghosting as a powerful 'vocabulary' for an 'epistemology that does not explain away the losses, [. . .] but incorporates those losses with an embodied ethics that does not rely on rationalist principles of an absolute and imaginary

justice but is not without reason'.[4] Rayner's definition comes out of theories
of theatrical ghosting as a repetition with difference that has affective and cognitive effects on audiences. According to Herbert Blau and Marvin Carlson,
the theatre is haunted by characters, gestures and properties, among other
material aspects of performance, that return again and again, like spirits of the
dead, to animate action onstage.[5] Yet Rayner's vocabulary also resonates with
another strain of performance studies, one that understands ghosting in terms
of 'genealogies of performance [that] document – and suspect – the historical
transmission and dissemination of cultural practices through collective representations'.[6] Joseph Roach, Diana Taylor and Leo Cabranes-Grant, among
others, have examined ghosting in colonial contexts, in which theatrical and
cultural performance reaffirms, challenges or simultaneously reproduces and
rearranges structures of privilege and oppression.[7]

Drawing on these different notions of ghosts and ghosting, I embrace
an epistemology of loss within a broadly materialist and bluntly historicist
framework. Specifically, I examine instances in which Shakespeare – as work
and as icon – frames performances of New Mexico's colonial past and thus
amplifies voices of this fraught history. Human residence in New Mexico
began more than eleven thousand years before the first Europeans arrived
in the region. The ancient peoples and cultures that thrived in the area and
that left behind evidence of complex civilisations, such as the ruins at Chaco
Canyon (a UNESCO World Heritage site),[8] were followed by nomadic
and Pueblo Indians, including the Apache and Navajo. Spanish ventures to
the region began in the late 1400s, and in 1598, Juan de Oñate marched on
what would become Neuvo México, overpowering Indigenous communities
and establishing a colonial seat that moved to Santa Fe in 1610. As soldiers,
missionaries and settlers continued to arrive, martial and ideological conflicts
with Apache and Pueblo tribes became common, culminating in the Pueblo
Revolt of 1680, which left thousands of Spanish dead and forced survivors to
flee the area. A ceremonial reconquest in 1692 restored colonial rule, which
lasted until 1821, when Mexico won its independence from Spain. The same
year witnessed the establishment of the Santa Fe Trail, which catalysed 'a
reorientation of perspective', according to historian Henry Tobias, in which
'an east–west axis of interest cut into the traditional north–south axis'.[9] This
reorientation solidified after the Mexican–American War (1846–48), with
New Mexico becoming a US territory in 1850; and again after the introduction of the railroad (1879–80), with the territory becoming the forty-seventh
state in 1912. During this more than half-century of military, commercial
and political expansion, the United States embarked on systematic campaigns
to displace and/or assimilate Indians and Mexicans in the region. Driven by
waves of confrontation and conversion, trade and technology, the colonisation
of New Mexico produced ghosts speaking diverse languages.

This chapter looks at performances in which Shakespeare is deployed to make these ghosts heard. A theatrical adaptation, stagings of American mythologies, and current-day local and global performances all reflect the complex role of Shakespeare in New Mexico's theatrical and cultural self-awareness. Even as Shakespeare's plays and iconic status authorise performances of New Mexico's colonial history, Shakespeare also contributes to the perpetuation of a selective historiography. The voices of the past speak from various Shakespearean stages, but these performances also demand that we listen for voices that remain forcibly silenced.

Spectral Adaptations

My first example is *The Merchant of Santa Fe*, a 'radical adaptation' of Shakespeare's *The Merchant of Venice*, written in New Mexico in 1993.[10] The play was commissioned by La Compañia de Teatro de Albuquerque, an Albuquerque-based theatre company founded in 1977, and written by the troupe's artistic director Ramón A. Flores in collaboration with playwright Lynn Butler Knight and with input from the community in the tradition of the Chicano teatro movement.[11] Set in colonial New Spain circa 1670, with a dramatis personae of Catholics, crypto-Jews and Native Americans, *The Merchant of Santa Fe* gives voice to some but certainly not all of the ghosts created by Spanish colonialism.

In the 1623 folio of Shakespeare's plays, *The Merchant of Venice* is listed among the comedies; yet, like a Renaissance revenge play, it registers the demands of the past on the present. And although no ghosts come onstage in *The Merchant of Venice*, a spectral presence is palpable in the romantic plot line. Lamenting the casket test by which a man must win her hand in marriage, and thus her wealth, Portia points to a potent if unseen paternal force: 'I may neither choose who I would nor refuse who I dislike; so is the will of a living daughter curbed by the will of a dead father.'[12] The demands of the past on the present are evident not only within the dramatic fiction but also in the play's performance history. After the Holocaust, it became virtually impossible to stage *The Merchant of Venice* without taking into consideration its place in the centuries of anti-Semitic violence that culminated in the murder of six million Jews.[13] Perhaps ironically, given its role in perpetuating racism over time and space, Shakespeare's play offered New Mexicans an opportunity to give voice to some of the regional victims of this global history.[14]

A key moment in this history began in Iberia in 1492 with the expulsion of Jews who refused conversion to Christianity. In the sixteenth and seventeenth centuries, some of the tens of thousands of these *conversos* came to the northernmost reaches of colonial Spanish America. Here, they might become crypto-Jews, secretly maintaining their ancestral Jewish identity while outwardly conforming to Catholicism and thus avoiding Inquisitorial prosecution for heresy. In the 1980s, fervent scholarly inquiry and local and national media attention brought this hidden history into the open and raised new questions about identity politics and resource allocation in New Mexico.[15] These revelations and debates spurred the commission of *The Merchant of Santa Fe*. The play attempts to speak to and for the ghosts of New Mexicans, past and not-so-past, who seek to retain their faith, culture and identity in the face of persecution.

In *The Merchant of Santa Fe*, this spectral presence coalesces around Portìa, who, unlike her Shakespearean namesake, is the descendent of Portuguese Jews. Neither the other characters nor the audience is fully aware of Portìa's crypto-Jewish identity until the final moments of the play when she reveals her ancestry to Rafael, the play's Bassanio character. Portìa's revelation puts a spin on her introduction to the play. Rafael relates his first sight of Portìa 'at Mass last New Year's Eve' where her eyes, 'lit with an inner fire', distracted him from the Gloria.[16] He also dubs her 'my Lady of the Apples', a reference to Manzano, the estate that she inherits from her father and whose name means 'apple tree' in Spanish.[17] But his epithet is also suggestive of female hagiography and, for New Mexican audiences, Our Lady of Conquest (or La Conquistadora) specifically.[18] This statue of the Virgin Mary has resided in Santa Fe, New Mexico, since the early seventeenth century, and the local audiences of *The Merchant of Santa Fe* might imagine her presence in the church where Rafael first sees Portìa. At the start of the play, Rafael wants to know 'que pasión brillaba en esos ojos negros' ('what passion shines in those black eyes'). At the play's end, he learns that the most likely answer is not fervent Catholic faith but a secret Jewish history. When Rafael realises that his bride descends from Portuguese Jews, Portìa tells him: 'Shhh, amor. Welcome to the family.'[19] Although she is identified with the Holy Mother of the Catholic Church in New Mexico, Portìa ties her identity to an earthly Jewish family whose story must be told in whispers.

Another story of Jewish ancestry is related in hushed tones by Lieutenant Manzanares, a character that has no counterpart in Shakespeare's play. Manzanares sings 'Durme, durme, hermoso hijico' ('Sleep, sleep my beloved son'), a traditional lullaby with lyrics in Ladino, a Judeo-Spanish language less well known than its Judeo-German cousin, Yiddish.[20] He then explains that he learned the song from his mother, who came 'from an old converso family', and who would sing it 'on Friday nights' when the Jewish Sabbath begins.[21] When a pair of Catholic zealots overhear Manzanares singing and accuse him of being a hidden Jew, Manzanares defends himself by 'making the sign of the cross' and explaining that his father 'was an Old Christian hasta los meros huesos' ('down to the very bones').[22] Like Portìa, Manzanares performs a Catholic zeal that may or may not be authentic but certainly serves to conceal crypto-Jewish lineage. Just as importantly, neither character's per-formance of Christianity precludes them from giving voice to ghostly family histories and practices. In this way, *The Merchant of Santa Fe* enacts a rehearsal of crypto-Jewish identity that, according to some scholars, continues to be told, generation after generation, through to the present.[23]

Energising this intergenerational haunting is a traumatic history of perse-cution. Portìa, Manzanares and other crypto-Jewish characters conceal their identity for fear of discovery by the Inquisition. The single tribunal in the Spanish Americas sat in Mexico City, more than nineteen hundred kilometres as the crow flies from Santa Fe, and it was expected to exercise bureau-cratic control over a geographically vast and increasingly populous empire. Moreover, as Stuart B. Schwartz writes, conditions in many parts of New Spain created 'a vibrant culture at odds with the dominant ideologies of Church and state'.[24] *The Merchant of Santa Fe* thematises the distance between its New Mexican setting and the colonial capital and enacts both the dissent and the tolerance that Schwartz describes. Nonetheless, the Inquisition haunts the lives of crypto-Jews in the play. As characters read from official records and recount local instances of interrogation, torture and execution, *The Merchant of Santa Fe* resurrects the Inquisition's material presence in colonial New Mexico. Shakespeare is reworked to tell familial and communal stories, both written and spoken, of enduring identity and its violent oppression.

Even as it gives voice to the crypto-Jewish ghosts of colonialism and espe-cially the Inquisition, *The Merchant of Santa Fe* simultaneously acknowledges and silences Native American victims of Spanish conquest. The play's dramatis personae includes two Genízaros, or enslaved Plains Indians who were taken from their tribes as children and indoctrinated in Spanish culture.[25] This indoctrination is palpable in the play's linguistic diversity. While the majority of the play is in modern-day English, several characters deliver lines in the Spanish dialect that developed in New Mexico and southern Colorado, and Manzanares is not the only crypto-Jewish character to speak Ladino. But Indigenous languages go literally unheard in *The Merchant of Santa Fe*. When Làzaro, the Lancelot Gobbo character, 'bluff[s]' knowledge of Apache to a would-be employer, gabbling 'Alshecoathe ne nazat shquack',[26] the play not only exposes the silence enforced by colonial and Inquisitorial ideologies but also replicates and perpetuates it. The intergenerational effects of this silencing are evident in the character of Nerisa, who rejects her Apache lineage along with the epithet Genízara when she marries a Spaniard. Descendants of New Mexico's Genízaros, like descendants of colonial crypto-Jews before them, are currently spurring research that aims to discover histories of assimilation and its aftermath.[27] Yet *The Merchant of Santa Fe* does not give as full voice to these Indigenous ghosts as to the spirits of New Mexico's European past.[28]

I dub *The Merchant of Santa Fe* a spectral adaptation because the play repeats colonialism's silencing of colonised peoples in the American Southwest. Admittedly, later in New Mexico's double colonial history, some colonisers were themselves forcibly adapted into the dominant culture. Yet in its representation of an earlier period in this history, the play gives a megaphone to the colonisers but not the colonised. In doing so, it effectively if unwittingly perpetuates histories of trauma that include suppression of native languages and ways of being. Although Shakespeare's work helps exorcise one ghostly presence in New Mexico, it remains haunted by structures of privilege and oppression that it also replicates.

Ghost Town of Shakespeare

In the southwest corner of New Mexico, close to the borders with Arizona, Texas and Mexico, lies a quintessential ghost town named Shakespeare.[29] The town, including its name, has a storied past. Once a watering hole called Mexican Spring, it became a stop for stagecoaches with the establishment of the transcontinental mail route in 1857. The American Civil War saw it as a Confederate fort, although it witnessed no battles, and at the end of the war, the settlement was newly baptised Grant. In 1869, after silver deposits were discovered in nearby hills, William C. Ralston, founder of the Bank of California, decided to invest in the settlement and bestow his name on it. Ralston became a happening town, according to popular account, with the requisite number of saloons but without a church, school or sheriff's office. When silver deposits proved less deep than expected and diamonds purportedly unearthed in the Pyramid Mountains were revealed to have been salted, Ralston fell into disrepute and waned. In 1879, Colonel William G. Boyle and General John Boyle bought the original mines and renamed the town Shakespeare.

Whereas the settlement's previous names attest to natural, military and financial resources, its last and current name reflects the cultural resource that is Shakespeare. According to Rita Hill, who purchased the town of Shakespeare with her husband, Frank, in 1935, the Boyles named the town Shakespeare both as a tribute to their English origins and as an attempt at rebranding after the financial scandal of Ralston. In *Then and Now, Here and Around Shakespeare*, a thin book that is part local mythology, part family history and part walking tour, Rita Hill writes:

> Since the old Burro Mines at Ralston City meant swindle and crooked work to so many people, these men renamed the camp to please their English ears and the main street became Avon Avenue in the town of Shakespeare. It was advertised as if it were a new camp and old buildings were remodeled and called 'new'.[30]

While certainly reasonable, this explanation does not take into account Shakespeare's significance in the late nineteenth-century United States. In 1879, to call a mining town Shakespeare was to identify with 'Anglo-American monoculture', in which Shakespeare had growing popularity, both among the 'literati' and in 'mass culture'.[31] At the same time, the name appropriates the English author, conveying gentlemanly legitimacy and advertising a self-made man.[32] Simply put, the name Shakespeare reflected many values associated with the so-called American frontier.

The Hills embraced the power that the frontier mythos shared with the name Shakespeare. Before and after Rita Hill wrote and self-published *Then and Now*, the Hills used performance to promote the town and to raise funds for its restoration. Rita, Frank and their daughter, Janaloo, conducted walking tours in the costumes and personae of the frontier. Then, in 1962, Rita conceived of a grander theatrical endeavour, entitled 'Shadows in Shakespeare':

> We wrote a series of scenes – monologs [*sic*] – women who went down to the spring at Shakespeare, for water, through the years. These were women of the types which, we know, were here and some were patterned after real women though, of course, we used no names.[33]

In her own self-published book, in a chapter entitled 'A Horseback Trip to California and Other Theaterly Adventures', Janaloo describes taking her mother's show on the road – and she attempts to explain its failure.[34] One factor that Janaloo does not consider, however, is the omission of Shakespeare's plays from 'Shadows in Shakespeare'. Indeed, the scenes appropriated none of Shakespeare's characters, lines, plots or theatrical devices, such as gender cross-dressing. Shakespeare lent the town mythology and legitimacy but not, it would appear, a dramatic legacy or a performance practice.

The result was to silence the very ghosts that the Hills intended to make audible. 'Shadows in Shakespeare' reflects a sincere if naïve effort to give voice to the past. Rita wrote and Janaloo impersonated 'types' of women from Shakespeare circa 1856–1962: an Anglo pioneer, a dancehall girl, the daughter of a Mexican cantina owner, 'a young' and 'very flirtatious matron', a 'hysterical', older Mexican woman, and Janaloo at ten years old and again as an adult.[35] On the one hand, 'Shadows in Shakespeare' feels socially progressive. Written and performed by women, the drama focuses exclusively on the lived experiences of women of various ethnicities, ages and situations. On the other hand, 'Shadows in Shakespeare' perpetuates oppressive logics by occluding histories and populations that precede US hegemony.[36] The character that opens the show – an Anglo pioneer woman in 1856, the year before stagecoaches arrived – is, to all intents and purposes, representative of Frederick J. Turner's 'frontier thesis'. Introduced at the end of the nineteenth century, Turner's frontier thesis conceptualises US expansion and settlement in celebratory and jingoistic terms. Anglo-American people and institutions, he wrote, '[adapted] to the changes involved in crossing a continent, in winning a wilderness, and in developing at each area of this progress out of the primitive economic and political conditions of the frontier into the complexity of city life'.[37] Although this thesis persists in the popular imagination, critics have pointed out its reduction of the complexities of US imperialism to streamlined narratives of teleology, sovereignty and consent. What recent scholarship makes clear is the way that the myth of the frontier energised 'articulations of national identity and territoriality' that, as Mark Rifkin shows, simulated, regulated and silenced competing voices.[38] These competing voices included both Mexicans and Native Americans residing in New Mexico upon its US annexation in 1846. Appropriating historical tensions between these populations, the US government asserted its jurisdictional authority by not only replicating the methods of colonial land grants and forcible displacement but also recasting Mexicans as white in opposition to Indian otherness. In 'Shadows in Shakespeare', Shakespeare the icon becomes complicit in this whitewashing of the past in a manner that reveals a historical need to perceive the United States as geographically and culturally unified.

Whether packaged as manifest destiny, civilising process, acquisitive individualism or democratic development, the frontier thesis omits the silencing of entire populations by political, economic and social institutions. In the final chapters of *Then and Now*, Rita Hill acknowledges this silencing when she registers ghosts who haunt Shakespeare, New Mexico, yet whose stories remain untold. Taking the reader on a chorographic tour of the town, in a manner reminiscent of John Stow's 1598 *A Survey of London*, Hill relates the town's history through a combination of architectural description and local legend. Stories of murder and execution, peeping Toms and drunken brawls, become mapped onto Shakespeare's main drag, Avon Avenue. This virtual tour and *Then and Now* conclude in a two-room building. The older of the rooms is 'an Indian type construction of mud and rock in forms. The lintels over the door and windows are cedar poles and the ceiling is the original one of yucca stalks covered with dirt'.[39] Rita finds 'this room [. . .] most interesting of all' because it feels haunted by the men who sheltered, died and killed there: 'there are more stories its walls could tell, if they could talk, than those of other buildings. Someday, some way, we may know some of these stories. Perhaps the ghosts will break their silence and tell us things we wish to know.'[40] What has gotten in the way of these ghosts breaking their silence is Shakespeare's iconic presence.[41] Representative of Anglo-American identity and authority, Shakespeare perpetuates narratives of displacement, assimilation and exclusion, even when the name is catalysed to unsettle these same narratives.

What's Past Is Prologue

On 8 April 1916, the editors of *La Estrella*, published in Las Cruces, New Mexico, informed readers about a performance of *As You Like It* on 22 April at the New Mexico College of Agriculture and Mechanic Arts, now New Mexico State University, in commemoration of the tercentenary of Shakespeare's death.[42] One hundred years later, in February 2016, a copy of the 1623 *The Workes of William Shakespeare* (the 'First Folio') came to Santa Fe, New Mexico, as part of a national tour organised and sponsored by the Folger Shakespeare Library in commemoration of the four hundredth anniversary of Shakespeare's death.[43] The arrival of the tour, *First Folio! The Book That Gave Us Shakespeare*, at the New Mexico Museum of Art was met by a rich repertoire of events, including a roundtable with theatre practitioners, scholarly lectures and an art exhibit, that put Shakespeare's works in local and regional contexts.[44]

First Folio! in New Mexico thus tapped into contemporary enthusiasm for site-specific Shakespeare. In Albuquerque, in Santa Fe, and throughout the state, audiences have supported regional, university and youth performances of Shakespeare's plays. The 2010s witnessed an emphasis on stagings that bring Shakespeare's plays, and thus audiences, into a variety of New Mexican spaces. For example, in 2010 Lauren Albonico, a graduate of the University of New Mexico's Department of Theatre Arts and Dance, spearheaded 'Shakespeare on the Rail'. On select trains of the New Mexico Rail Runner, a commuter system that runs between Santa Fe and Albuquerque, local actors staged – and, as of summer 2019, have continued to stage – scenes from Shakespeare's plays, 'fully immers[ing] the performance into the space in which it takes place', as Albonico told a reporter for the *Santa Fe New Mexican*.[45] Also in 2010 the Vortex Theatre, an Albuquerque theatre established in 1976, inaugurated its annual Shakespeare festival. Originally called 'Will Power', the festival was renamed 'Shakespeare on the Plaza' in 2014, when performances were moved from the Vortex's black box theatre to an open-air stage in Albuquerque's Civic Plaza.

These site-specific performances have begun to take on contemporary social and political issues, pairing local places and current events to highlight the relevance of Shakespeare in modern-day New Mexico. In 2016, for example, Shakespeare on the Plaza staged a 'New Mexican version' of *Much Ado about Nothing* that highlighted New Mexico's Spanish heritage,[46] and director Dennis R. Elkins framed his 2018 plaza production of *The Merry Wives of Windsor* in the context of the #MeToo movement. In a similar vein, in 2017 Aux Dog Theatre in Albuquerque's Nob Hill neighbourhood inaugurated a 'new Bardian branch of annual productions' named Shakespeare 505, which nods to New Mexico's area code.[47] That summer, director Vicki

Liberatori staged *Much Ado about Nothing* in a way that layered New Mexican places and cultures. The play was set in current-day Placitas, an idyllic village situated between Albuquerque and Santa Fe, and was staged at the Aux Dog and in Nob Hill's Triangle Park. Changes to the play text, such as the addition of 'by Our Lady of Guadalupe' and the use of Hispanic dialects, highlighted the connections between locale and local ways of being.[48] In 2018, again under Liberatori's direction, Aux Dog set *Measure for Measure* in Albuquerque to highlight 'crime and political corruption in our own state'.[49]

This list of site-specific and/or presentist performances would seem to suggest the appropriation of Shakespeare – both as work and as icon – to the exploration of New Mexican geography, history and culture, both past and present. If *First Folio!* created additional opportunities for New Mexicans to learn about Shakespeare and his local resonance, it also risked replicating New Mexico's colonisation by European and American monoculture. Robin Williams, founder and leader of the International Shakespeare Center Santa Fe, cited *First Folio!* as a source of new support for building 'Santa Fe's very own Globe Theatre, offering world-quality presentations of Shakespeare's works, drawing fans from around the country and even farther afield'.[50] Williams's comment is striking for two reasons. First, to borrow Martin Orkin's terminology, it values metropolitan Shakespeares, such as the Folger Shakespeare Library and Shakespeare's Globe Theatre, over local ones.[51] The implication is that New Mexican institutions for the study and performance of Shakespeare are insufficient, less legitimate, and in need of infusion by elite, urban Anglo-American expertise. Second, Williams's proposal privileges a centralised Globe Theatre for a global audience over distributed, site-specific stages for local audiences. This vision of Shakespeare in New Mexico is void of New Mexicans, who would likely be displaced from the stage by professional actors and from the playhouse by elevated ticket prices.[52] Such displacement would replicate New Mexico's imperial history in a new mode.

Theatre, like ghosts, needs living, non-actorly actors to take action on behalf of the past. 'Theatre [. . .] can both represent and exhibit action,' Rayner writes, 'but in any political, pragmatic, or even personal sense, theatre is a force without obvious or immediate consequence, which is not to say it is inconsequential. But ghosts do not have the power of action. Hence, they call upon the living to act for them.'[53] In New Mexico, Shakespeare – from the staging of *The Merchant of Santa Fe*, to the Hills' amateur theatricals, to recent local productions – is frequently used to act on behalf of the region's ghosts. Indeed, Shakespeare serves explorations of New Mexico's colonial history and its implications for identity politics, national mythologies, and economic and cultural priorities in the state. It is precisely these repeated enactments of the past in the present, rather than exorcism or restitution, that ghostly voices demand and that Shakespeare helps, albeit imperfectly, to deliver.

By listening for Shakespeare's ghosts in stagings of New Mexico's double colonial history, we may also better hear the state's spectral presence in histories of national and global theatre, including Latinx Shakespeares. 'By simply placing New Mexico at the center rather than the periphery of theatre history,' Brian Eugenio Herrera shows 'how theatrical performance in New Mexico has, for more than four hundred years, stood as both a part of, yet also emphatically apart from, global theatre history, ever and always a local elaboration of national and international performance traditions.'[54] Shakespeare in New Mexico is a pivotal part of this history, as the examples explored here demonstrate: *The Merchant of Santa Fe* carries forward the 'capacious syncretism' that Herrera identifies with *nuevomexicano* colonial drama; the Hills' all-female production offers another example of territorial-era, ethnically inclusive amateur theatrics; and the recent emphasis on local Shakespeare complements the 'translocal networks' of late twentieth-century New Mexico's theatre scene.[55] Multilingual, women-forward, site-specific: these appropriations and performances of Shakespeare in New Mexico may feel radical, but they are of a piece with the state's longer theatre history. Following Herrera's lead, then, we might productively place *nuevomexicano* Shakespeare at the centre of our conversations about Latinx Shakespeares, where it may provide an enduring yet dynamic model of listening for the diversity of voices within and beyond Spanish-language communities and thus of politically engaged, socially progressive Latina/o theatre-making.

Notes

1. Earlier versions of this essay were presented at Université Paul-Valéry, Montpellier 3, under the auspices of Études Montelliéraines du Monde Anglophone (EMMA), and at the New Mexico Museum of Art, as part of *First Folio! The Book That Gave Us Shakespeare*. Databases consulted for the keyword search include Chronicling America: Historic American Newspapers (Library of Congress), America's Historical Newspapers and America's Historical Hispanic Newspapers (NewsBank), and the New Mexico Newspaper Project (University of New Mexico).
2. Thomas H. Guthrie, *Recognizing Heritage: The Politics of Multiculturalism in New Mexico* (Lincoln: University of Nebraska Press, 2013), 5.
3. Alice Rayner, *Ghosts: Death's Double and the Phenomena of Theatre* (Minneapolis: University of Minnesota Press, 2006), xxvi.
4. Rayner, *Ghosts*, xxviii.
5. Herbert Blau, *Take Up the Bodies: Theater at the Vanishing Point* (Urbana: University of Illinois Press, 1982); Marvin Carlson, *The Haunted Stage: The Theatre as Memory Machine* (Ann Arbor: University of Michigan Press, 2003).

6. Rayner, *Ghosts*, 25.

7. Joseph Roach, *Cities of the Dead: Circum-Atlantic Performance* (New York: Columbia University Press, 1996); Diana Taylor, *The Archive and the Repertoire: Performing Cultural Memory in the Americas* (Durham, NC: Duke University Press, 2003); Leo Cabranes-Grant, *From Scenarios to Networks: Performing the Intercultural in Colonial Mexico* (Evanston, IL: Northwestern University Press, 2016). Mounting a case for a networked approach to intercultural performance, Cabranes-Grant 'recommend[s] that we keep in mind that working *together* and working *against* are coexisting gestures, not alternative ones' (4, original emphasis).

8. Thomas H. Guthrie discusses the ways that 'heritage interpretation and preservation', including UNESCO World Heritage site designation, participate in processes of recognition that often function as a 'counter-intentional form of domination' in New Mexico and the Southwest more broadly (*Recognizing Heritage*, 6, 5). In this essay I identify Shakespeare's participation in similar processes.

9. Henry J. Tobias, *A History of the Jews in New Mexico* (Albuquerque: University of New Mexico Press, 1990), 33.

10. Ramón A. Flores, '*Merchant of Santa Fe* Concept Paper' (unpublished manuscript, 17 March 1993), 1.

11. Elizabeth Klein and Michael Shapiro, 'Shylock as Crypto-Jew: A New Mexican Adaptation of *The Merchant of Venice*', in *World-Wide Shakespeares: Local Appropriations in Film and Performance*, ed. Sonia Massai (London: Routledge, 2005), 31–9; Marissa Greenberg, 'Rethinking "Local" Shakespeare: The Case of *The Merchant of Santa Fe*', *Journal of the Wooden O*, 12 (2012): 15–24.

12. William Shakespeare, *The Merchant of Venice*, in *The Norton Shakespeare*, 3rd edn, ed. Stephen Greenblatt, Walter Cohen, Suzanne Gossett, Jean E. Howard, Katharine Eisaman Maus and Gordon McMullan (New York: W. W. Norton, 2016), I.ii.20–2.

13. Edna Nahshon and Michael Shapiro (eds), *Wrestling with Shylock: Jewish Responses to The Merchant of Venice* (Cambridge: Cambridge University Press, 2017).

14. Marissa Greenberg, 'Critically Regional Shakespeare', *Shakespeare Bulletin*, 37.3 (2019): 341–63.

15. For a summary and assessment of this controversy, see Michael P. Carroll, 'The Not-So-Crypto Crypto-Jews of New Mexico: Update on a Decades-Old Debate', *Religion*, 48.2 (2018): 236–51.

16. Lynn Butler Knight and Ramón A. Flores, '*The Merchant of Santa Fe*, Draft 3B' (unpublished manuscript, 1993), 12.

17. Knight and Flores, '*The Merchant of Santa Fe*, Draft 3B', 12.

18. Fray Angélico Chavez, *La Conquistadora: The Autobiography of an Ancient*

Statue (Paterson, NJ: St. Anthony Guild Press, 1954; rev. edn, Santa Fe, NM: Sunstone Press, 1983, 1997, 2011).

19. Knight and Flores, '*The Merchant of Santa Fe*, Draft 3B', 127.

20. Emmanouela Kavvadia, 'Aspects of Contemporary Jewish Music in Greece: Case of Judeo-Spanish Songs of Jewish Community of Thessaloniki', PhD dissertation, Goldsmiths College, University of London, 2005–6, 27.

21. Knight and Flores, '*The Merchant of Santa Fe*, Draft 3B', 20–1.

22. Ibid. 23.

23. Stanley M. Hordes, *To the End of the Earth: A History of the Crypto-Jews of New Mexico* (New York: Columbia University Press, 2008).

24. Stuart B. Schwartz, *All Can Be Saved: Religious Tolerance and Salvation in the Iberian Atlantic World* (New Haven: Yale University Press, 2008), 125.

25. Andrés Reséndez, *The Other Slavery: The Uncovered Story of Indian Enslavement in America* (Boston, MA: Houghton Mifflin Harcourt, 2016).

26. Knight and Flores, '*The Merchant of Santa Fe*, Draft 3B', 42.

27. Simon Romero, 'Indian Slavery Once Thrived in New Mexico. Latinos Are Finding Family Ties to It', *New York Times*, 18 January 2018.

28. Indeed, while the play includes extensive New Mexican Spanish and a smattering of Ladino, no Indigenous languages appear in the script.

29. The following history is based on accounts of Shakespeare, New Mexico, in H. Glenn Carson, *Ghost Sites of Southwest New Mexico* (Deming, NM: Carson Enterprises, 1991); T. M. Pierce (ed.), *New Mexico Place Names: A Geographical Dictionary* (Albuquerque: University of New Mexico Press, 1965); James E. Sherman and Barbara H. Sherman, *Ghost Towns and Mining Camps of New Mexico* (Norman: University of Oklahoma Press, 1975); Philip Varney, *New Mexico's Best Ghost Towns: A Practical Guide* (Albuquerque: University of New Mexico Press, 1987); and Norm Weis, *Helldorados, Ghosts, and Camps of the Old Southwest* (Caldwell, ID: Caxton Printers, 1977).

30. Rita Hill, *Then and Now, Here and Around Shakespeare* (n.p.: n.p., 1963), 13. An alternative genealogy is offered by Michael Jenkinson, who contends that Colonel Boyle was a 'Shakespearean scholar', implying that the choice of name reflects literary rather than economic interests (*Ghost Towns of New Mexico: Playthings of the Wind* [Albuquerque: University of New Mexico Press, 1967], 113). I heard something similar when I visited Shakespeare in August 2015: Colonel Boyle, our tour guide explained, was 'a lover of the Bard'.

31. Kim C. Sturgess, *Shakespeare and the American Nation* (Cambridge: Cambridge University Press, 2004), 2, 21.

32. Fran Teague, 'Shakespeare and America', in *The Oxford Handbook of*

Shakespeare, ed. Arthur F. Kinney (Oxford: Oxford University Press, 2012), 719–34.

33. R. Hill, *Then and Now*, 24.

34. Janaloo Hill, *The Hill Family of Shakespeare: How a Cowboy and a Schoolmarm Got Married and Saved a Historic Ghost Town* ([New Mexico]: J. Hill, 2001), 165–97.

35. R. Hill, *Then and Now*, 24–5.

36. Dydia DeLyser, '"Good, by God, We're Going to Bodie!" Ghost Towns and the American West', in *Western Places, American Myths: How We Think about the West*, ed. Gary J. Hausladen (Reno: University of Nevada Press, 2003), 273–95.

37. Frederick J. Turner, 'The Significance of the Frontier in American History', *Annual Report of the American Historical Association* (1894): 119–227. Available at https://www.historians.org/about-aha-and-mem bership/aha-history-and-archives/archives/the-significance-of-the-fron tier-in-american-history (last accessed 13 November 2020).

38. Mark Rifkin, *Manifesting America: The Imperial Construction of U.S. National Space* (Chapel Hill: University of North Carolina Press, 2009), 13.

39. R. Hill, *Then and Now*, 47.

40. Ibid. 48.

41. In a continuation of this practice, the Hills have become spectral presences in this history: 'Ghosts of the Past' tours in Las Cruces, New Mexico, feature residents impersonating 'historical ghosts', which turn out to be now deceased Anglo-American residents, including Janaloo Hill. 'Ghosts of the Past Event This Weekend at NMFRHM', *Las Cruces (NM) Sun-News*, 24 October 2014, NewsBank.

42. 'New Mexico State News', *Estrella*, 8 April 1916, Readex. This article appeared in English and Spanish, but the language(s) of the performance are unknown.

43. 'First Folio! The Book that Gave Us Shakespeare', Folger Shakespeare Library. Available at https://www.folger.edu/first-folio-tour (last accessed 13 November 2020).

44. Venues throughout Santa Fe and Albuquerque hosted talks, performances, film viewings and concerts. See 'Calendar of NM Events', Folger Shakespeare Library, New Mexico Museum of Art. Available at http://archive.nmartmuseum.org/shakespeare/calendar.html (last accessed 20 June 2020). For a potent critique of the *First Folio!* tour's claims to inclusivity, and especially the inclusion of Latinx perspectives, see Kathryn Vomero Santos, '¿Shakespeare para todos?' (forthcoming).

45. Flo Barnes, 'Shakespeare on the Rail on Board, Enjoy the Bard's Immortal Rhymes', *Santa Fe New Mexican*, 2 June 2010, ProQuest.

46. Set in Spain during the Spanish Civil War, the performance featured

flamenco dancers from local dance school Casa Flamenca. Kathaleen Roberts, 'Shakespeare on the Plaza – "Much Ado" and "The Tempest" Presented in Free Shows', *Albuquerque (NM) Journal*, 5 June 2016, NewsBank.

47. Kathaleen Roberts, 'Shakespeare, Updated – Aux Dog's "Much Ado" Set in Modern-Day New Mexico Theater', *Albuquerque (NM) Journal*, 7 April 2017, NewsBank.

48. For details of the production, I draw on Matthew Yde's review, 'Updated "Much Ado" a Fresh, Novel Approach to Classic', *Albuquerque (NM) Journal*, 16 April 2017, NewsBank.

49. Kathaleen Roberts, 'Aux Dog Updates Bard's "Measure" – Theater Gives Play a Contemporary Albuquerque Setting', *Albuquerque (NM) Journal*, 8 April 2018, NewsBank.

50. Jackie Jadrnak, 'Visions of Shakespeare – Center Named after Writer Looks to a Future Where Santa Fe Lures in Fans for World-Class Productions', *Albuquerque (NM) Journal*, 1 January 2016, NewsBank.

51. Martin Orkin, *Local Shakespeares: Proximation and Power* (Abingdon: Routledge, 2005).

52. For one example of the displacement of regional actors, see Adam Hansen and Monika Smialkowska, 'Shakespeare in the North: Regionalism, Culture and Power', in *Shakespeare on the Global Stage: Performance and Festivity in the Olympic Year*, ed. Paul Prescott and Erin Sullivan (London: Bloomsbury, 2015), 101–32. To enable more New Mexicans to attend Shakespeare performances, local theatres such as the Vortex have begun to admit audiences free of charge to their summer festivals.

53. Rayner, *Ghosts*, xx.

54. Brian Eugenio Herrera, 'To Imagine a *Nuevomexicano* Theatre History', in *Theatre and Cartographies of Power: Repositioning the Latina/o Americas Theatre*, ed. Jimmy A. Noriega and Analola Santana (Carbondale: Southern Illinois University Press, 2018), 85, 86.

55. Herrera, 'To Imagine', 88, 93, and *passim*.

9

Diálogo: On Translation and Adaptation

Henry Godinez and José Luis Valenzuela
Facilitated by Carla Della Gatta

In this conversation, José Luis Valenzuela and Henry Godinez draw from their extensive experience as actors, directors and theatre professors to discuss how translation and adaptation have factored into their journeys with Shakespeare. While both artists are firmly grounded in US theatre-making practices, both of them were introduced to Shakespeare through European aesthetics, be it a workshop with Patrick Stewart or directing work in Europe. These experiences helped foster an appreciation for the Shakespeare canon and have led to both theatre-makers engaging with Shakespeare throughout their storied careers. Still, Valenzuela's and Godinez's journeys speak to the intersections of Latinx theatre and Shakespeare. It is quite literally impossible to separate the two.

Carla Della Gatta: How did you get your start with Shakespeare?

Henry Godinez: When I was in college, as an undergraduate. The first Shakespeare play I did was *A Midsummer Night's Dream*. I played Bottom. I kind of fell in love with it. I also did *The Taming of the Shrew*, which was not as pleasant of an experience. I played Baptista. But then a really cool thing happened. I went to this tiny Catholic liberal arts university, and somehow our professors got Patrick Stewart to do a workshop with us. I got to do a scene playing Petruchio from *The Taming of the Shrew* and get notes from Patrick Stewart and listen to him talk and hung out. It was life-changing. That's how I got into Shakespeare.

In my last semester of graduate school, I was in a production of *Richard III*. I was directed by an eccentric Romanian director named Alexa Visarion that the school had brought in to direct in our last semester of graduate school. He blew me away. Because he spoke so little English, he didn't give a damn about iambic pentameter. It was his first time directing outside the Iron Curtain, so it was all about the passion and the subversive metaphor that he was employing around *Richard III*. Consequently, in terms of performance, we had become little acting machines and good little Shakespeare robots, little voice and speech machines, and he would literally say, 'No, it's necessary for life, for love, for art.' That's all he knew. All he cared about was the passion of Shakespeare. And I loved it. It was the best thing that could have happened to me at the end of three years.

José Luis Valenzuela: In my early years as a theatre professional, my experience with seeing Shakespeare in the United States was complicated because I did not see the relationship Shakespeare had with a modern audience. I was working in Chicano theatre where the audience was directly involved with our work, and I was trying to figure out how Shakespeare spoke to us as a community. It was not until I went to Europe to assist my mentor on Shakespeare productions that I began to understand the immense beauty and amazing humanity in Shakespeare's work. Interestingly, the Shakespeare productions we were doing were not in English – but in German, Norwegian and Swedish. My exposure and work on those Shakespeare productions – ironically translated from their original English – began my appreciation for Shakespeare's masterful storytelling and an amazing capacity for humanity.

Carla: A lot of your directing has been in Latinx Theatre, and your acting with Shakespeare, at least recently. Why is it important to work in both, and how does that affect your process?

Henry: When I was a young actor, I would do whatever people would hire me to do. The first four years out of grad school, I did some Shakespeare. Then in 1988, I did *Romeo and Juliet* at the Goodman with Michael Maggio, with Phoebe Cates and Michael Cerveris in the leads. Then Barbara Gaines cast me as Iachimo in *Cymbeline* at what is now Chicago Shakespeare Theater (CST; then called Shakespeare Repertory). My relationship with Barb started there, which went on to span many years and many productions. The following year, I reprised my role as Tybalt in another production. It was Michael Maggio's production, set in Little Italy, in 1917/18, right after World War I. I was Tybalt and had a moustache and wore beautiful suits. The second time I performed it that year, we were at the Old Globe. The San Diego critic used veiled racist comments, referring to me as the 'hot-blooded Tybalt', which is typical Latino code words for a Latino actor. Like 'fiery' and other terms.

As a director, after starting Teatro Vista, I became focused on championing new Latinx work. Teatro Vista did a co-production with the Goodman of *Cloud Tectonics*. That went well, and eventually the Goodman asked me to come on to the collective, and so my position at Goodman became about championing Latinx work.

I was fortunate to direct some Shakespeare along the way, some for Barb, some for freelance – Oak Park Festival Theatre. I directed a short *Romeo and Juliet* for CST at Grant Park. There were three or four summers in a row in the early 1990s, mid-1990s, when CST would do a free outdoor Shakespeare in the Park, which was great because it has a huge stage for thousands of people [in the audience]. One summer Barb asked me to co-direct *Romeo and Juliet* with her. She was busy and travelling, so I did the bulk of the directing. And then I was asked to direct *A Winter's Tale* for Kansas City Rep, which was then called Missouri Rep. At Oak Park Festival Theatre, I directed the Scottish play. It was right after the death of Kurosawa, the Japanese film-maker. The production was inspired by Kurosawa's work, by *Throne of Blood*. Those are some that I have done.

Carla: Does your process for engaging with Shakespeare differ from your process with other playwrights?

José Luis: The Chicano theatre, where I began my career, had a personal relationship with its audience. We could not create plays that would not cultivate that vital relationship. When I approach Shakespeare or Ibsen I am aware that I have to find an entrance to the play that engages the audience on a human level.

The majority of the playwrights that I work with are living playwrights, so I have a very intimate and collaborative relationship with them and their play. From that relationship, I know what the playwright desires their play to communicate with the audience. With Shakespeare, it is a different process because he is not alive, and it becomes, in a way, more challenging to have that personal intimacy because I have to investigate how Shakespeare speaks to people in contemporary times. I do not do theatre for theatre people, I do it for non-theatre people – an audience often new to the theatre, and that is what I am interested in as a director. When I approach Shakespeare, I need to discover how the story and characters speak to this contemporary audience, who may not know Shakespeare's work. How do you incorporate Latinx themes into a Shakespeare production/adaptation? I do not work with adaptations of Shakespeare, I work with Shakespeare's text. When I use Latinx themes (which are similar to other cultures) in my productions, they ask questions about how we get close to our own understanding of ritual, spectacle, human emotion and understanding of our own world within Shakespeare's poetry.

Henry: In 2014, I played Henry, the old king, at Notre Dame Shakespeare. When I did that, I hadn't played Shakespeare in a long time, I hadn't per-formed in a long time. Most recently, last year, I played Camillo in Bob Falls's production of *The Winter's Tale* at Goodman. I had always wanted to do a Shakespeare with Bob. Bob had seen the production of *Richard III* I was in in graduate school. When I met [him] a couple years later at Wisdom Bridge Theatre, which he was running at that point, he told me he saw it, and thirty-some-odd years later we finally worked together on a Shakespeare play. It was a great experience.

I don't pursue acting anymore; I don't care about it that much, except for when it comes to Shakespeare. Because it is infinitely perfectible. There is so much possibility in it. It seems like a contradiction, but it's this strange dichotomy where you have structure and rules, but the real fun of playing Shakespeare is when you can be so prepared with the rules, that you are free to break the rules. Just like Shakespeare did. He would set up rules, and he would break them, for emphasis. To me, that process is infinitely perfectible. And Shakespeare taps into the most essential things about being human, that no other playwright is able to do. There are some, for me, Latinx playwrights that get really close, such as José Rivera and Octavio Solis. For me, I think José gets the closest of anyone.

Carla: José Luis, how do you feel your extensive work directing Latinx theatre and being the artistic director of a Latinx theatre informed your experience directing Shakespeare at a non-Latinx theatre company such as Oregon Shakespeare Festival (OSF)?

José Luis: My approach to Shakespeare, Ibsen or any playwright is to treat their play like a new contemporary play that speaks to an audience today. My identity is Latinx, specifically Mexican, so I have a whole cultural background that informs my work. If the play, for example, calls for a funeral, I know how Mexicans do funerals: we cry, have music, and throw ourselves on the floor. It is not necessary for anything to change in the text, because the playwright is only asking for a funeral. Whatever play I direct, I am always informed by who I am as a human being. Treating the play as a new play in a dramaturgical sense lets me understand the humanity of the characters inside the text. Many times I do add moments or begin the play at a different time in order to answer the question, 'why this production of this play at this specific moment in time?'. I do not think that the text has to be adapted to speak to a contemporary audience in terms of the text. I think the original text can speak to a contemporary audience if you approach the production as if it is a contemporary play.

Carla: And, Henry, how did you get involved in translating Shakespeare for the 2008 bilingual *Romeo and Juliet*?

Henry: Chicago Shakes contacted me and asked me if I knew a playwright that would be interested in doing a bilingual translation/adaptation. I thought of Karen [Zacarías] right away. We had just worked on *Mariela in the Desert* at the Goodman. She's a wonderful playwright and a disciplined writer, and she's bilingual. We have a great working relationship, and I loved the idea of balancing Shakespeare with a female voice. Elizabeth Peña played Lady Capulet, and it was a wonderful experience.

I think that some gets lost in translating Shakespeare into Spanish, but not that much. I was really proud of what Karen and I did in translating *Romeo and Juliet*, and Karen did the bulk. I was more of a sounding board. I thought she did that beautifully, maybe it is due to her experience with [seventeenth-century poet] Sor Juana. Like good translations of Lorca – it will never be the same. That's why I am always thankful that I can speak English and Spanish, because it isn't the same.

Carla: Today, many Latinx playwrights are adapting the classics and taking up issues not specific to the Latinx community. Is it important, even today, for Latinx artists to focus on Latinx stories?

Henry: Like the English language, I think that Latinx theatre deserves both extraordinary works from the canon, whether that be Spanish Golden Age – Lope de Vega, Calderón, Tirso de Molina – or Federico García Lorca. When I think of the beauty of Shakespeare in English, what Shakespeare means to the English language, I think Lorca (with Cervantes as a close second) is the equivalent in Spanish. Because once you speak or hear Lorca in Spanish, you never want to hear it in English, you never want to *speak* it in English. I guess speaking it is the thing. I have had the good fortune to be in a rotating Spanish/English (Spanish one night, English one night) production of *Blood Wedding*. After performing it in both languages, [you can feel that] the Spanish is masterful. Like Shakespeare, the onomatopoetic value of the words, the rhythm, the imagery is there. It's just that Lorca didn't have the life, the opportunity, to be as prolific as Shakespeare. The plays we do have are just amazing. And yes, Luis Alfaro and others are adapting the Greeks, as Cherríe Moraga was doing so much earlier. Octavio [Solis]'s work is deeply influenced by Shakespeare. You can feel it in the rhythmic quality, the poetry of his text. The scope of his plays is very Shakespearean. A play like *Santos and Santos*, it is totally Shakespearean.

José Luis: This is a complicated question because I am not a fan of adaptations. When relying on adaptations, you have to follow Western ideals to make the play succeed. I think there is a greater need in our community for contemporary playwrights to tell stories that have not yet been told. However, the importance of creating a unique voice coming from within the Latinx community and a new approach to storytelling is still in development. As theatre artists, we still need a lot of nurturing from the culture itself to establish our own contemporary and relevant style. I don't feel that we need to borrow the structure or stories from classical texts.

10

Shakespeare Through the Latinx Voice

Michelle Lopez-Rios

You taught me language; and my profit on't
Is, I know how to curse. The red plague rid you
For learning me your language!
      William Shakespeare, *The Tempest*

Love, murder, ghosts, politics and scorching poetic language: do these words
bring to mind the world of Shakespeare or that of Latinx theatre? Both
Shakespeare and Latinx plays utilise rhythm, sounds, high stakes and multilingual text to create profound storytelling. The performance of Shakespearean
text through the Latinx voice offers a unique experience that resonates with
modern audiences, foregrounding a Latinx cultural and historical perspective
that offers one more way to personally connect to plays written over four
hundred years ago.

I use the term 'Latinx voice' to describe the influence of the Latinx artist
as actor, director, playwright, designer or producer. Directors orchestrate a
collaboration among the artistic team and company to reveal a specific time,
place and perspective. The contributions of artists are inextricably linked
to the complex composition of who they are and how they approach the
material and task at hand. And so, there are many ways that the Latinx voice
may influence the production of Latinx Shakespeares. Here, I call on two such
productions – *Measure for Measure* at Chicago's Goodman Theatre and *Julius
Caesar* at the Oregon Shakespeare Festival (OSF) – to illuminate this potential
range of influence. I also bring into conversation Luis Alfaro's *Mojada*, a
non-Shakespearean Latinx production that ran in rep with *Julius Caesar* at
OSF, to further expand on the possibilities of the Latinx voice.

I speak from the perspective of the voice and text director (sometimes
called a voice or dialect coach), a role that may not immediately come to mind
when one names the collaborators on a production. The person in this role

contributes a wide range of vocal expertise, such as healthy vocal use, dialects, clarity of language, knowledge of archaic language, regional pronunciation of text, and so on. Scott Kaiser of OSF concisely describes the mission of this work as, 'to encourage the full expression of the language of the plays through the actor's voice'.[1] The voice and text director helps shape the sounds in the text to create the vocal landscape of the production.

This vocal landscape includes regional sounds, cultural expression, pronunciations, translations and anything else specific to the meaning or expression of the language. Navigation of the vocal landscape in Shakespeare is central in the rehearsal process and includes an incredible amount of work on the text. The performer must clearly tell the story with full emotional availability using both poetry and prose. World-renowned Shakespeare director John Barton describes this process as a barrier that actors must address: 'First, that the heightened language in a text has to be found by the actor and not just taken for granted. And secondly, that a right balance has to be found between the naturalistic and heightened elements in that text.'[2] In describing his work with Barton on Shakespeare's *Henry V*, fellow director Trevor Nunn notes that success was achieved when 'the poetry was not an end in itself. The words became necessary'.[3]

The vocal landscape is just as central to the success of storytelling in many Latinx plays. In response to a question about what makes a play Hispanic, José Rivera highlights the importance of language:

> Latin culture is very specific – a belief in family, a willingness to think magically, a passion for love and sex, a code of honor and respect [. . .] these things, more than food and music, are what define Latin culture for me. So a lot of Latin theatre in the US is very passionate, very invested in the musical possibilities of language, very willing to use nonrealistic methods of storytelling. What makes a play Hispanic? The emotional and cultural and aesthetic sensibility of the creative artists involved.[4]

Much like Shakespeare's text, the Latinx lens requires actors and directors to unleash poetry, prose and multiple languages with ease as they explore the politics of the day.

In 2012, I met with artistic director Robert Falls of the Goodman Theatre in Chicago to discuss coaching his upcoming production of *Measure for Measure*. He was interested in my experience with both Latinx theatre and Shakespeare. Though I began my theatrical career as an actor, I eventually turned to directing and coaching a wide range of projects including several plays at the Houston Shakespeare Festival. I am also the co-founder of the Royal Mexican Players (originally from Houston), which has brought many new Latinx works to life. In my conversation with Falls, I quickly confessed that I was not a Shakespeare scholar, but I am a coach who likes to dig into the language and make sure the story is clear and accessible to the audience.

Measure for Measure is a dark comedy about Claudio, who sends Isabella, his sister and a novitiate, to plead for his life before the moralistic Angelo. Angelo becomes infatuated with Isabella and astonishingly proposes that, if she sleeps with him, he will spare her brother's life. Falls believed that the themes of religion, power and justice resonated strongly with a modern audience, and that the play was a 'world not unlike our own: flawed, excessive but always compelling – and inhabited by people who are achingly, vibrantly and recognizably human'.[5] Shakespeare set his play in Vienna, but Falls was setting his production in New York City during the 1970s, 'an era in which economic challenges, urban flight and the sexual revolution transformed what had been arguably the greatest city in the world to one of the most troubled'.[6] He cast the play to reflect not only 1970s New York but also present-day Chicago. He believed that my diverse background would help create a vocal landscape that was true to the text, the concept of the production and the diverse voices performing the characters.

He cast the siblings Isabella and Claudio as a Latinx family. Actress Alejandra Escalante was charged with bringing to life the complex character of the virtuous nun who must decide whether to accept Angelo's horrific offer to trade her virginity for her brother's life. After research and discussion, the actors and I decided that the family would be specifically Dominican New Yorkers. The actors took on the rhythms and sounds of the Dominican New York dialect and spoke a few of the lines in Spanish. I was struck seeing the character of Isabella through this lens. I have experienced Shakespeare productions set in various locales that incorporated dialects and particular cultures. However, the fierce loyalty to God, religion and family made sense to me more than it ever had in this play. Rivera's words about Latinx culture echoed in this discovery: 'a belief in family, a willingness to think magically, a passion for love and sex, a code of honor and respect'. Claudio's passion for Juliet, Isabella's love for God and, most importantly, the crucial sibling relationship were amplified. The chilling, familiar feeling of fighting an oppressive institution hit closer to home. As a Latina, I found this Shakespeare text resonating within me in a whole new way.

I wasn't alone in the connection to the piece. Theatre critic Scott Morgan noted that the 2013 production 'largely succeeds at making Shakespeare's play from the early 1600s feel much closer for adventurous audiences of today'.[7] Critic Brian Hieggelke echoed this sentiment in his review, concluding, 'the clarity of the ideas that Falls teases out of the work creates a contemporary relevance'.[8] Falls used the individual voices of the actors to find specificity in the characters that allowed audience members to connect to the story and relate it to the present day.

In 2017, I served as the voice and text director at OSF for Shakespeare's *Julius Caesar*, as well as, concurrently, *Mojada: A Medea in Los Angeles* by Luis Alfaro. OSF has been a leader in putting equity and inclusion at the centre of its practice. According to artistic director Bill Rauch, as of 2017 the acting company was close to 70 per cent actors of colour.[9] However, the commitment to inclusion did not stop with the artists onstage. The staff, directors and designers that came together to collaborate were also diverse.

The cast of *Julius Caesar* reflected this commitment to inclusion, with African American, Asian and Latinx actors in lead roles. I prepared for rehearsal like I prepare for any Shakespeare piece. I began discussions with director Shana Cooper on her vision for the piece and the way that she wanted to tell the story. She was incredibly passionate about making the language, relationships and story as clear and real as possible in each and every moment. She was interested in each actor's individual and authentic voice. I researched meanings, pronunciations and interpretations, and I collected as much information as I could in preparation. Then, once we started rehearsing, I worked with each actor to fully express the language through their own unique voice.

Three Latinx actors were cast in the production. Unlike *Measure for Measure*, however, the production did not focus on the race or ethnicity of the actors or characters. The role of Caesar was played by Latino actor Armando Duran. We explored the language for clarity of thought as Caesar gains so much honour and respect that he is offered a crown. We explored love as Caesar negotiates his wife's wish to stay home after she has a horrific dream. Finally, we explored family as Caesar is betrayed by his family of military brothers. Unlike *Measure for Measure*, our time was not focused on dialect. We were working to unleash the actor's voice, which means, in part, having the freedom to express this voice fully, including (for Latinx actors) their Latinidad.

At the same time, I was working with the actors in Luis Alfaro's *Mojada*, a modern retelling of Euripides' *Medea*. The play is set in the Los Angeles neighbourhood of Boyle Heights and follows members of a Mexican family through their terrifying journey from southern Mexico to the United States. Once in the States, they must face the trauma of their journey and their undocumented status. True to the OSF mission, the playwright, cast, director, assistant director, set and costume designer, lighting designer, sound designer, dramaturg and voice and text director were all Latinx.

Mojada is written mostly in English, but it also incorporates Spanish and Nahuatl. Director Juliette Carrillo sought a seamless flow between the three languages that allowed the cultural specificity to be present in each conversation. The vocal landscape had to capture a variety of Mexican characters, from Armida, a Mexican immigrant who had fully assimilated to the United States, to Tita, a curandera or healer who teaches the ways of her Indigenous culture. There were conversations that would most likely have taken place in Spanish or Nahuatl but that were spoken in English for the sake of the audience. And though the main characters are from southern Mexico, the English text is strongly influenced by the rhythms and cadence of a Boyle Heights dialect. Finally, there are harrowing screams and cries at climactic moments in the piece.

I had prepared for *Julius Caesar* and *Mojada* differently. Initially, *Mojada* felt familiar to me as a Mexican American who had lived in Los Angeles for many years, while *Caesar* was further away, and the preparation was more academic. However, as I went back and forth between these two politically timely pieces I was struck by the similarity in the work. Both pieces required a strong understanding of the past (Ancient Rome for *Caesar* and the Ancient Greek inspiration for *Mojada)*. Both pieces resonated powerfully in the United States, where millions of people were marching in protest against the newly elected president, and where immigration was a volatile topic. Language barriers in both plays had to be dismantled so that the story could be told clearly. Themes of love, honour and ghosts reminded the characters of their past. Both pieces required me to be fully present with actors as they allowed for the full expression of the poetry and prose through their unique voice. We made the language necessary.

Artists from both productions shared that having a Latinx voice coach was crucial to their process and also unusual in their experience. For *Mojada*, I believe that there was an advantage to having a shared, shorthand understanding about the culture and the language. The Latinx artistic team was intimately familiar with the culture, language and characters. For *Caesar*, the advantage was less a matter of specifics and more a matter of the authenticity of one's voice. If a person's voice is Latinx, then having a Latinx voice coach may in some way give permission for the authentic voice to fully come out.

The response to both OSF pieces was positive, and audience members related to the timeliness of the stories. Theatre critic Bill Choy said about *Julius Caesar*, 'What is so impressive is how clear and concise the language is, so the audience knows what's going on, and the motivations of these characters, as the words of the Bard come vividly to life.'[10] And critic T. J. Acena wrote, '"Mojada" is a bilingual show; the characters slip effortlessly between English and Spanish. They do so without translations, but this doesn't pose a problem. The actors' delivery ensures the intent is always understood.'[11]

Master voice teacher Patsy Rodenburg professes that a person must be 'passionate, political and curious'[12] to engage with Shakespeare's text. These same touchstones are vital to many Latinx plays. It is no surprise, then, that exploring Shakespearean text through the Latinx voice offers a unique connection for artists and audience. The passion and curiosity about the words and world of the play allow performers to access the human story and tell it in the most specific way. Latinx artists are bringing their authentic voice to Shakespeare.

There is no longer a need to fit the 'idea' of what the character or play should be. Latinx artists are beautifully realising the roles by bringing their authentic voices to the productions both on- and offstage. This authenticity provides audiences a unique opportunity to engage deeply with Shakespeare's text.

Notes

1. Mandy Rees (ed.), *Shakespeare around the Globe: Essays on Voice and Speech* (Cincinnati: Voice and Speech Trainers Association, 2005), 23.
2. John Barton, *Playing Shakespeare: An Actor's Guide*, foreword by Trevor Nunn (London: Methuen, 1984), 25.
3. Trevor Nunn, foreword to Barton, *Playing Shakespeare*, viii.
4. José Rivera, interview by Michelle Lopez-Rios, 15 April 2003.
5. Robert Falls, 'Why *Measure for Measure?*', *OnStage* (Goodman Theatre playbill), 29.3 (March–May 2013): 1.
6. Falls, 'Why *Measure for Measure?*', 1.
7. Scott C. Morgan, 'Risk Pays off in Goodman's Daring Disco-era *Measure*', *Daily Herald* (Arlington Heights, IL), 21 March 2013.
8. Brian Hieggelke, 'Review: Measure for Measure /Goodman Theatre', *New City Stage*, 18 March 2013. Available at https://www.newcitystage.com/2013/03/18/review-measure-for-measuregoodman-theatre/ (last accessed 16 November 2020).
9. Joan Lancourt, 'Equity and Diversity Starts at the Top', *American Theatre*, 15 February 2018. Available at https://www.americantheatre.org/2018/02/15/equity-and-diversity-starts-at-the-top/ (last accessed 16 November 2020).
10. Bill Choy, 'Oregon Shakespeare Festival Review: "Julius Caesar" A Powerhouse of a Production', *Siskiyou Daily News* (Yreka, CA), 11 March 2017.
11. T. J. Acena, '"Mojada" Beautifully Fuses Greek Myth with a Modern Immigration Story', *Oregon Live*, 13 November 2017. Available at https://www.oregonlive.com/art/index.ssf/2017/11/mojada_portland_center_stage.html (last accessed 16 November 2020).
12. Patsy Rodenburg, *Speaking Shakespeare* (New York: Palgrave Macmillan, 2002), 13.

Part III: Shakespeare in Latinx Classrooms and Communities

11

Shakespeare With, For and By Latinx Youth: Assumptions, Access and Assets

Roxanne Schroeder-Arce

I like watching high schoolers perform Shakespeare, but not so much adults. I like to see young people relating to the story and sometimes with adults, it's just too well rehearsed. I think with the right coaching, Shakespeare can be accessible and exciting to watch – for everybody. In theatre class, I learned a Shakespearean monologue, but my teacher had us relate what was going on back then to our own personal experiences. I've also seen some plays based on Shakespeare, written in modern times which is great so young people can understand and appreciate the stories.

Genevieve

Genevieve is my 14-year-old daughter. Ethnically and racially, Genevieve identifies as Latina, Indigenous and White. Here, Genevieve illustrates the need for those seeking to engage Latinx youth with the work of Shakespeare – as artists and audience members – to consider best practices in making the work accessible and relevant to young people. After hearing from an expert in this conversation (a young person), I sought out varying perspectives from adults doing the work. While Genevieve articulates the need for artists to consider making Shakespeare relevant and accessible, the artists below articulate how they are responding to this need.

Through framing interviews with three Latinx theatre-makers, this chapter examines methods of exploring Shakespeare with, for and by Latinx youth. The interviews serve as case studies offering insight into the intersections of Shakespeare, Latinx youth identity and theatre education. In his 2016 article 'Stranger Shakespeare', Ruben Espinosa offers: 'Encouraging our students to think about race, ethnicity, xenophobia, and difference not only in Shakespeare, but also through Shakespeare – to cultivate the idea that what they see is something worth seeing – is our obligation.'[1] This chapter explores how different artists employ their artistic practice to encourage such thought among youth and offers a look at efforts in different theatre education settings, where teachers/writers/directors employ culturally responsive pedagogy and artistry while they teach, write and direct plays by, for and with Latinx youth.

Specifically, this chapter examines the work of José Cruz González, Christopher Fernandez and Briandaniel Oglesby, and their respective work as playwrights, directors and theatre educators in different regions of the United States. González is a well-known Chicano playwright who has published many plays for young audiences. In the interview below, González discusses two Shakespeare-inspired plays he was commissioned to write, sharing the goals and journeys of the plays as well as his relationship to Shakespeare and his approach to adapting his work for young audiences. Fernandez teaches at a high school in the Rio Grande Valley of Texas, where most of the student body is Latinx. He has chosen to direct several Shakespearean plays with his students and speaks in his interview about how he explores this work with his students on stage and in the classroom, and the joys and challenges of that work. Oglesby often devises work inspired by Shakespeare with his students of many races and ethnicities at the school where he teaches in Austin, Texas. In his interview, Ogelsby shares how his own identity and experience and that of his students impacts his practice and the plays that he and his students write and produce. Collectively, this chapter and these artists speak to myriad ways to engage youth with Shakespeare and the many considerations for doing so effectively.

Rewriting Shakespeare: An Interview with José Cruz González

José Cruz González was born in Calexico, the son of migrant farm workers. González has published many plays, including *The Highest Heaven* (2002), *The Sun Serpent* (2014) and *Tomás and the Library Lady* (2018). I have long been a fan of González and I was delighted to have an opportunity to ask him questions about his plays for youth and family audiences in relation to Shakespeare.

Roxanne: In thinking about your prolific career and journey as an artist, where does Shakespeare come into the story?

José: Well, it comes early from being an undergraduate student at UC San Diego and taking acting classes there. Our instructor was Eric Christmas, who was a Shakespearean actor, and we rehearsed and performed *A Midsummer Night's Dream* in class. That experience planted a seed in me because of Shakespeare's heightened language and storytelling.

Roxanne: So, your interest in classical work was planted as a seed for you as an actor, which hung around and later infiltrated your playwriting?

José: Right. Many years later, I adapted for the stage Homer's *The Odyssey* in a one-act play titled *Odysseus Cruz* for South Coast Repertory's outdoors production of *California Scenarios*. I loved adapting and reimagining this epic story and placing it in a Latinx context. In my interpretation, Odysseus Cruz returns home to Mexico through the Sonoran Desert only to face his ghosts, the people he left behind as a coyote in the desert to die. *The Odyssey* made a huge impact on me as a high school kid. The story just resonated with me deeply.

Roxanne: So, that's the classical connection. What about adapting Shakespeare? How and when did your Shakespeare-inspired plays come about?

José: *Invierno* came in 2010 and *Forever Poppy* would follow several years later. *Invierno* was inspired by *The Winter's Tale*. It premiered at PCPA, the Pacific Conservatory of the Performing Arts, in Santa Maria, California. With *Invierno*, I was able to reconceptualise *The Winter's Tale*, setting it in California just prior to the Mexican–American War. The play blended multiple languages including Samala (Chumash), Spanish and English. One of the wonderful things that we were able to do was to work with Nakia Zavala of the Chumash community. She has been working to reconstruct the Samala language which hasn't been spoken since 1965. For *Invierno*, we were able to incorporate some Samala language in the play. The play begins with a Chumash woman and two teenagers. The play was a chance for me to tap into important history, which I love.

Roxanne: And *Forever Poppy*? What was the spark for that play?

José: *Forever Poppy* was inspired by visiting my brother-in-law and his partner in Mendocino, California. They have a magical place in the woods. Over a hundred years before, the trees were cut down and now they have returned. Some of the remaining tree trunks were turned into performance stages. Everywhere they took me seemed like the fairie woods of *A Midsummer Night's Dream*. I came away inspired: 'I'm going to write about this.' And that's how *Forever Poppy* was born. I thought, 'What if William Shakespeare's last descendant was a person of colour?' I wanted to celebrate the idea of mixed heritage. And, so that's when the play opened up for me. And then, of course, I could reference all Shakespeare's plays and sonnets. I wanted to create something new while reaching back to the past.

Roxanne: Yes, well, I am glad you did. My daughter read it with me. You know she knows many of your plays. And we were talking about how different it is from the other works of yours that we have read, and then the similarities.

José: Oh, really, what are those?

Roxanne: I am supposed to be interviewing you! But, I will tell you that one thing that stands out is how each of the actors plays many roles. In several of your plays, people become multiple characters. Not unlike Shakespearean actors. You must have a palette of actors for your work.

José: That's a really good point and I can address one reason why. *Forever Poppy* has many characters, but I've written it for only six actors to play all the characters. I want to give actors an opportunity to soar playing diverse characters and using different accents. I love the theatricality of it.

Roxanne: And I think young people, young audiences, especially love that. Seeing the magic – being in on the magic.

José: Yes, the whole family. And different entry points. I try to write for both the seasoned theatre-goer and the first-time theatre-goer no matter what age. I love the alchemy. For the Latinx community it may be their first time seeing themselves reflected on stage. Our communities are so hungry for stories. They don't get often those opportunities. I want the families to be there sharing the experience together.

Teaching Shakespeare: An Interview with Christopher Fernandez

Christopher Fernandez, like González, also reaches youth through engaging Shakespeare, but Fernandez's work is as a teacher/director working directly with his students at Sharyland High School in the Rio Grande Valley in South Texas. Fernandez grew up in Canutillo in West Texas. While I haven't gotten to see any of the Shakespeare plays he has directed, I have gotten to see him working with his students. His passion as a teacher shows through in the interview.

Roxanne: Christopher, could you walk me through your trajectory?

Christopher: I grew up and went to school about as far west as you can go in Texas. In fact, my school was on the other side, west of the Rio Grande but still in Texas and still in the United States. We kind of had this mentality that we were from the other side. We literally were from the other side of the river and I think it made us, ironically enough, at least in our theatre department, work harder. It was something that we all understood – that we weren't going to be given anything and I think a lot of it was because we didn't have an auditorium. We practised on our cafeteria floor. But we knew we were a bunch of spark plugs and we just did it. We just didn't know how much of a spark we were really providing not only for our community, but what we would later eventually learn for the state. And what I mean by that is we participated heavily in the Texas One-Act Play Festival and we made it all the way to the state competition.

Roxanne: Where did Shakespeare come into the picture for you?

Christopher: One year we did *A Midsummer Night's Dream* and I will be very honest – that was my first time being exposed to it. And no matter how eager and zealous I was, and nothing against my director at that time, but it just didn't, it didn't stick with me or I wasn't bit by the excitement of what I was doing, or the innuendos and the somewhat rudimentary nature that Shakespeare naturally has embedded in his plays wasn't brought to my attention. And so we literally were up there trying to do British accents and perform Shakespeare. It wasn't until I actually got into graduate school that I realised, wow, we were so far from what was actually intended in the first place. And what Shakespeare wanted to do and why these plays even existed during the Renaissance time period. A lot of it was written for the common man and for the basic individual with very little learning and I feel like that was a big component that was missed when I was learning Shakespeare in high school.

Roxanne: Alright, so there you were in high school, you're exposed to Shakespeare and then, when did you start really engaging with Shakespeare more deeply?

Christopher: I was very fortunate. I had a British teacher named Charlotte Cornwell, who was a resident at the Royal Shakespeare Company. She brought all of that expertise. We'd go and hang out in her swimming pool and we would talk. We would talk theatre and of course everything always went back to Shakespeare and all of the greats. And it was just a wonderful cultural experience where I saw intellectuals normalise and humanise Shakespeare in such a rudimentary way that I became instantly addicted. So being around that type of culture and being exposed to how simple it can be, if you just learn and apply yourself from the jump the right way. I was very fortunate. I ended up playing Macbeth in *Macbeth*. I also got to revisit *A Midsummer Night's Dream* where I played Demetrius.

Roxanne: Could you talk about how much Shakespeare you've produced/ directed at Sharyland High and why you choose to do it there, specifically given your school's demographic?

Christopher: Yes, absolutely. There are about 1,600 students and 92 per cent of them are Latinx. So I have Caucasians as well as Black students in my programme which allows me to really run the gamut as far as the plays that we pick as well as in the casting. So I'm very fortunate in that aspect to have that type of diversity, but our school is predominantly Latinx and our pro-gramme reflects those demographics. My introductory-level Theatre Arts has a two-week time period dedicated to nothing but Shakespeare. It starts with the Sonnets. It starts with vocabulary. Really breaking down the most funda-mental components that could potentially derail or discourage the students right off the bat. I like to give them a foundation of what Shakespeare is, the historical implications of what was going on at the time; I humanise him. That happens at the introductory level before students are even allowed to get into the production. The classes that I teach are tiered, and one of the prerequisites of getting into those production classes is that you must go through Theatre

Arts Training first which allows me to then take all of that knowledge that we've studied and that has been previously presented to them. And the text – what's being said and then how to go about staging and moving comfortably authentically and genuinely while performing Shakespeare.

Roxanne: Given who your students are and what they bring into the room, how they relate to the material, how does that inform how you approach Shakespeare, specifically at Sharyland High?

Christopher: Yes, the approach is tiered in a way where once those initial teachings have been established, then we can begin to personalise, we can begin to identify correlations between a character's traits and objectives in relationship to things that happen in our lives. It can be something as simple as Romeo and Juliet's love affair. Their age, in particular their rebellious nature, talking to them and asking them questions that aren't going to necessarily reveal too much on their part and put me in a funny place but definitely help them connect. But that language sometimes creates a barrier. And it's that barrier that I'm looking to break down by helping draw connections. But when we get down to the nitty gritty, like in *A Midsummer Night's Dream*, for example, and like when Hermia is set to marry Demetrius, but truly is in love with Lysander. We get into that, we get into prearranged marriages and how that's still very prevalent in Mexican culture, even though it's not as forefront now, and may be even slightly taboo in some places, it still exists. And so being able to start there. Some cultural experiences that are unique to the Mexican Latinx culture resonate still, even within a Shakespearean play. So, I choose very carefully what it is that we explore because at the same time we're still in high school, so I can't cut too deep. I can't get too personal. It's a very fine line between making sure that you're hitting Shakespeare's objectives and capturing the essence, or relationship to their experience, but not crossing the line and going too personal where you're going to open up potentially Pandora's box and maybe even potentially lose the kid because of too much emotional baggage. It's just a very careful set of words and choices that must be made in relationships to what the text is saying because it can get very real and very relevant very fast. That's what makes Shakespeare so wonderful. He literally can transpose his work from culture to culture and from place to place. And there's really a lot of similarities that he reflects in his text.

Roxanne: That's wonderful. So, going back to some of the ideas about why you do Shakespeare, and even how much Shakespeare you have produced with your students. Why do you do Shakespeare there at Sharyland high school?

Christopher: As far as teaching Shakespeare at Sharyland High School in a curriculum setting, it is present every semester. Whether we're putting up a production or not, we are going to dabble in Shakespeare. That's going to be the creating of the base. The foundation that we can then begin to launch off of. And here's why. The reason why I feel having Shakespeare taught at Sharyland high school predominantly is that there is a greater opportunity that students are going to have more confidence in their education and more confidence in their academic abilities. Once they feel like they understood, if not conquered, Shakespeare and his language, it gives them a great sense of belonging – when a play or reference to Shakespeare comes up and they can chime in. Or they're in their English class and they know exactly what iambic pentameter is, they understand the purpose of soliloquy, and they are called upon to or volunteer to read out loud in class. Whether they're going to go on and be actors or actresses to me is pointless; what's happening here is we're setting up lifelong learners.

Roxanne: So, beyond academics and the art of theatre, how would you say Shakespeare helps your students with, as you say, 'lifelong learning'?

Christopher: We're setting up students to be more confident in how they present themselves to the world once they leave the safe walls of Sharyland High School. And that to me is worth more than having a successful production. We also put productions up in order to help recruit. We put productions up so that honestly, we can invite the entire Middle School over to our auditorium and perform for them so that those young scholars can look at the school that they're about to attend in a year or two and say, 'Oh my gosh, I need to up my game.' Because these people are up here doing it and doing it well and I'm just not where I need to be. So a lot of it is advertising the school, promoting the school. In an academically rich and culturally rich way that is promoting academic excellence and not suppressing it, rather giving students an opportunity to shine. And challenging them within themselves to do more, as opposed to saying 'now there's easier things as a teacher to go out and teach. Let me go and teach these things instead'; the end game is creating academic wealth in typically underprivileged and underserved communities.

Devising around Shakespeare: An Interview with Briandaniel Oglesby

Briandaniel Oglesby grew up in Northern California. He identifies as queer and mixed race; his father is white and his mother is Latina. Oglesby teaches theatre at a small alternative private junior and high school called Skybridge Academy in Austin, Texas. Oglesby started teaching at Skybridge six years ago, coming directly out of the MFA in Playwriting programme at the University of Texas at Austin.

Roxanne: You've said that you are passionate about making work with and for your students. When you talk about creating the plays with your

students and for your students and your community, what are their identities
and their ideas? What do they bring into the classroom?

Briandaniel: We have a large LGBT population at our school. They
bring that into the space. The stories that are reflected here oftentimes have
LGBT themes in them. I think that is what is missing in American theatre
and, in particular, educational theatre. I think that a lot of educational theatre
replicates older values, particularly older commercial values which you could
sell to a sort of a bland audience, a Broadway-centric audience. I think that
we, people who are producing theatre with young people, should truly be
making it with them. And that will result in not just their stories being on
stage because it's not just about their stories, putting up a mirror, though that's
useful. But it's not the only thing you can do. You're also sort of reflecting
their identities in different kinds of stories and imaginative stories in different
worlds in different places. You're creating space for them and acknowledging
them and demonstrating to them that they are legitimate.

Roxanne: So, you are devising work, and reflecting the students' perspectives and identities. And you have developed some work inspired by
Shakespearean plays?

Briandaniel: The play we devised that is most directly adapted from
Shakespeare was an LGBT *Romeo and Juliet*, essentially. One of the projects
that I brought in was Shakespeare plot twists and the kids really enjoyed reimagining and adapting these plot twists. These were junior high kids. There's
a little bit of currency that went into that – Shakespeare, that's a thing we've
heard of. One of the stories they came up with was a princess who couldn't
marry another princess because there was a king who didn't like that. They
have LGBT friends. They have LGBT relatives. Some of them were LGBT,
and so that really sort of piqued their interest and so the kids and I elected
to combine those to do a Shakespeare adaptation that was LGBT. They also
wanted a story that didn't have a single protagonist, but I knew going into
it that it needed to have a really strong plot. *Romeo and Juliet* has a plot that
is both very recognisable and built like a barn. And it doesn't just have one
single protagonist.

In order to do this, I knew I needed to have at least two students who could
play Romeo and Juliet. I had everyone close their eyes and raise their hands.
And I asked who wanted or who would be willing to play Romeo and Juliet –
the same-sex couple. And that's how I ended up with two boys playing these
parts. And so next was creating the script. There are a lot of games that we
play to adapt the original material to our own vision and world. We started
to create character voices that we did activities like hot seating. We unpacked
the play in a dramaturgical way. It made a lot more sense in a modern context
of why families would not want two people to be together, so it added an
extra social force to push them apart. So that was the one big part that was

most directly adapted. We changed the ending because I was very aware that the trope of killing your gays is kind of toxic. And I didn't want it to just be a gay romance and they die at the end. So there's a way that we get to keep our cake and eat it too. And so at the very end, they just make the potion. The poison potion that Romeo takes was just a knockout potion, it's just an extra little bit of conspiracy story at the very end.

Roxanne: Could you share a little about the other Shakespeare-inspired projects you have devised with your students?

Briandaniel: We also did *The Untitled Pirate Play* which matches up things from elements from *the Tempest* from *Treasure Island* and from all of these other well-known nautical stories. But I was very consciously taking stuff from *The Tempest*. We also did *And Then, She Picks Up the Sword* which was inspired partly by *A Midsummer Night's Dream* and that one is also queer. Basically, there's a wedding between a prince and princess who do not want to get married, much like the beginning of *A Midsummer Night's Dream*. Both run away from the wedding into a forest and the story pushes against the idea that they are going to fall in love with each other. It's a traditional trope that the people who do not want to be together wind up together at the end that seems very Shakespeare. I was aware that the Prince needs a friend, not to get married. The Princess falls in love with a female knight who's there to save her and take her back to reintegrate her into the society. Other magical things happen in the forest. There are dreams that sort of can infect you and hurt you or there's creepers who can go into your dreams, all those kinds of all sort of very much drawn from these Shakespearean tropes. I think the idea of people going into a forest and then just stumbling into each other is also very much built off those old romantic comedies.

Roxanne: You talked about some of what Shakespeare brings and why you engage with Shakespeare. But how did you come to Shakespeare and what is your relationship to to Shakespeare's work?

Briandaniel: I came to it in sixth grade when we did *Julius Caesar* in my Spanish immersion class. I remember we did it on a playground and that was a lot of fun. And I'm sure that no one could hear us. Because we're doing it on playground. I'm sure we performed for other people. I'm sure it was an edited version because I can't imagine a sixth-grade class doing a three-hour *Julius Caesar*, which I think is funny. Also, I encountered Shakespeare when there was this sort of aborted attempt at doing *Midsummer Night's Dream* that someone in the neighbourhood was trying to put together. Then, Acme Theatre Company in Northern California at Davis, where I grew up, has an adult artistic director and it's a student or high school run theatre company and they have a great apprenticeship programme so they can pass on the the content knowledge from generation to generation to generation. And they would do Shakespeare. They would do Shakespeare in the Park every spring.

And they had a programme that would have the high schoolers teach junior high and younger students. That was a major fundraiser for them. But it was also part of the way that they would grow artists. That theatre company models how Shakespeare is introduced to younger people.

Roxanne: Do you ever have tensions around engaging Shakespeare as an educator, given your identity and even political outlook?

Briandaniel: As a playwright I have tension with it. I think that Shakespeare, because it's something you have to decode, can feel like you're like breaking a code when you do it, and that can feel very satisfying. I have had a shifting relationship over the years, because I can't see more Shakespeare because I don't see myself in these plays and when I do it feels very artificial. He's occupying energy and time and space and that is not going to new playwrights, that's not going to people who are reflecting and encountering the world as it is now. And yet I also see the value in having a shared cultural touchstone that people can draw upon, and in my case, both make fun of and reimagine. You say 'gay Romeo and Juliet' and people get exactly what you mean, and then you add on 'with 12-year olds'. People go, 'wow',' because they know what that means. And you add on 'in Texas'. It adds another layer of wow factor to it and it is valuable to have that reference point. But it's problematic. Absolutely it is. It's very white-centred. Shakespeare is easier to decode if you've been taught how to decode it and it's easier to decode if you're reading it in English and English is your native language. There are definitely problems in it as well.

Roxanne: Why do you continue believing in devising Shakespeare with young people? What do you want to say to other educators who are doing or considering doing this work?

Briandaniel: Well, I think the biggest thing that I want to say is that there is a lack of work out there for Latinx young people that reflects their stories and identities. We have to incorporate them into it and I think that my process is one that can be used as a model, or at least an inspiration. Theatre teachers can become theatre-makers and work with young people in bringing them in to make work that reflects their identities. Shakespeare is both the thing that we should detonate and blow up but also, it's a great tool for adaptation that allows you to save time when you are creating work for people. Adaptation saves you a lot of time. And it allows people to sort of get on the same page when you're in a devising process very quickly and efficiently. Shakespeare is very much the thing that takes over theatre. It's helpful to reimagining what is possible with known material that you can draw upon.

I also hope that this sort of model will inspire more − not just theatre teachers − to imagine themselves as collaborative playwrights with young people, but also for playwrights to imagine they could collaborate with young people to reflect their stories. To incorporate them into their work.

Shakespeare was not just a one brilliant human being, like, he was working with a group of people. My work with my young people oftentimes fits more in that kind of realm than the traditional playwright-centric model of there's a brilliant playwright who then makes a play and then other people do it.

Conclusion

Talking to these three Latinx artists about the varying ways that they engage youth in Shakespeare helped me to recognise the many considerations for artists undertaking this work. Responding to these considerations can look very different for different practitioners: a playwright writing to engage the intergenerational audience; a teacher-director helping youth to simultaneously translate culture and language; a teacher-deviser crafting plays with a critical consciousness of who is in the room and how they are (self)represented. Ultimately, as Genevieve helped articulate, first and foremost, these artist educators must consider accessibility and relevance for the youth they wish to engage, exploring identity on multiple levels as they tell, retell and revise Shakespearean texts with, for and by Latinx youth.

Note

1. Ruben Espinosa, 'Stranger Shakespeare', *Shakespeare Quarterly*, 67.1 (2016): 51–67.

12

Celebrating Flippancy: Latinas in Miami Talk Back to Shakespeare

James M. Sutton, with Catherine Socarras Ferrell, Ana Menéndez, Josie Urbistondo, Yasbel Acuña-Borrero, Cristina Rosell, Carla Rosell and Sophie Herbut

I have been teaching Latinx students Shakespeare for twenty-five years at Florida International University (FIU), Miami's public research institution. Since its opening in 1972, FIU's students have mirrored the diverse population of Miami-Dade County and southern Florida. Consequently, although FIU enrolls Caucasian, African and African-diasporic, and Asian students, most of our students are Latinx. Primarily they are Caribbean Latinx, claiming origins in Cuba, the Dominican Republic or Puerto Rico. Many more, though, have ties to Mexico and Central or South America, including Nicaragua, Honduras, Guatemala, Colombia, Venezuela, Peru and Argentina. Thus, like Miami, FIU's Latinx composition is a mosaic rather than a monolith of Latinx peoples.[1]

When I started to think about the ramifications of teaching Shakespeare to Latinx students for this volume, I informally asked about twenty alumni whether they would be willing to reflect on their experiences of encountering and (re)appropriating Shakespeare, both during and after their time studying at FIU. The responses I received were complex and thoughtful, plumbing both the many dissimilarities (linguistic, cultural, temporal, class) and surprising points of contact between themselves and Shakespeare. Neither by design nor by intention, the respondents were overwhelmingly Cuban American *women* who had excelled in their studies and continued for advanced degrees in literature, journalism, creative writing and education. The resulting essay, co-created and co-written by eight individuals, melds my own perspective – white, monolingual, Anglo-American, male – with the viewpoints of seven Latina co-authors. The first six alumnae, all second- or third-generation Cuban Americans, graduated from FIU prior to 2006; their thinking about Shakespeare has developed, in both professional and personal settings, over many years. The seventh and final voice belongs to a recent alumna of Venezuelan birth; her exilic testimony, less seasoned by time, and coming from a very different place in terms of class and privilege, provides a useful counterbalance to her Cuban sisters' seemingly sunnier attitudes towards, and appropriations of, Shakespeare. With compelling urgency, she highlights the continuing struggle that many Latinx students today – immigrants, refugees, exiles – face when they meet Shakespeare in the United States. My hope is that our collaborative piece underscores the surprising and highly significant role Shakespeare can play in lending agency to Latinas in Miami, and thus contributes to a wider scholarly conversation – both within and without the confines of this volume – concerning how Latinx peoples might claim ownership over Shakespeare.[2]

Throughout the essay, I attest to the 'flippancy' of the approach taken here. Despite the risk inherent in the word – especially given the nature of current political and media discourse in America – I embrace 'flippancy' due to its playfulness and its broad range of meanings. I repeatedly term the transaction that allows a Latina to connect meaningfully to Shakespeare a 'flip'. In doing so, I intentionally gesture at a range of possible manoeuvres that allow Latinas to gain access to and control over the author and his works. Most often, it indicates some (over)turning of the text, a form of strong reading that permits the Latina entry into the works on her terms, from her perspective. And, although 'flip' suggests an epiphanic moment, a discrete second in time when this transaction occurs – a 'flip of the switch' – I would counter that insofar as the student's 'flip' remains largely invisible or unremarked, it is in fact pro-cessual, gradual and often hard won. Additionally, I embrace the ambiguity of the term, insofar as a 'flip' can be (spatially) backward or forward, switched off and on: Latinas can and should be enabled to engage and disengage, connect and disconnect, from Shakespeare. I also assert that while the appropriative strategies outlined here are not necessarily particular to Latinas. the individuality and vivacity of the narratives lend them an authenticity and urgency worth heeding.

The 'flipped' nature of this chapter – students/alumnae lead, as their professor follows behind, commenting and curating – closely mirrors the 'flippant', highly dialogic/discursive approach to Shakespeare within a partially 'flipped' classroom that I propose as best practice when Latinx students encounter this canonical author. Although not a complete adherent of 'flipped learning', my Shakespearean pedagogy at FIU is often playful, unscripted, collaborative and student centred, and it assumes that much of their learning takes place prior to, and outside of, the space of my classroom.[3] Fittingly, this chapter concludes by reviewing the etymology and history of 'flippancy', arguing that both the original positive connotations of the word 'flippant' and its later, pejorative meanings have *everything* to do with how Latinas read, appropriate and understand Shakespeare in Miami.

Finding Their Place at the Table

The 'flippant' nature of conversation between a Latina and Shakespeare is beautifully rendered in the heretofore unpublished poem, 'A Place at the Table: Shakespeare, Latinx, Miami and Me', written by Catherine Socarras Ferrell, an educator and creative writer from central Florida who attended FIU from 2003 to 2005. When asked to reflect on the quadrant evoked in her subtitle, Catherine wrote:

> I crave picadillo and chicken pot pie.
> I'm sort of Latina,
> Spanish Cuban French Irish conglomeration,
> a mixed up something.
> Am I Wonder Bread or pan Cubano?
> Raised to speak español,
> pale of skin and dark of hair.
> Round hazel green honey eyes.
> Moved to Miami
> where I am a gringa.
> Moved to Miami to go to school.
> My vowels and /l/s are flat and clipped like a northerner
> but I say y'all
> and sometimes I think in Spanish.
>
> And Shakespeare beckons,
> a bridge between,
> a world unto himself.
> Humor, sadness, longing, loss –
> familiar themes in a strange world,
> a world in which I've never been home.
>
> I didn't belong there, and I didn't belong here,
> but in this room I belonged.
> In this room I had a place.
> Hard plastic seat with sometimes a desk attached,
> and you at the front of the room.
> Your eyes two kind smiles beaming out at me,
> believing I understood,
> challenging me to understand,
> nurturing new understandings.
> Fostering fluency in a language I didn't know I loved,
> nascent within me.
> A language born long ago, the play-fellow of the Bard.

And I fell in love
With this language
Because it was new
And old
And established
And delicious
And it understood me
And sometimes I understood it.

You invited me to sit at the table,
a square divided in four.
and I thought and I wondered and I had questions.

Who sits in those quadrants?
I sit here, over there is Latinx, there is Miami, and right here is that fellow
     with the pen.

And I had been invited to sit.

Back then the squares were separated by semesters
(hard plastic chairs with sometimes a desk attached)
and the menu came in pieces.
A sonnet here, a play there,
if you're in the mood for tragedy order now.

That was then.
Now I have aged and fermented enough
To pop
And these words will out
And the language still pops up
when I need it
And bridges wor(l)ds for me when I feel I don't belong.
And I can still see you there,
Smiling eyes
Beaming and believing,
You and me and Shakespeare and Miami.

And now you have invited me to partake once again.
But this time the squares are conjoined.
I sit at the big square table
and this is good.
The menu has fused and I peruse and muse and

decide I would like
Picadillo and chicken pot pie.

I wonder what Shakespeare will order.

You approach the table and this time I smile out of beaming eyes.
I offer you a glass of vino tinto,
aged and rich and effervescent
with anticipation.
And you sit.

Gracias por todo
Mil veces
Gracias por todo.

Catherine identifies herself as a 'conglomeration, / a mixed up something'. Her hybridity is particular and precious to her, but such hybridity is common among FIU's Latinx students, who find themselves suspended between two or more places 'in a strange world' – in a theatre of absurdity and difference – searching for a place to call 'home'. Catherine may not experience exile or immigration firsthand, but in Miami these burdens of inheritance ('Spanish Cuban French Irish') resonate, and even her internal language (code-)switches from 'northern' English, to southern dialects, 'y'all', to her first language, 'Spanish'. Catherine finds that she belongs in the Shakespeare classroom – 'in this room I had a place' – precisely due to the bridge created by Shakespeare's own (foreign) language, 'the play-fellow of the Bard'. Neither the playwright's life nor his times pull her in and root her; rather it is 'the thing itself', this 'new', 'old', 'established / And delicious' language, that provides Catherine a home, because 'it understood me / And sometimes I understood it'. His topsy-turvy, high-low, hybrid tongue enables her to pause and compose herself: at the table with Shakespeare, 'I thought and I wondered and I had questions'.

This is the remarkable and unpredictably meaningful 'flip', the reflection of self that allows the hyphenated Latina to find herself (and not find herself) within Shakespearean language, not just then but now too, since 'these words will out / And the language still pops up / when I need it / And bridges wor(l)ds for me when I feel I don't belong'. This became life-long learning for Catherine, a continuously unfolding gift, providing her 'fluency in a language [she] didn't know [she] loved', as she discovered that 'you and me and Shakespeare and Miami' represented a quadratic equation that we might solve together.

'Fostering fluency', 'beaming and believing': though a gross simplification of our work, Catherine's formula aptly captures what those of us who profess

Shakespeare at FIU have long done to promote the success of our Latinx students (and others). Teaching well here entails exploring the plays with liveliness, depth and integrity, celebrating the language nimbly, and getting out of the way so that the meaningful 'flip' might occur, whether within class or outside of it, during or well after the temporal confines of the semester. Negotiating with or appropriating Shakespeare – the shared effort to understand his language 'new [. . .] old [. . .] established and delicious' – can prove hard work, but the lessons learned can be long lasting. Our Latinx students hunger for language, thirst for plots, stories and characters that they might appropriate and remix into their own *ficciones* – and Shakespeare, among others, can provide this to them.

Acclaimed author, journalist and educator Ana Menéndez, who graduated from FIU in 1992 and went on to earn her MFA at New York University (NYU), well represents such hard-won borrowing. She recalls being haunted by Shakespeare's words and characters, then and now. She writes,

> I studied Shakespeare in the late 1980s [. . .] before the idea of 'remixes' hit the general culture. But even then, I could intuit something in Shakespeare which [seems] modern, but we know is the way art has always been made: by layers of accretion and appropriation. [T]his narrative remixing works in both directions, back to Holinshed and Brooke and forward to us. [. . .] I was a child when I first heard Shakespeare spoken, which is why in my mind [. . .] he's always associated with José Martí, the Cuban poet [of] my childhood. Poetry is language performing heroic feats. That [. . .] is what haunted me about Shakespeare through [many] years [. . .] even graduate school: Language. Its infinite delight. Its playfulness. Its personality. Characters who spoke in blank verse! [. . .] The rat-tat-tat of madness. The incantations of witches. It was magic, tun[ing] my ear for the music in ordinary stories. Shakespeare continues to speak to me for this reason. I compare him to Bach, whose music becomes eternal precisely because of its ability to shape-shift through time and place.[. . .] This to me is the definition of the classical: work that – far from being diminished – is strengthened by the bruising contact of other contexts.

Blending, remixing, appropriation: these are the go-to reading strategies of the Latina attempting the conversion of Shakespearean noise into 'music'. For this daughter of Cuban exiles, José Martí and Shakespeare conjoin, united in crafting 'language performing heroic feats'. This is the 'flip' for Ana, a marriage of Latin and Anglo, of Cuban Spanish and Elizabethan English, which revivifies both authors, and in turn gifts her with voice; hers, too, is of 'infinite delight [. . .] playfulness [. . .] personality' and life-long learning: 'Shakespeare continues to speak to me.' Most important is her assertion that Shakespeare, like all things 'classical', is not lessened by encountering the alien and foreign, but rather 'strengthened by the bruising contact of other contexts'. The remix quickens; it provides the exile, or the daughter of exiles, a bridge connecting past and future; it becomes a new (linguistic) home: 'We have heard the chimes at midnight';[4] 'In Cuba I Was a German Shepherd'.[5]

This blending of old and new, English and Spanish, Elizabethan and Cuban – the 'Elicubethan' – emerges repeatedly as these alumnae reflect on the resonance of 'Shakespeare to me, here in Miami'. Josie Urbistondo, who graduated from FIU in 2004 and went on to NYU (MA) and the University of Miami (PhD) to study Caribbean literature, finds in Shakespeare a bridge over the troubled exilic waters of the Florida straits. Recalling generational burdens, she composes herself through Shakespeare:

Initially, a Latinx young woman approaching Shakespearean language may feel overwhelmed; but for second generation Cuban Americans like myself, political dramas feel less dramatic, more like reality. [. . .] I relish[ed] the [. . .] hyperbolic narratives of exile [. . .] encountered at the kitchen table. They're just not in iambic pentameter.
   ¿Como pesa ese libro? Y las palabras tan chiquitas. ¡Te vas a dañar tu ojos!
   Memories flood – food simmers on the stove, a thick tail of steam dances above the pots. The promise of sustenance, and the aroma of Cuban coffee forever lingers in the air as I first meet Shakespeare. My grandmother [. . .] was more preoccupied with how reading such tiny print would hurt my eyes. Abuelaca's wisdom resided not in books but in her resilience and grit: she had immigrated to the States younger than I was then, with two young daughters, no English and an aversion to the word 'revolution'. My childhood and young adulthood came after the *miseria*, as she called it: exile, second chances and immigration are precisely what you purchase so as to avoid the taste of misery. Thirty years later [. . .] at my aunt's kitchen table, as conversations about America and Cuba swirled, I read *The Tempest, As You Like It, A Midsummer Night's Dream, Hamlet, Richard the Third*. [. . .]
   Storylines and plot twists intertwine with real life. Suddenly, Cuban dictators and the Elian crisis superimpose upon Richard the Third and 'the winter of our discontent'. The fate of a nation and the innocence of the young: the reign of King Edward IV, the 'princes in the tower', and contemporary Cuban American politics meld together.
   Fast forward [. . .] twenty years, and my family is more American than Cuban. Now my mom and aunt serve as our bridge to a culture we have inherited but never lived, always feeling its nostalgic absence. [. . .] [Still,] Shakespeare helps me examine how we come to grips with loss, love, tragedy – with how we learn to take our position within the mysteries

of being Cuban, and American, and human. I will teach my daughter to revere the power of the pen, to love Shakespeare's wisdom, and to boldly live her identity, no matter how many hyphens she possesses.

'At my aunt's kitchen table'. For Josie, the location of learning is not the institutional space (Catherine Ferrell's classroom table, 'a square divided in four') but the nostalgic home, full of flavour and aroma, provided to her by the women who came before: abuela, aunt and mother. She reads Shakespeare as they fret about her, Cuba, Miami. And her 'flip' occurs: 'plot twists intertwine with real life', Richard III's poor nephews and young Elian Gonzalez equally bear witness to innocence, lost. Two decades later, she is now a mother of a young daughter, and such 'home lessons' continue. She honours her grandmother by educating her daughter – likely at her own kitchen table – about the mysteries of the hyphen, 'the power of the pen', and 'Shakespeare's wisdom'. Her exilic dreams exemplify the best of lifelong, 'flipped' learning.

For some Latinas, the hybridity of Shakespeare's writing is so powerful that in their act of flippant appropriation, he seems to lose all – or most – of his Englishness, his Elizabethan/Jacobean flavour. 'Shakespeare is Cuban, for all we know. I remember reading the plays in college and immediately identifying some of the characters as members of my family or my community,' Yasbel Acuña-Borrero attests. Yasbel, who graduated from FIU in 2003 and earned her MFA at the University of Miami, continues,

> Shakespeare [. . .] breaks down the human condition [to] make it relatable to every society – including but not limited to the Latin community. Core human emotion – love, jealousy, insecurity, vulnerability – take the form of characters, and those characters exist in every corner of the earth. I think of Othello and [. . .] Iago. [. . .] Who doesn't know an 'Iago'? Or an 'Othello' for that matter? Who has not seen that plot unfold in their community? [. . .] What I am trying to get at is how relevant [such] interactions are, how these characters wrestle with one another and themselves to show the audience members that they are not alone. Because Shakespeare is so fundamentally universal, there are so many renditions of his plays that take place in modern Latin settings. The connections are inevitable and omnipresent.

Let me take this discussion a step further and venture that Shakespeare understands Latinxs in more ways than we could imagine (or should I flip that and say that Latinxs understand Shakespeare in more ways than we could imagine?). If you think about it, Shakespeare was writing telenovelas long before they were called telenovelas. Take [. . .] *Twelfth Night* – a storyline straight out of Univision: twins separated by a shipwreck, mistaken identity, betrayal, and of course, a wedding. [. . .] I, for one, couldn't get enough.

Every time Shakespeare is mentioned, the issue of language [. . .] come[s] up. Some may wonder if non-native English speakers struggle with the language. In my case, no [. . .] not more than any other college reading. I would get absorbed in the plot and then [. . .] find beauty in the language. Shakespeare speaks our language, and I don't necessarily mean Spanish; he speaks the language of the fighting class – those fighting to get ahead, doing whatever it takes to make it, pushing for progress. [. . .] This drive, this hunger, is truly characteristic of the Latinx community, and we see it manifested in so many of the plays. Shakespeare nods at us Latinxs, winks at us. Yup, Shakespeare is definitely Cuban.

For many Shakespearean scholars, Yasbel's claims of the author's universality would be troubling, in need of challenge.[6] I often do this work of pushing back when, in class, my students make such assertions about Shakespeare's purported timelessness and his assumed greatness, canonicity. But on closer inspection, Yasbel is not making any such propositions about the author's universal reach. Rather, she is framing Shakespeare as 'definitely Cuban'. She is not saying that Shakespeare is Dominican, or Puerto Rican, or some sort of everyman. Rather, playfully erasing his Englishness, she 'flips' him and thereby possesses him, bringing him home to her: 'Latinxs understand Shakespeare in more ways than we could imagine!' Far from passively permitting his works to construct her, to interpolate and remake her, she actively and confidently grasps him, and hence reshapes him to her own particular ends. His plays inscribe 'love, jealousy, insecurity, vulnerability' in a manner that, for her, powerfully evokes Cuba. Why would I, her white Anglo English-speaking professor, violently strip away this deep and lasting connection – this remix, this 'bruising contact' – with Shakespeare? When she asserts that the author 'speaks the language of the fighting class – those fighting to get ahead, doing whatever it takes to make it, pushing for progress', she has found treasure: revolutionary Shakespeare as mouthpiece of the exile, the immigrant, the stranger, the first-gen Latinx student struggling to make it through college. Would I dare steal this treasure from her in a fit of academic political posturing? Let it be.

Due to the wide and diverse ancestries of Latinx individuals in Miami, many of our students at FIU don't present as Hispanic at all; they could pass for 'Anglos' very easily. This hybrid identity – internally, native-born Latinx, externally 'white' – can stir up strong feelings of cognitive dissonance within them, a sense perhaps of 'passing strangeness'.[7] Alongside Richard III, Iago and Viola, if for very different reasons, they might well say, 'I am not what (who) I am'. For Cristina Rosell, Shakespeare became part of the solution to this bifurcation, a link that helped her bridge her deep Hispanic roots and seeming 'whiteness'. Cristina, a 2005 graduate from FIU who went on to NYU (MA) and Louisiana State University (LSU; PhD) to study Renaissance literature, writes:

> I was in seventh grade [. . .] when I first experienced the beauty of Shakespeare. Baz Luhrmann's *Romeo + Juliet* had just come out in theatres [. . .] a good friend of mine [. . .] asked me continuously to explain what was going on. I never stopped to consider that the language was different or difficult – it just made sense to me. I appreciated the poetry – the sounds, the words, the imagery. Somehow, Shakespeare felt familiar.
>
> Growing up in Miami [. . .] the daughter of Cuban immigrants, I was saturated in Hispanic culture. [. . .] My mother often spoke to me in Spanish, and I could only communicate with my grandparents if I spoke their language. Although I identified (and continue to do so) as Hispanic, this was [. . .] difficult [. . .] for me, partly because I have never looked 'Hispanic'. I have blonde hair, fair skin, and hazel eyes. I do not speak English with an accent. Strangers and family members alike called me 'gringa' during most of my adolescence – an act that impacted me profoundly. I felt like I had no claims to my own culture.
>
> Throughout my formative years, I worked assiduously to excel in my Spanish classes and thus prove my innate 'Hispanicism'. In elementary school, I recall reading *Lazarillo de Tormes*. [. . .] Later, I studied the work of Jorge Luis Borges, Pablo Neruda, Gabriel García Márquez, José Martí, and Octavio Paz. [. . .] During high school, I [studied] Shakespeare and savored his plays [:] [. . .] *Romeo and Juliet* [. . .] *The Taming of the Shrew, Macbeth* and *Hamlet*. I learned about the Romantics and the Victorians, and my heart swelled. [. . .] Meanwhile, my paternal grandfather, a Spanish professor whom I loved but who intimidated me, constantly corrected my Spanish whenever I spoke to him. My maternal great-aunt, a professor of Spanish literature, did the same. She, however, introduced me to the poetry of Sor Juana Inés de la Cruz. Her husband, a professor of Spanish Golden Age poetry, discussed Miguel de Cervantes with my sisters and me.
>
> This was [. . .] my adolescence – continually immersed in, yet excluded from, my own heritage.
>
> When I arrived at FIU, I knew I was going to major in English. [. . .] My older sister, also majoring in English [. . .] told me about [. . .] Shakespeare, [and] I decided to give [it] a chance. In a very significant way [. . .] Shakespeare's comedies altered my trajectory [. . .] here [. . .] I felt at home, learning how to unpack Shakespeare's language. I took so many courses on Shakespeare and early modernism at FIU that [at] NYU, my cohort often joked that I should teach the classes myself. They were surprised to learn

that I was Hispanic. Similar experiences occurred at LSU. In Louisiana, however [. . .] I began hosting dinners for my friends. These were some of my happiest moments, cooking traditional Cuban fare and discussing what it means to be a Hispanic studying Shakespeare and company as opposed to Caribbean Literature. [. . .]

What I have come to realise is that Shakespeare is a part of my identity as much as and in negotiation with my Hispanicism. I make no apologies for choosing to study his works. It is through the distance, the perspective afforded me by his poetry and plays, that I have been able and willing to access and explore my heritage. [This] heritage [. . .] of the Cuban refugee [is] always around me, shaping me; inside me, nourishing me; a part of me, yet held apart. I am Hispanic, but I am also a Shakespearean.

Cristina clearly credits Shakespeare for helping her join two seemingly oppositional ethnic identities, the 'gringa' and the 'Hispanic'. Working with him permits conversation – 'negotiation' – between these two facets of herself, with clarity gained through 'distance', 'perspective'.

However, there is something else happening here as well, and though this breakthrough – 'flip' – lurks just beneath the surface of her words, it signals a no less significant intervention that I believe Shakespeare's plays might offer Latinas. The presence of male authority – *machismo* – powerfully surrounds and contains Cristina's attempts to prove she is 'Hispanic'. As an adolescent, she reads *Lazarillo de Tormes*, studies Borges, Neruda, Márquez, Martí, Paz: all gifted poets, all men. Her great-uncle 'discusses' Cervantes. Her paternal grandfather 'corrects' her Spanish. Though her great-aunt tries to smuggle in a woman's perspective, the poetry of seventeenth-century proto-feminist Sor Juana Inés de la Cruz, this effort remains muted among so many voluble men. Ironically, strangely, Shakespeare – another verbose white man, but Anglo, not Spanish or Latino – provides the necessary distance, permitting her voice to resonate. Note that Tina says not a word concerning Shakespeare's gender, personhood or historicity: it's the works (and words) that matter. In this regard, her singular reference to the comedies is significant, since here Shakespeare's most vocal, expressive women reside. Furthermore, three of the plays she recalls – *Romeo and Juliet*, *The Taming of the Shrew* and *Macbeth* – feature witty, brilliant, brave women. 'Flipping' the negative trajectory of Juliet, Katherine and Lady Macbeth on its head, Cristina finds her voice, ideas and agency unleashed in reading them. Through appropriating Shakespeare (one among many possible authors), the Latina can gain volubility and credibility, learning to speak nimbly and quickly, flippantly. Through his language and words, she might gain access to crystalline Juliet, vociferous Katarina, crafty and clever Lady Macbeth. Cristina embarks on a sparkling conversation – one that will last a lifetime – with these heroines, and their flesh-and-blood sisters, early modern authors such as Sor Juana and Aemilia Lanyer.[8]

Cristina has also been talking about such themes with her older sister, Carla Rosell, for some time. Carla, who obtained her FIU degree in 2003 and continued her studies of Shakespeare and Elizabeth I at NYU (MA) and the University of Illinois (PhD), is keenly interested in questions of gender, sexuality and power – namely, how women, then and now, might claim agency and voice when surrounded by strong (and self-conceited) men who attempt to dictate proper codes of speech, decorous behaviour and sexual practice. In what follows, Carla evinces that the 'flip' connecting students to the plays is not, in Miami or elsewhere, always about race and ethnicity. Nimble playfulness concerning sexuality and gender can also powerfully beckon students into the plays: hybridity, queerness, hyphenated existence take on many forms, in life and in Shakespeare's plays. Carla recalls:

At FIU, I was fortunate enough to take several courses with professors who made the material come alive. [. . .] Their passion [. . .] sparked my own. I went on to take five Shakespeare courses, though I never approached the material through the lens of my Hispanic identity. I simply fell in love with the stories themselves. I found the characters' plights relatable.

There is one character that has always held a special place in my heart, *Twelfth Night*'s [. . .] Viola. I remember being instantly drawn to [. . .] her vitality and quick wit. [. . .] But more than that, her predicament spoke to me. I was fascinated by how she could travel between Duke Orsino and Olivia's courts, one of only two characters afforded this freedom. Yet despite her mobility, she seemed trapped in a liminal space. Neither court was fully home. Mourning her brother's loss and having fallen in love with Orsino, she was then forced to woo another woman on his behalf.

Her speech at the end of Act II, where dressed as Cesario she reveals her love to a still unsuspecting, obtuse Orsino [. . .] still moves me. Yes, she admits her feelings under the pretence of a lost family member, yet this admission is still an act of bravery. Reading this speech helped me realise something I had suspected for a long time, yet had not really wanted to confront: I am a bisexual woman. Not an easy thing to face when one grows up in a conservative Hispanic household like the one in which I was raised. Yet Viola's speech gave me the courage to face this knowledge. This moment, more than any, cemented my love for Shakespeare.

Shakespeare may not have written with a Hispanic audience in mind, yet the beauty of his work is that it transcends time periods and ethnic differences. Having chosen to study early modern literature as a profession [. . .] I [. . .] now better [. . .] appreciate how he approaches differences, [yet] it is the likenesses that keep me coming back. In many

ways, Shakespeare's characters feel like old friends, none more so than
Viola.

'Bruising contact': Shakespearean literature and language discloses secrets,
forces truth, on Carla: she does not conform to the heteronormative woman
that her 'conservative Hispanic household' 'raised' her to be. Viola, her friend,
demonstrates that with mobility, flexibility and voice comes also the responsibility to be brave, authentic and honest. Smiling patiently at her grief – the
potential loss of parents and home – Carla embraces a newly shaped form of
exile when she admits, 'I am a bisexual woman'. Like Catherine, Ana, Josie,
Yasbel and Cristina, Carla too finds a share of self-possession, perspective and
voice through conversing with Shakespeare. In discovering their place at the
table with him, wrestling with his language, they negotiate and in part shape
their own identities.

Flipping the Script: From Cultural Capital to Cultural Clash

In fall 2006, coincidentally after these six Cuban American women had
graduated from FIU, the faculty of our department voted through a new
curriculum for our majors, which, among other interventions, decentred
Shakespeare. Our decision to remove the Shakespeare requirement from
our major was fitting, both in terms of national trends in English studies
and, more importantly, in relation to our local context. Given the nexus of
demands and constraints placed on our students – economic, cultural, familial,
institutional and political – there was then and is now *no* justifiable reason
to *compel* study of this canonical figure and the age of European expansion
he purportedly represents. Rightly, our majors are now required to engage
with 'multicultural' and/or 'multiethnic' literatures as the centrepiece of their
literary inquiry.

   With the curricular script flipped – a response to both our location and
our students' origins and diverse perspectives – 'flippant' critique rather than
unexamined acceptance of Shakespeare's place has become our starting point.
The encounter between our Latinx students and Shakespeare, though now
volitional rather than enforced, has become more complex and charged. If
Catherine, Ana, Josie, Yasbel, Cristina and Carla all seem to acquiesce in
some manner to his siren call (perhaps in part because they encountered him
at FIU when he was held up as the centrepiece of English literature), our
current students are frequently much more conflicted in their approach to
him, more likely to find his plays 'boring', irrelevant, even offensive. Despite
such obstacles, though, many Latinx students, when encouraged to grapple
with him on their own terms, find the struggle meaningful – if not revelatory.

Therefore, I wish to attend to a young woman for whom the 'course' of Shakespeare 'never did run smooth', whose 'flip' of, or into, Shakespeare was tentative, fraught, hard won. The 'flippancy' celebrated throughout these pages is never easy. For our freshest 'strangers' newly arrived on these shores, we need to recall that Shakespeare might well represent precisely what they fled back home: authoritarian privilege, power, class conflict.[9] Consider, in this light, the adversarial relationship of Sophie Herbut towards Shakespeare. This Venezuelan exile, born in Valencia, came to Miami with her parents at age four. She attended local public schools, and she graduated from FIU in 2016; she went on to earn an MA in journalism in 2017. Speaking of Shakespeare, she asserts:

> Growing up in a predominantly Latinx community, I had it was engrained within me in school, by classmates, teachers and our culture, that reading Shakespeare was a sign of privilege, wealth, opulence, and high status. In my lower-middle-class suburb, all those characteristics were resisted and unwanted. There was nothing to boast about if you could quote Shakespeare; in fact, doing so brought unwarranted embarrassment. In addition to being majority Latinx, many of us were first-generation Americans or immigrants, so English was not our first language. Shakespeare symbolised the high class of white English speakers, not so much the common, working-class, immigrant communities from which we came.

Sophie's home life was secure and comfortable, and she was nurtured through its innate hybridity. Her father, with advanced degrees in engineering and criminal justice, delighted in strumming classic Venezuelan music on his guitar, her sister painted, and 'my mother filled the house with pictures and projects and her bohemian energy. My household was a place of tolerance and expression, and an integral part of my identity.'

In 'stark contrast', her schooling assaulted her Latinx, hyphenated character, and 'Shakespeare' represented the lynchpin of this subtractive, violent education:

> Despite the privilege of [my] being a Latinx immigrant in Miami, the school curriculum was abundant with English and American authors, so the atmosphere was not conducive to taking pride in, or understanding, the identity of the majority of students. These were not just cultural, linguistic, or race impediments; class factored in too. My neighbourhood was lower middle income, yet many of the writers we read were white, upper-middle-class men, and many wrote about the lands where we, or our parents, had been born as a destination for adventure, unconcerned about the lives of real people who lived there. Latin America was always pictured

in their texts as a conquered land, a land of revolution and jungle, with savage inhabitants tending towards cannibalism. We were the children of those savages, reluctantly forced to read about white men who had come to save us.

Shakespeare was symbolic of this internal culture war. Teachers told us to revere him, praise him, read him, and quote him as though that would guarantee improved reading levels and better testing scores. He represented opulence, royalty, wealth; we were called delinquents and degenerates; unsurprisingly, the combination never worked for us.

Sophie and her high-school classmates repeat firsthand the unpleasant play-book of *The Tempest*: as cursing is the only profit taken from the language Prospero offers to 'sa(l)vage' Caliban, alienation and embitterment blossom when Sophie's teachers force Shakespeare on them, the 'delinquent' and 'degenerate' children of Caliban. Shakespeare becomes the site of class(room) struggle, writ large. The harmonious remix, hyphenated Shakespeare, a 'place at the table': none of these are available to Sophie, who finds only disconnection and anger towards this mouthpiece of Anglo-American 'opulence, royalty, wealth'.

So, who or what brought Shakespeare and Sophie into conversation, however tenuous and uncomfortable that connection might have been? Who made Shakespeare (somewhat) palatable to her? A cursing woman, an exiled monarch, Queen Margaret, unrepentant widow speaking 'flippant' yet bitter truth to power in *Richard III*. For Sophie, Margaret proved the 'relatable' character that unlocked 'the combination [that had] never worked for' her. She recalls:

Margaret defied the traditional narrative that Juliet fell into. She was aggressive, witty, unapologetic, and her story resonated with me because of her similarity to my mother, a lower-middle-class single woman who fought through a failing country, an alienating new country, a different language – all micro-wars in themselves – to provide a successful future for her daughters. Reading Queen Margaret, I imagined her as any woman. She could have been a struggling Latinx mother as well as a queen fighting for her son's rightful claim to the throne of England. That perspective, which lent itself to diversity, that lifted the character away from her environment as she spoke a universal language of motherhood instead, freed Shakespeare from the chains of privilege and class. In *Richard III*, through Margaret's agency, I came to understand Shakespeare differently.

In conflict and defiance, anger and 'micro-wars', Sophie tentatively, momentarily locates herself within Shakespeare. Just as Margaret flouts Richard – 'Oh, let me make the period to my curse'[10] – so too her mother confronts countries both 'failing' and 'alienating', and Sophie finds the courage to 'understand Shakespeare differently', on her terms, with wit, without apologies. Sophie's perspective provides a fresh lens by which to view the 'bruising contact' of the ongoing encounter between Shakespeare and Latinas in Miami: class(room) struggle leads her to replace cultural capital with valuable culture clash. Her words, in alignment with Margaret's, also testify to the agency that 'flippant' discourse can provide when the 'lowly' speak truth to power, allowing them to find their deserved place at the table. She 'leans in', and demands our respect.

'Jacquie be nimble, Jacquie be quick': Reclaiming Flippancy

When it was first coined, the adjective 'flippant' did not possess the largely pejorative connotations that it carries today. The *OED* dates the word's first appearance to 1605, in the fifth act of George Chapman's comedy *All Fools*. Although such meanings are now obsolete, throughout the seventeenth and into the eighteenth centuries, 'flippant' signified movement or bodily carriage that was 'nimble', 'easily moved or managed, light to the hand; pliant, flexible, limber'.[11] Applied to the 'tongue', it connoted 'nimble' speech, defining, as in Chapman's original coinage, individuals who spoke 'freely', who were 'fluent, talkative, voluble'. Another now-obsolete meaning was 'sportive, playful'. These original positive meanings were replaced in the later eighteenth and nineteenth centuries by today's negative connotations, such as being 'impertinently voluble' and 'displaying unbecoming levity in the consideration of serious subjects or in behaviour to persons entitled to respect'. From here on, all later derivatives of 'flippant' are pejorative, including the noun form, 'flippancy', which the *OED* dates to 1746 and defines as a 'disposition to trifle, frivolity [. . .] volubility.' Furthermore, these scornful associations are primarily assigned to one gender: impertinent women. 'Flippancy' becomes the new code word for 'shrewishness': the project of taming, silencing and controlling women continues unabated from the eighteenth and nineteenth centuries to the present day.

In attempting here to reclaim and celebrate the 'flippant' and the 'flipped', I have sought to return 'flippancy' to its original positive constructions: to be 'nimble', 'limber' and 'quick'. I have also intentionally located these traits exclusively in Latinas as they converse with Shakespeare in Miami, in order to push back strongly on the problematics of shrewishness that 'flippancy' later constellates. When Latinas learn to talk back to the Bard, they embrace the 'flippant' as it was originally understood. Following in the footsteps of Shakespeare's comic and tragic heroines (though refusing either silence or death as their 'rightful' ends), remixing his language and his ideas, and putting these resources into conversation with their own linguistic and cultural origins, these women become 'nimble', lively or 'quick' in motion, 'fluent' and fleet of tongue, 'sparkling, sportive and playful' in discourse. Especially today, in a place like Miami, such speech and action must not be censored.

Through writing this chapter, I have realised that 'flippancy' rightly defines and structures my own teaching practices in the Latinx Shakespearean classroom at FIU. By adopting the 'flippant' and the 'flipped' in our conversations about Shakespeare, I aim, for all my students, Latina and otherwise, to inculcate productive attitudes towards this canonical author, the better to strategically possess him on their terms. Furthermore, given who our Latinx students are at FIU – predominantly exiles (or the children and grandchildren of exiles) and immigrants (both documented and undocumented) – I assert that a display of 'unbecoming levity in the consideration of subjects or in behaviour to persons entitled to respect' is an absolutely appropriate and highly fruitful form of pushback when these students encounter Shakespeare in South Florida. 'Flippancy' is precisely that habit of mind that enables them to own Shakespeare, to 'flip' him from 'mine' to 'theirs'. Such practices embody a form of the 'flipped' classroom, a space where student learning becomes active, flexible and lifelong.[12]

When 'Jacquie' 'flippantly' jumps over the candlestick, she acquires confidence and illumination as she leaps. Rather than being burned or lit aflame, she traverses the candle, moving into a new space, a new home, whence she sees with clarity. She glances back, to perceive where she came from; she looks forward, dreaming of where she might go. Fresh perspectives open up to her, thanks to the candle she has just leapt. 'Jacquie': every Latinx student I have or will encounter at FIU. The candlestick: Shakespeare. 'Flippancy': how we jump, nimbly and quickly.

Notes

1. Sarah Mahler, introduction to 'Monolith or Mosaic? Miami's Twenty-First-Century Latin@ Dynamics', special issue of *Latino Studies*, 16.1 (2018): 2.
2. Carla Della Gatta, 'From *West Side Story* to *Hamlet, Prince of Cuba*: Shakespeare and Latinidad in the United States', *Shakespeare Studies*, 44 (2016): 151–6; Ruben Espinosa, 'Stranger Shakespeare', *Shakespeare Quarterly*, 67.1 (2016): 51–67.
3. Robert Talbert, *Flipped Learning: A Guide for Higher Education Faculty* (Sterling, VA: Stylus, 2017).
4. William Shakespeare, *Henry IV, Part II*, in *The Norton Shakespeare*, 3rd edn, ed. Stephen Greenblatt, Walter Cohen, Suzanne Gossett, Jean

E. Howard, Katharine Eisaman Maus and Gordon McMullan (New York: W. W. Norton, 2016), III.ii.93–4.

5. Ana Menéndez, *In Cuba I Was a German Shepherd* (New York: Grove Press, 2002).

6. Kiernan Ryan, *Shakespeare's Universality: Here's Fine Revolution* (London: Bloomsbury Arden Shakespeare, 2015).

7. Ayanna Thompson, *Passing Strange: Shakespeare, Race, and Contemporary America* (Oxford: Oxford University Press, 2011).

8. Cristina Rosell, 'A Poetics of Temperance: Gender, Genre, and Meaning-Making in Early Modern England', PhD dissertation, Louisiana State University, 2019, 146–85.

9. Espinosa, 'Stranger Shakespeare'.

10. William Shakespeare, *Richard III*, in *The Norton Shakespeare*, 3rd edn, ed. Stephen Greenblatt, Walter Cohen, Suzanne Gossett, Jean E. Howard, Katharine Eisaman Maus and Gordon McMullan (New York: W. W. Norton, 2016), I.iii.234.

11. *Oxford English Dictionary*, s.v., 'flippant, *adj.*'. http://www.oed.com (senses 1, 2a, 2b, 3, 4) (accessed 5 June 2020.

12. Talbert, *Flipped Learning*.

13

Diálogo: On Making Shakespeare Relevant to Latinx Communities

José Cruz González and David Lozano

In this conversation, directors and community-focused artists José Cruz González and David Lozano discuss the varied ways they have appropriated Shakespeare in community settings. Coincidentally, both were introduced to the world of Shakespeare performance by performing Bottom in traditional takes on *A Midsummer Night's Dream*. Yet, their work as professional theatre artists has been anything but conventional when it comes to Shakespeare. From community-engagement projects featuring lost Native American languages to physical theatre riffs off *The Tempest*, both González and Lozano demonstrate how Shakespeare can be remixed to become relevant to Latinx audiences today. Although the productions they discuss are distinct, they all share the same goal: to be relevant to Latinx audiences who might not otherwise see themselves represented in a traditional production of one of Shakespeare's plays.

José Cruz González: What has drawn you to Shakespeare?

David Lozano: That's not an easy answer. I first became passionate about Shakespeare as a performer. The experiences as a performer are so robust because of the language, the complexity of the characters, and the veracity of the actions. As a physical comedy actor, I really was able to dive into some of the comedy and, specifically, the clowns, such as was the case when I played Bottom in *A Midsummer Night's Dream* in college. Later, when I became the artistic director of Cara Mía Theatre Co. in Dallas, when we did decide to produce Shakespeare, I was looking at the universal qualities that are so extraordinary that they break out of any cultural parameters. In that way, Shakespeare can resonate at an outdoor festival in the park that has been around for over sixty years and also at a $15 million LORT [League of Resident Theatres] theatre. It's adaptable. I always look for these universal qualities that just grab us and shake us to our core no matter what our cultural centre is. And so, for me, it's when Shakespeare just jumps off the page and lights me up with its fire, and then, when I begin to reflect on how our audience can have the same experience, I know that it's a play that I want to produce.

José: I had a similar experience performing Bottom in an acting class in college, which was really my first introduction to performing Shakespeare. But, as a kid, I had several experiences watching Shakespeare. My school in my little town would take us on field trips to the American Conservatory Theater in San Francisco to see Shakespeare – that was my first introduction to Shakespeare. And I didn't know anything about what they were talking about – I had no clue what they were saying, but I still remember thinking it was really cool because I was able to relate to the physical comedy and the play on words here and there. It reminded me of Cantinflas and Charlie Chaplin.

David, you directed *Romeo and Juliet* at Cara Mía in 2013, which was the company's first ever Shakespeare production. What motivated you to do so?

David: When we did *Romeo and Juliet*, the process began much like any other play. I was just looking for plays, and, to be honest, I rarely look to Shakespeare when I look for plays for Cara Mía to produce because I believe that our own playwrights need to be produced and that our own stories need to be told. I really shy away from non-Latinx writers, but there was something about that specific moment in time where I felt compelled to look at our plays. At the time, Cara Mía was only producing two plays a year in a 296-seat proscenium. We were caught in a moment in time in our history in which our plays needed to be culturally specific, but they also needed to have a broad reach and impact. We had just produced *The Magic Rainforest*, which was a play that brought in a lot of people. It involved all kinds of design opportunities. It was multigenerational, and we brought in schools and had large groups of youths who saw the show. After that success, we looked at what we were going to produce next, and again, *Romeo and Juliet* just jumped off the page.

José: Did anything trigger you to look at *Romeo and Juliet*?

David: There was one thing that really triggered the idea. I was sitting at dinner with my mother-in-law and my wife, Frida Espinosa-Muller, who is also in the Cara Mía ensemble. While we were at dinner that night, my mother-in-law would start singing Mexican boleros to my wife, who would then sing back. They were at dinner just singing these classic love songs to each other, and I asked myself what kind of story would inspire people to just sing to each other, and in that moment, it occurred to me to look at *Romeo and Juliet*. When I reread the play, it took [me] in a different direction than previous times I had read it. The impulse and the passion between Romeo and Juliet was clearer.

José: What did you specifically see in it that made it clearer?

David: What I saw in it was two kids from every single generation of every single culture for thousands of years. I saw Romeo and his friends as those punks that roam around town and pick on people like the nurse and Peter. I saw the obnoxious and aggressively machista jokes that they play on each other, not to mention the sexual references. I also saw the fierce patriarchal household of Juliet. That was our point of departure. We dug into the idea of Romeo as a kid who runs the streets with his friends getting into trouble. And then Juliet comes from a wealthier house. What does it mean when this is basically a town in Texas?

José: Did the production explicitly say it took place in Texas?

David: No, we didn't explicitly say that. We didn't want to be explicit about transposing the play to a literal time and place that is near to us. Even so, the idea was that what if it's a suburb of Dallas that is majority Latinx.

José: How did you build the show from there? What was your process for integrating Latinx culture into the story?

David: Well, bilingual people have roots in our communities, so all of the characters were bilingual. For instance, the nurse became a nana and spoke primarily Spanish. Those lines were written by our company member Frida, who also played the character. It seemed like the nurse was finally funny for our audiences because Frida changed the terminology completely. She didn't stick a piece of wormwood in her bosom; she put a chile at the edge of her breast to wean the child off of nursing. We also added a lot of things into the characterisation, such as Chilango Spanish, that just lifted the character off the stage. Not to mention that she was brilliantly portrayed by Frida.

José: How did audiences receive the work? What was the audience feedback like?

David: The most emblematic response was from a college student, a young woman who was just graduating, who came up to me and said it was the first time she had ever understood this play while watching it.

José: That's awesome! So you were able to find a way to reach the audience, again taking Shakespeare and making it your own. Like taking a classic car that comes from Detroit and converting it into a lowrider. It still has its original form, but it has been transformed into something that is so culturally specific.

David: Exactly. What about your professional experiences with Shakespeare?

José: I have two experiences with Shakespeare. Many years ago, when I was running the Hispanic Playwrights Project at South Coast Repertory (SCR), I began working with playwright Edit Villarreal. She wanted to do a contemporary version of *Romeo and Juliet* that I would later direct. I helped her develop the play at SCR, and we eventually premiered it at Cal State LA, where I was teaching. The play began its life as *R and J*, but it eventually became *The Language of Flowers*. It was a story about Juliet being an upper-middle-class Chicana from the Westside of Los Angeles and Romeo being an undocumented house painter. Edit didn't use Shakespearean language. It was entirely contemporary language. It was really something.

The other Latinx Shakespeares I did was *Invierno*, which was inspired by *The Winter's Tale*. *Invierno* premiered at PCPA (Pacific Conservatory Theatre) in 2010. To write the play, I looked at the years around 1846 during the Mexican–American War and how that affected people in California. I looked at Spanish and Mexican cultures that were here in California at the time. I looked at the conquest battles that saw the United States take possession of lands that did not belong to it. I also weaved in California's Indigenous population, specifically the Chumash culture and the Samala language. We were able to work with the Chumash community in California's central coast to help bring back the Indigenous language that had been lost. Ultimately, we tapped into that community, and it was the first time that the language had been spoken in about one hundred years. The fact that we were able to do that onstage was a pretty awesome experience.

So those are my two experiences with Shakespeare in terms of a Latinx perspective.

David: Those are incredible and ambitious projects.

José: They really were. We had a wonderful time. Have you done any other Shakespearean work? Or, are you interested in doing more Latinx Shakespeares with Cara Mía? I know that you're committed to producing new work from Latinx playwrights, which is really important, but, for instance, there are some ways to merge the two. One of the things that Luis Alfaro has been doing with classic Greek plays is that he adapts those through a contemporary Chicanx lens. Do you think you would ever commission writers to do that? Or, do you take the lead with the artists and ask them what they are interested in creating?

David: I love Luis Alfaro's work and his series of plays on Greek tragedies. They are extremely powerful, and we would absolutely produce those plays. Even so, as a producer who primarily commissions work and, specifically, develops new work, I would need to see a really persuasive idea to consider a classical work not written by a Latinx writer. For instance, our first collaboration with El Laboratorio de la Mascara from Mexico City was actually an adaptation of *The Tempest* made from masks and object manipulation. It was a severe cutting that focused on movement and the essence of the story in a very bare-bones way. From the beginning, it was an interesting experiment for us. We never presented it in Dallas – only in Mexico. I remember when we did it in Mexico, I kept questioning how it would connect with our audiences in Texas, especially with regard to our mission and our identity.

Fast forward to 2019. For the first time in years, I have come across a Shakespearean play that I could consider and reposition to make it accessible to our mission and our moment – *The Merchant of Venice*. Talking to you,

José, and hearing the descriptions of your plays and how you have reinvented Shakespeare's plays has made me reconsider some things. This is not something we have looked at because I am a bit of a purist when it comes to Shakespeare. I look at the play itself to see what it reveals. Elise Thoron, who is in the Cara Mía ensemble, was commissioned by Oregon Shakespeare Festival's *Play on!* to write a translation of *The Merchant of Venice*. I remember reading it in two sittings; during the second sitting, I picked it up in Act IV. I was reading Shylock, and I said to myself 'this is a militant character here', and I felt like Shylock could be a Latino Jew. I was bowled over by the intensity of Thoron's translation because of the cutting and the editing. It was still essentially Shakespeare's original language, but I was pulled into that play in a way I hadn't been before. Now I am looking at it as a possibility for a future reading or a production at Cara Mía. It was the intensity of Shylock's position in his society and his fervent and militant reactions to the other characters that drew me in. I feel like if Cara Mía were to perform this play for our audiences, who are really more diverse than just Latinos – our audience is majority Latinx, but more so an audience that is engaged by human and civil rights conversations – I think this play could be very explosive.

José: That's really awesome. I have one last connection to Shakespeare that I want to tell you about. I write for young people as well as for families and adults. I have a Theatre for Young Audiences piece called *Forever Poppy* that I wrote a number of years ago. First, I wrote it as a book, and then I adapted it into a play. It was developed in 2018 at the Kennedy Center through its New Visions, New Voices programme. *Forever Poppy* questions [what might have happened] if Shakespeare's lineage had continued on and what that would be like if his lineage included a child of colour. The play looks at the possible Shakespearean bloodline of a (Latina, African, Native) mixed-race child. On her journey of discovering her lineage, she comes to learn that she is the last living descendent of Shakespeare. *Forever Poppy* will have its world premiere at Childsplay in Tempe, Arizona, during the 2021–22 season.

David: I want to ask you one last question. Do you think it is important for Latinx theatre artists to do Shakespeare, maybe even more than other historically canonised playwrights?

José: I think it's an individual thing in terms of the artists. Sometimes you have the producers pitching ideas to artists. That's one thing. But I think, for me, in terms of my own journey, I start to look at how I can try something that I maybe haven't tried before. In the case of *Invierno*, when I read *The Winter's Tale*, I saw it through the lens of California, through the lens of Latinidad. It was all right there so I was able to take Shakespeare and make it my own. It is inspired by his work, but it is still my own. I think my own experiences are similar to other artists who every now and then will want to try something different. They will want to put it through their lens and see what they can learn about themselves and about their work. Shakespeare is always going to be done, no matter what, and so it will always be there for the artist's choosing.

David: That's powerful. I hear you talk about your work, and I hear such an immersion into a project that it becomes a reinvention of the work. It places it in a new context, which I believe is extremely powerful, especially because your work is so community driven.

José: That's right. Given our communities and, in particular, our work on a lot of community-based projects, we are always dealing with a lot of communities that don't even know what theatre is. To have these communities come to a theatre space that oftentimes they have felt excluded from for many reasons and then all of a sudden see themselves reflected onstage and in the language is a really powerful thing. Of course, we have a long way to go, but the work you are doing, David, with Cara Mía, and the artistry and commitment to the community – what you are doing is sacred work. That's what I believe, and I applaud you.

David: I appreciate that, José. What a pleasure to speak with you. You're a legendary playwright and I am humbled at how warm you've been to me in the past and the impact you have made on generations of playwrights.

14

Romeo y Julieta: A Spanish-Language Shakespeare in the Park

Daphnie Sicre

In 2006, while I was a high school drama teacher in Miami, Florida, I was approached and asked to direct Miami's first ever Spanish-language production of Shakespeare in the Park – *Romeo y Julieta*. The request came to me by way of one of my students, Steven Rodriguez, on behalf of Colleen Stovall, the artistic director of Shakespeare Miami (formerly the Miami Shakespeare Festival). Colleen had been directing Shakespeare in Peacock Park in Coconut Grove, Miami, and had expressed an interest in mounting a Spanish-language production of *Romeo and Juliet*. The only problem was that she did not speak Spanish. Steven, who had been cast in her *Taming of the Shrew* and was her intern at the time, suggested my name.

I am fluent in Spanish and had directed theatre productions in this language before, but I had never directed Shakespeare in Spanish. I had also only directed scenes and monologues from Shakespeare's work, never a full-length production. Fortunately, in 2004, I had spent the summer taking workshops with the Royal Shakespeare Academy and the Globe Theatre. Thus, I embraced the challenge and jumped right on board. Needless to say, mounting *Romeo y Julieta* was a crash course in translating a classic to Spanish for various Latinx audiences. From casting concerns to translation choices to local weather conditions, the challenges were many. But overcoming all these challenges was worth the learning experience, especially since this production introduced many local Latinx audiences to a classical work in their native tongue for the first time, and for free.

I met with Colleen, and we finalised the production dates for the summer. We quickly started production and casting meetings. She also contacted the Miami-Dade Division of Arts and Culture, which had held various free concerts at the West Miami Dade Park but had never helped produce any Shakespeare in the Park productions. With the help of the Miami-Dade Division of Arts and Culture as well as the City of Miami Parks and

Recreation, Shakespeare Miami agreed to host three nights of Shakespeare in the Park in Spanish, for free, at Tropical Park as part of the newly formed *Noches Tropicales*.[1] *Romeo y Julieta* ran from 21 to 23 July 2006, as part of this series. With the support of Mayor Manny Diaz, and donations from local and non-local businesses for lumber and costumes, our production was set. But before we could start, we needed a cast, and I needed to pick the right script.

The first major challenge was casting. Everything about Shakespeare Miami was on a volunteer basis. Neither I nor the actors would be paid for our role in the production. This also meant that we could not cast union actors, thus limiting our acting pool selection in Miami. Colleen and I created a casting call in both English and Spanish that we posted through multiple outlets, from *Craig's List* to *Backstage*. We also posted on several Spanish casting sites. We asked for Latinx actors fluent in Spanish as well as actors who understood and would be willing to act in Spanish. Unfortunately, the response was very low, likely a result of the online casting exposure not being as far reaching as it would be today, as well as the volunteer nature of the production. I turned to various high school teachers across the area and asked them to share this opportunity with their Spanish-speaking students. We also approached students at University of Miami and Florida International University (FIU). Given the age of most of the characters in *Romeo y Julieta*, high school and college theatre students were the perfect casting choice.

We had no response from students at the University of Miami, but several FIU and high school students showed up to audition. Some community members came out to audition as well, which was perfect, as we needed strong actors to play the friar, the nurse, and Romeo and Juliet's parents. Most of the community did not have experience acting, but they still wanted to give it a try, and thus they came out and auditioned. Our nurse was a white American actress who had learned Spanish in high school and college. She spoke Spanish with a noticeable American accent but was charming in the role of the nurse. She had previously performed with Shakespeare Miami and had worked with Colleen. Our friar was a complete surprise: he had never acted before but was probably one of the most talented actors I had ever worked with. The actor that played Juliet's father was an improv actor who wanted to give dramatic acting a try, and he made all of our rehearsals a blast. Juliet was a former FIU film student who looked young enough to portray a fourteen-year-old, and Romeo was Steven, the student who initially contacted me about the production. Despite the age difference and the actors' unfamiliarity with each other, our Romeo and Juliet shared a powerful chemistry. Once onstage, the friar and the nurse excelled in all their scenes, becoming audience favourites.

We managed to cast every role in the show despite the low turnout of trained actors. However, after we cast Romeo's parents, they both dropped out due to the demands of the rehearsal schedule. We also had a couple of other actors who played minor roles drop out for various reasons. This is community theatre where no one gets paid, and individuals who have not previously acted in a professional setting often do not realise the importance of regularly attending rehearsals. Although we broke up the rehearsals into scenes, the schedule still proved too demanding for some. What we were not ready for was having the actress who played Romeo's mother drop out the week the play opened! Without an actress, and with only one week until opening, we ended up cutting most of Romeo's mother's lines from the play. But we still needed a Lady Montague for Mercutio's death and Romeo's banishment. With no other options, I stepped up, memorised the lines, and played the role for the crucial scenes.

Overall, we ended up casting seventeen actors, from ten different countries: Colombia, Venezuela, the Dominican Republic, Costa Rica, Mexico, Cuba, Peru, Ecuador, Brazil and the United States (including one actor from Puerto Rico). In all my years of directing, that is the only time I have had the pleasure of working with so many Latinx and Latin American actors in one play. I loved that everyone came from all over the Americas – as came out in performance through the different Spanish accents – and that they were all here to put on this production for the community. However, the diversity of the cast created problems with the script and the Spanish language used.

Choosing the script was not an easy process. As the only fluent Spanish speaker on the production team, I had to select the script. In 2006, Amazon and other online book retailers did not have as many options as they do now. I could not just search online for Spanish-language translations of *Romeo and Juliet*. I called my family in Spain and asked them to go to a couple of bookstores and purchase copies of the play. I received seven different translations in the mail. It took me a couple of weeks to read all them. I wanted to find a translation that kept the rhythm and the rhyme of Shakespeare's words. It was important that the translation retain the iambic pentameter as well as the richness and flow of the language. My favourite script was Pablo Neruda's 1964 translation, a beautiful, poetic adaptation in which Neruda intertwined his own language and made it his own. Yet, because the translation contained neither the fluidity nor the metre of Shakespeare's text, I had to find another version. If I wanted to keep the same integrity of Shakespeare's words, I needed to pick a translation closer to his original script.

Next, I landed on a 2003 translation from Colección Letras Universales, which seemed most useful because it provided a bilingual translation side by side with the original. This text was written in conjunction with the Shakespeare Institute at the University of Birmingham in Stratford-upon-Avon, and it pulled from an English version that was similar to the First Quarto from 1599 (Q2) and 1623 (F). It maintained the metre and rhyme of the English. As soon as we started table work, however, we discovered that this script was not ideal. The page layout helped with translations, but the actors' diverse backgrounds made it complicated to define some of the words in the script as well as to pronounce certain words. It became clear that even though we all spoke Spanish and were predominantly Latinx, there were too many unknown Spanish words in the script. It was the curse and blessing of casting diverse Latinx actors from all across the Americas. The Spanish used was similar to the 'old Spanish' used during the 1500s and 1600s in Spain, difficult to understand in much the same way as Elizabethan English. We often found ourselves using *No Fear Shakespeare* to translate the English, just to then translate it back to the Spanish. Had we had a Spanish-speaking dramaturg or a vocal coach or even someone to work on dialect, we might have been able to use this version, but given that we were all volunteers, this script was not working. Thus it became very tedious. After a couple rehearsals, the cast asked whether there was another translation we could use.

At that point, I decided to bring in Ángel-Lui Pujante's 1993 version. As one of the leading Spanish translators of Shakespeare, Pujante's craft is evident. The difference was like night and day. Coincidently, several actors shared that they had read that version when they were in middle school or high school, which was a revelation to me. Personally, growing up in Spain, I had not read Shakespeare's work before I came to the United States. In contrast, several of the actors came from Latin American countries whose governments mandate (translated) Shakespeare as part of the curriculum. The Pujante script helped unify the cast. It was written in the most universal, approachable language and was thus easier for the cast to memorise. It also provided useful Spanish annotations. I kept the Colección Letras Universales version available as well, though, for its annotated notes and side-by-side translation. This working method with the two scripts proved useful for the actors who did not speak Spanish fluently.

After the table work, we started our rehearsals. Since we were performing in the park, our rehearsals were outdoors. This led to a consistent challenge in Miami, where the rainy season extends from April to July, and the hurricane season extends from June to November. June to July is the intersection of these two seasons, when the frequent midday storms can last up to four hours. Unfortunately, our rehearsals (which took place in the late afternoons and early evenings, after the actors were done with work or school) often coincided with these storms. We were lucky, however, in our choice of rehearsal location. Rather than rehearsing at Tropical Park, where the performances would take place, we rehearsed at Peacock Park (site of previous Shakespeare at the Park productions), which was closer for everyone involved.[2] Fortunately, Peacock Park not only had a rehearsal space similar to the two-storey stage that would be built for the production; it also provided us with refuge during the rain. Tropical Park had no such sheltered spaces.

Rain or shine, the show was going to happen! Unfortunately, the weather did not want to cooperate. The set was built a week before opening, and its construction was followed by daily bouts of rain. It rained so much that our first performance was cancelled. Although the rain had stopped by the scheduled start time, there was so much water accumulated in the soil that no audience member would have wanted to sit in the mud for three and a half hours to watch a production of Shakespeare – even a free one.

Fortunately, we opened the next day, 21 July 2006, and we were able to perform three shows for the community. Hundreds of people showed up. They brought their blankets, chairs and bright smiles. The *Miami Herald* wrote a feature on us, describing our production as the focal contribution to *Noches Tropicales*, what would become a centre for cultural arts in West Miami-Dade. Thanks to our production, *Noches Tropicales* was officially launched. Although *Noches Tropicales* has not since produced another Shakespeare in the Park, the programme is in its thirteenth year as of 2020, and it still brings free Latinx arts to audiences in the park. [3] More importantly, this experience brought the cast closer together, and many of us have kept in touch to this day.

Overall, the process of mounting *Romeo y Julieta* was an incredible learning experience: from casting Spanish-speaking actors from across the Americas, to spending weeks finding the perfect translation for the cast, to mounting a production in the park in the middle of the rainy season in Miami. All the challenges were worth it, in the end, in order to mount Miami's first ever free Spanish-language Shakespeare in the Park.

Notes

1. *Stars at the Park Noches Tropicales* is an annual programme of Miami-Dade Parks that provides local communities with culturally relevant entertainment for families.
2. Tropical Park is a 275-acre park west of South Miami near Palmetto Expressway and Bird Road, whereas Peacock Park is a 9.4-acre park in Coconut Grove closer to Biscayne Bay.
3. Colleen took a break from producing plays and rebranded the Miami Shakespeare Festival as Shakespeare Miami. She still produces plays in the park, but she has not since produced one in Spanish.

15

Politics, Poetry and Popular Music: Remixing Neruda's *Romeo y Julieta*

Jerry Ruiz

In spring 2016, Stephanie Ybarra, then the director of special artistic projects at The Public Theater, approached me about directing a staged reading of Pablo Neruda's 1964 play *Romeo y Julieta*. Ybarra oversaw The Public's Mobile Unit programme, which tours performances of Shakespeare's works to correctional facilities, homeless shelters and community centres across New York City's five boroughs. Familiar with my extensive history of working with Latinx and Spanish-language artists and audiences, she entrusted me with spearheading this project.

The Mobile Unit, re-established under the leadership of artistic director Oskar Eustis in 2010 after a thirty-year hiatus, aims to overcome the various barriers that communities and individuals might face in accessing Shakespeare. As The Public Theater contemplated ways to reach non-English-speaking communities, it looked back to its own rich tradition of Spanish-language performances during Joseph Papp's tenure as artistic director. In fact, in the 1960s, Papp wrote to Pablo Neruda seeking permission to tour a version of his Spanish-language translation of *Romeo and Juliet*. Neruda assented.

In summer 2016, following the Mobile Unit's current formula of stripped-down stagings and ninety-minute versions of Shakespeare's texts, we held public readings of an abridged version of Neruda's work. The initial readings took place at an after-school programme for high schoolers in Brooklyn and at a church in the Jackson Heights neighbourhood in Queens. This initial project would develop further over the next few years. As it did so, I gradually discovered the power of well-known popular music to illuminate Shakespeare's (and Neruda's) play for Spanish-speaking audiences.

Neruda's contemporaries in Chilean music, most famously Violeta Parra, had responded to the injustices of their day through powerful protest music. In our work, the sociopolitical context of Neruda's translation became intertwined with a contemporaneous musical sound track as an entry point for staging the play in Spanish. The project gradually blossomed into *Mala Estrella*, a streamlined version of the Romeo and Juliet story culled from Neruda's translation, and then combined with popular Latin American music and original Spanish-language songs.

Preparation of the Text of *Romeo y Julieta* for a Mobile Unit Staged Reading

Before I began assembling my script for the initial readings in summer 2016, Ybarra asked me to follow the performance parameters typically employed by the Mobile Unit: the performance should be about ninety to a hundred minutes in length, with approximately eight or nine actors playing all of the roles. These parameters enable the performance to be both portable and accessible. At the same time, they force a director to make some crucial choices about how to prepare the text.

As I began to cut Neruda's translation, I used another Mobile Unit script as a guide for approaching a ninety-minute run time while keeping the story clear and intact: dramaturg James Shapiro's cut of Shakespeare's original *Romeo and Juliet* text. This English-language production had taken place in spring 2016, not long before our staged readings. Shapiro, an eminent Shakespearean scholar, has prepared several cuts for the Mobile Unit. Having assisted on a production of *Much Ado about Nothing* that used one of his cuts, I knew that his work would always strive for narrative clarity and maintain the spirit of the original text.

Directorially, my way into considering *Romeo and Juliet* via Neruda began with the theme of exile. The discovery that Neruda had spent three years in exile in the late 1940s and early 1950s because of his affiliation with the Communist Party proved illuminating, given that Romeo ends up in exile after killing Tybalt. As such, Romeo's forced departure from Verona seems quite poignant, and I began to consider the larger sociopolitical realities of Neruda's native Chile in the mid-1960s. This angle seemed especially important given that Neruda carved out a significant career not only as poet but as a diplomat and political figure. He eventually returned to Chile, remaining active in politics. In fact, by 1970, his supporters wanted to nominate him as a presidential candidate, but he declined, instead endorsing pro-democracy leader Salvador Allende. Allende was eventually elected and then overthrown by Pinochet, whose regime some still blame for Neruda's mysterious death in 1973.

Part of what makes Neruda's telling of this story unique and important is his keen awareness of the power of social unrest to shape the personal lives of individuals living under unstable or unjust authoritarian regimes. Romeo and Juliet's romance becomes more than teenage rebellion: it is also an act of political subversion. Romeo's eventual exile takes on a deeper significance in a translation by a Chilean poet who found himself exiled. Moreover, it might resonate very deeply with a Spanish-speaking audience of immigrants and descendants of immigrants now living in the United States. This context was an essential part of my instructions to the actors on the first day of rehearsal, as well as in subsequent table work. I wanted them all to consider that Romeo and Juliet's love is truly dangerous and destabilising, and that their actions are not just romantic and heroic, but defiant. At the same time, I began to view the role of the prince in the play as that of an authoritarian, autocratic leader who essentially imposes martial law in Verona, in part to gain control of the escalating (and seemingly endless) feud between the Capulets and the Montagues.

Driven by a desire to capture the unrest and uncertainty of Neruda's time, I gravitated towards the music of his contemporaries: the great Chilean protest singer-songwriters Victor Jara and Violeta Parra. I invited Julián Mesri, the highly knowledgeable Argentinian musician and composer (as well as actor and playwright), to join us for the reading. I knew that his familiarity with this music would help me integrate appropriate musical content. In the end, we incorporated the ballad 'Muchacha Ojos de Papel' by Luis Alberto Spinetta to underscore the fateful first meeting between Romeo and Juliet, and Violeta Parra's iconic song 'Gracias a la vida' to punctuate the deaths of Mercutio and Tybalt. Mesri wrote original music for the prologue and turned the prince's final speech into an epilogue, both of which he sang.

The Latin American music, paired with Neruda's beautiful language, rendered many of the play's well-known passages new again. Romeo and Juliet's first meeting and the subsequent balcony scene – scenes that many theatre aficionados can recite by memory and that are replete with well-worn phrases such as 'O Romeo, Romeo, wherefore art thou Romeo?' and 'a rose by any other name would smell as sweet' – became novel again for a bilingual audience hearing them for the first time in Spanish. Additionally, the cast's awareness of the sociopolitical textures at play for Neruda and his original audiences brought Shakespeare's tragedy to life in a new and exciting way for our artists and audiences alike.

Adaptation: Development of *Mala Estrella/Star Crossed*

In summer 2017, Ybarra approached me again about continuing my work with the Mobile Unit on *Romeo y Julieta*. This time, The Public was collaborating with the New York City Parks SummerStage programme, which presents free performances in parks throughout all five boroughs.

The idea that emerged throughout my conversations with Ybarra was that music, especially songs known to a Spanish-speaking audience, could serve as a gateway into Neruda's translation of Shakespeare's story for SummerStage's Spanish-speaking audience, who are accustomed to enjoying live music but might not be as well versed in classical theatre.

Ybarra and I approached the highly acclaimed Argentinian performer Sofia Rei. Rei writes original music and also interprets well-known traditional songs from the Latin American canon in a contemporary style, employing elements of electronic music such as vocal loops. Rei eventually selected a number of songs, and through a series of conversations, we placed them strategically throughout the play. Many of these songs were from Chile or Argentina, with two Violeta Parra pieces, as well as Spinetta's aforementioned ballad 'Muchacha Ojos de Papel'. Rei sang all the songs herself, backed by her three-piece band. This decision was made for somewhat practical reasons, chiefly to allow us to cast the best Spanish-speaking actors available without having to worry about their singing abilities. Her voice, and the presence of the musicians, who added a significant amount of underscoring, hinted at the dynamic storytelling potential inherent in this approach. We billed the evening as *Los Desdichados*, or *Star Crossed*. The event, which used a cast of four in addition to the four musicians, offered select highlights from the love story at the centre of Shakespeare's play with various songs serving as connective tissue.

The following year, in 2018, The Public commissioned me to continue developing the project with Sofia Rei. Although we were satisfied with the four-actor version of *Star Crossed* presented in 2017, it had been limited to scenes between the two lovers and their respective confidants, the nurse and the friar, which rendered it solely a love story, stripping it of the sociopolitical context that served as our initial entry point into Neruda's text. Characters such as Mercutio (with his raunchy humour) and the foppish suitor Paris had been entirely absent, which may have meant a missed opportunity to connect with the audience through comedy.

For this third iteration, then, we added a fifth actor who would play Mercutio, the prince and Paris. The actress playing the nurse would also double as Tybalt, allowing us to depict the fateful fights between Mercutio and Tybalt and then Romeo and Tybalt; the actor playing the friar would also play Capulet and the comedic role of the servant Peter. Additionally, Rei would be further integrated into the dramatic structure of the evening, serving as the chorus at the beginning and end of the play. She became our primary storyteller, framing the evening more clearly. With Rei in this role – performing both love songs reflective of the central characters' journey and protest music evocative of the larger sociopolitical circumstances – we were able to successfully interweave those two strands of the story.

The song list remained largely intact from the previous version, with some key additions. In brainstorming this new version with Rei, I landed on a satisfying Spanish title for the project: *Mala Estrella*. This phrase was pulled from Neruda's translation of the play's famous prologue sonnet. When I mentioned this new title to Rei, she replied, 'that sounds like the perfect title for a *cumbia*'. Rei proceeded to compose a cumbia song with lyrics based on Neruda's translation of the prologue. An opening number in the cumbia style – which originates in Colombia and Venezuela, and combines African, Indigenous and European influences – firmly places these characters and their story in the Americas from the beginning. This number was performed following an abbreviated version of the fight between the Montague and Capulet servants, with Romeo intervening and Tybalt interrupting to clash with him. Rei also composed a song titled 'Reina Mab', which was combined with a condensed version of Mercutio's Queen Mab speech. The scene was staged with Mercutio and Romeo smoking marijuana before entering the Capulets' feast.

It so happened that some of our actors this time around could sing well, so Romeo ended up singing a snippet of 'Muchacha Ojos de Papel', Romeo and Juliet sang 'Jurame' (a romantic ballad by Mexican songwriter Maria Grever) as a duet, and the friar rapped his first speech as well as a subsequent monologue where he is giving counsel to Romeo. All these changes resulted in a work that felt complete and satisfying as a theatrical narrative buoyed by the constant presence of music, unlike the version from the previous summer.

Retrospect

There are some obvious challenges when introducing a primarily Spanish-speaking audience to Shakespeare's work. Language and cultural barriers may exist, and some of these audiences have likely not enjoyed the degree of familiarity with Shakespeare that even non-theatre-going English speakers usually have; indeed, *Romeo and Juliet* is commonly assigned as part of the curriculum in American high schools, and many English speakers have likely watched a film version at some point, even if they have never seen it in a theatre.

Fortunately, Neruda gifted us with a masterful Spanish translation of *Romeo and Juliet*, which served Ybarra, Rei and me as the foundational piece of our continued work on the material from iteration to iteration. The process of making Shakespeare our own and filtering it through our cultural experiences while adding both traditional and new music proved to be artistically rewarding. In our experience, popular music played a key role in making the story accessible to a Spanish-speaking audience, while underscoring the political resonance that Shakespeare's play would have had for a poet such as Neruda in his time, and that it continues to have for Spanish speakers in the United States, individuals who may well have left their homeland behind due to political unrest or economic uncertainty.

16

'Lleno de Tejanidad': Staging a Bilingual *Comedy of Errors* in Central Texas

Joe Falocco

The Comedy of Errors has a reputation as a knockabout farce whose plot depends on the confusion arising from a series of improbable coincidences. In this play, two sets of twins (two masters and two servants) are separated at birth. One master and one servant grow up in Ephesus, while the other pair grows up in Syracuse. On a fateful day, the 'boys from Syracuse' arrive in Ephesus, and chaos ensues as everyone mistakes them for their counterparts. Yet this farcical play also seriously considers the nature of identity. Its characters find that their sense of self is not defined in monistic isolation. Instead, their identity is contingent on relationships to family members and community. Thus, Antipholus of Syracuse discovers that to know 'Who he is' he must first understand 'Whose he is', by re-establishing a connection with his long-lost mother and brother.

I had long suspected that these two attributes of *The Comedy of Errors* – its reliance on comedic confusion and its exploration of the quest for identity – would lend themselves to a bilingual adaptation in which the characters from the two cities spoke opposing languages. The resulting linguistic chaos would enhance the play's farcical tone, while the theme of identity would hopefully resound with bilingual audiences, whose sense of self is often divided between two cultures and two languages. In 2014, I found myself teaching at Texas State University, a Hispanic-Serving Institution whose student body is roughly 40 per cent Latinx (a percentage that mirrors the population of Texas as a whole). It seemed the time had come to pursue this idea further.

My own knowledge of Spanish is imperfect and derives from my ability to speak, read and write Italian. As every speaker of both languages knows, the similarities between the two initially aid in comprehension but eventually cause more problems than they solve due to the high number of 'false cognates' – words that only appear to be identical but that in reality have divergent meanings. Since Spanish is much more prevalent than Italian in the

United States today – and given the population in San Marcos, where Texas State University is located – it made sense to use Spanish for this adaptation. I also see many (admittedly imperfect) parallels between the situation of Spanish-speaking immigrants today and my great-grandparents' generation, who came from southern Italy. Italian Americans, by and large, solved the riddle of assimilation by 'choosing sides' and wholeheartedly embracing their new American identity. But this is not the only answer to assimilation, and Latinx individuals need not make such a binary choice in the twenty-first century. They do not have to turn their back on Latinx language and culture in order to live in the United States. The characters in this adaptation, like many Latinx Americans today, find a way forward by uniting the English and Spanish sides of their identity.

Building the Script

To begin the process of adaptation, I found an uncredited public-domain Spanish-language version of the play online, which appeared to be a Castilian (as opposed to a Latin American) translation from the late nineteenth or early twentieth century. I then set about cutting and pasting dialogue from this translation into Shakespeare's original text.[1] The first major decision was which language the characters of each city should speak. The play is set entirely in Ephesus, and this city's characters speak roughly 60 per cent of the play's dialogue. I wanted very much for our script to be more than 50 per cent Spanish in order to counter a prevalent trend among the 'bilingual theatre' currently offered in Central Texas. In most of these productions, the dialogue is overwhelmingly in English, with an occasional 'pues' or 'que no' thrown in for 'Latin flavour'. There is certainly nothing wrong with theatre that targets English-speaking Latinxs, but such an approach limits access for the area's large Spanish-dominant population.

The challenge with making Ephesus the Spanish-speaking city, however, is that the government of this city is portrayed in Shakespeare's play as brutal and repressive. I therefore considered 'flipping the script' and making the characters from Syracuse undocumented Latinx immigrants in a hostile anglophone Ephesus that would resemble contemporary Texas. Such a concept would be even more tempting in 2020 than it had been in 2014, but this approach is not amenable to comedy. Nor, unfortunately, are there many alternative settings that could be drawn from the long, sad history of Anglo–Latinx relations in Texas to justify a farcical tone. That is why, for its next project, our creative team hopes to mount a bilingual *Romeo and Juliet* set in Texas in the 1850s, in which the Capulets will be long-time, Spanish-speaking Tejano residents and the Montagues will be English-speaking newcomers. For *The Comedy of Errors*, however, my desire to maximise the adaptation's Spanish content, and to avoid references to painful events in Texas's past and present, led me to adopt Cuba as the setting. This setting made sense – in part, because Shakespeare's play describes two nations that have been involved for many years in a low-level conflict with trade forbidden and families separated, a scenario that mirrors the situation that existed until very recently between the United States and Cuba.

In light of Duke Solinus's harsh and capricious policies, I chose to costume him as a guerrilla turned 'caudillo', or military strongman. Though somewhat of a cliché, this imagery has some historical justification across the Latin American political spectrum: from Noriega in Panama and Trujillo in the Dominican Republic to the Ortegas in Nicaragua and the Castros in Cuba. Dressed in combat fatigues and a red beret, our Duke Solinus resembled, more than anyone else, a young Hugo Chavez. This design choice was well received in both of our San Marcos productions (2015 and 2017). It remains to be seen, however, how this play would land if we succeed in taking this show to Florida, since that state has a significant Cuban and Venezuelan population that may not see the caudillo archetype as appropriate comic material. In Texas, because most of our performers spoke with Mexican accents, the play's setting served our purpose of remaining firmly Latinx while avoiding visual references to Tejano culture.

Once the linguistic preferences of each character had been determined, I cobbled together a rough draft of the script and sent it to my colleague David Navarro, in Texas State's Department of Modern Languages. David was kind enough to smooth over the rough edges created by my juxtaposition of English and Spanish dialogue, and also to 'Americanise' the script by removing the 'vosotros' form of address and other locutions not common to American Spanish. We staged a public reading of this draft in October 2014, using Spanish-speaking students and faculty along with a few volunteer actors from Austin. While readings of this kind are common for any new work, it was an especially important step for this bilingual adaptation since we needed to gauge the ability of both Spanish-dominant and English-dominant audience members to understand the text. Response to this reading was quite positive.

Navigating the Language Divide

In order to stage a full production in summer 2015, I applied for and received an Equity and Access Grant from the university. Crucially, the grant allowed us to access a larger pool of bilingual actors and to *pay* these actors rather than asking them to volunteer their time. With the money, we hired four bilingual actors from Austin and also built the production. To fill out our cast, David then set up a special topics course in the Department of Modern Languages, through which Spanish majors were able to earn academic credit by playing smaller roles.

As we looked forward to this summertime staging, however, several issues needed to be addressed. With any production of *The Comedy of Errors*, one must decide whether to use four actors for the two sets of twins (two Dromios and two Antipholi) or to have one actor play both servants and another to play both masters.[2] In the final scene, all four characters must appear onstage together, which leads many companies to use four actors the whole time. In my own career, however, I have found that having two actors play four characters better serves the play, since it prevents the audience from getting ahead of the production. 'Doubles' – typically student interns – can then be brought on for the play's final scene, by which point the audience has, hopefully, suspended its disbelief.

We therefore chose to have one performer play both Dromios and another play both Antipholi. This choice had the advantage of reinforcing our thematic desire to explore the division of identity through linguistic code-switching. The challenge was that we needed to cast two actors who were not only bilingual but who had an equal command of English and Spanish. Fortunately, in both 2015 and 2017, Austin-based actor Julio Mella was available to play the Antipholi. A native of Mexico City, Julio has lived in the United States for decades and speaks English with only a trace of an accent. Our Dromios (Eva McQuade in 2015 and Sergio Alvarado in 2017) were both more comfortable in English, but they were able to compensate for any deficiencies in their Spanish through the use of broad comic mime.

A more vexing challenge came in the play's first scene. For most of our adaptation, in any given scene some characters speak Spanish while others speak English. This practice mirrors a conversation pattern that is common in Central Texas, and the dialogue in our adaptation can be understood by anyone who speaks either language (and have special resonance for those who speak both). The first scene of *The Comedy of Errors*, however, contains a series of long speeches by Egeon that provide essential exposition. We needed all audience members, regardless of linguistic preference, to understand every word Egeon says. I therefore introduced the character of the 'bilingual soldier', who would translate everything Egeon says into Spanish.

In our October 2014 reading, this translation was done in a formal manner resembling what one would expect at a political summit or academic conference. Egeon spoke; the soldier translated. The result was dreadfully boring and caused the audience to tune out for most of this scene. For summer 2015, I therefore reverted to a strategy I had used in a production of *The Comedy of Errors* at the Shakespeare Festival of Arkansas in 2001. That production was set in postwar Italy during the time of the American occupation, when the US military ruled the south of the country in collaboration with organised crime.

Duke Solinus was a local Don, and an Italian American serviceman 'translated' Egeon's speech for him. Since none of the actors (or audience) spoke Italian, this scene was an exercise in what Dario Fo calls 'Grammelo': the comic mixture of a few words of a foreign language with characteristic sounds and broad gestures.[3] This approach had succeeded in 2001 in turning the tedious exposition of the first scene into a comic highlight of the production.

I decided to try something similar with our bilingual adaptation in Texas. Fortunately, I was able to rely on the comic talents of Jesus Valles as the bilingual soldier. Jesus is an Austin-based performer, who is skilful in clowning and fluent in both English and Spanish. Jesus wove a series of Latinx pop culture references into his recounting of Egeon's saga. Transcription cannot do this performance justice: Jesus was sensational and a highlight of the production.[4] Egeon's description of his 'wealth increased / By prosperous voyages I often made / To Epidamnum' was rendered by Jesus as 'Se volvió muy rico. Iqual que el Chapo'.[5] The phrase, 'That by misfortunes was my life prolonged, / To tell sad stories of my own mishaps', became 'Asi que le cuento un historia muy larga, como *La Rosa de Guadalupe*'.[6] These interpolations were, by Jesus's own description, 'lleno de Tejanidad' ('full of Tejanidad') and served to put our Central Texas audiences at ease through a series of shared cultural references. If we ever take the show to Florida, we will need find similar common denominators among that state's more diverse Latinx population.

In preparation for our summer 2015 production, we did another public reading in January of that year, featuring the contracted professional actors along with student volunteers. We found that more work needed to be done to replace Castilian words with Latin American ones that were more accessible to our community. David Navarro's efforts have been tireless in this regard, and the script has continued to evolve in each iteration, from our first reading in 2014 to the most recent staging in 2017. One small example must suffice. When Dromio complains that he has been transformed 'both in mind and in my shape', Luciana taunts him in the Shakespearean text with 'If thou art changed to aught, 'tis to an ass'.[7] The public domain translation rendered this line as, 'Sí en algo te has convertido, es en asno'. The problem is that none of our actors had ever heard the word *asno*. David therefore changed it to *burro*, which even our anglophone audience members understood. While most theatrical works are composed in a collaborative manner, this project was even more dependent on this kind of shared authorship, since we were working from a variety of linguistic and cultural perspectives (David is a native of Spain; our actors were Latinx; and I am white). As we began rehearsals in summer 2015, we discovered that our student actors (almost all of whom were heritage speakers, having grown up speaking Spanish) found Shakespeare in translation as daunting as many English-speaking undergraduates find the Elizabethan original. 'We just don't use that many words when we speak

Spanish', was a common lament. Ultimately, however, the company rose to the occasion with the help of David's skilful coaching.

Looking Back on the Performance

The 2015 production was a great success. Admission was free and open to the public. We got the word out in part through the bulletin of the local Catholic church. The demographic in attendance differed significantly from a typical theatre audience, which tends to be predominantly white and over fifty. Our public, instead, was majority Latinx and represented a much broader age range. Many families brought their children, who appreciated the play's broad comedy and fast pace. It was especially rewarding to see several generations of a single family in attendance, with everyone able to appreciate the show despite their linguistic preference.

Due to budgetary restrictions, I played the role of Egeon myself in 2015. For me personally, the pay-off of this production came in the play's final scene. Egeon, sentenced to death for journeying to a forbidden country, is overjoyed when he sees his long-lost son. He does not realise, however, that the man he assumes is Antipholus of Syracuse is actually Antipholus of Ephesus, who does not recognise him. Although Egeon insists, 'But tell me yet, dost thou not know my voice?', his son still does not know him.[8] Egeon then laments:

> Not now my voice! O time's extremity,
> Hast thou so cracked and splitted my poor tongue
> In seven short years, that here my only son
> Knows not my feeble key of untuned cares?[9]

In our production, this moment was all the more poignant because the father and son were, literally, speaking different languages. This exchange seemed to me to represent a sadly archetypal moment in the American experience, in which immigrant parents (and especially grandparents) are unable to speak to their descendants because they do not share a common language. I remember how my own father, whose parents had forbidden the speaking of Italian in their home because they wanted to become 'American', had been unable to communicate with his grandmother. My hope was that the resolution of this adaptation, in which the Spanish and English sides of the family are reunited in a new 'nativity' following decades of separation,[10] might lead our students and younger audience members to realise that they do not have to make the same mistakes my family made. They do not have to forget Spanish in order to learn English. Instead, their identities can be fully realised through the union of these two languages.

When we staged our bilingual *Comedy of Errors* in 2015, the newly

announced DACA (Deferred Action for Childhood Arrivals) and DAPA
(Deferred Action for Parents of Americans) programmes seemed to herald
a breakthrough in immigration policy, and the Obama administration had
recently announced steps towards rapprochement with Cuba. We believed
our theatrical efforts to be on the right side of history. In early 2016, I therefore applied for an NEA Challenge America grant that would allow us to
mount a better-funded version of our script in 2017. We got the grant, but,
alas, when the time came to stage this second production the world seemed
very different. Ever since the presidential election in November 2016, the
Texas State campus has suffered a series of ugly incidents involving the distribution of racist propaganda. Immigration raids have swept up many people
in Central Texas, and some of my students who previously felt safe under
DACA now no longer know where they stand in terms of their immigration
status. I debated cancelling our 2017 production, since I feared it might create
a target-rich environment for Immigration and Customs Enforcement (ICE)
or for racist protestors. In the end, the show went on (as it must), but I can't
help wondering whether our bilingual adaptation and its message of multicultural inclusion represents the shape of things to come, or whether I will
instead look back on this staging as the failed harbinger for an age of tolerance
that might have been. Perhaps this question will be answered if we are able
to mount our bilingual *Romeo and Juliet* after the 2020 election, in a cultural
moment that once again contains the potential for hope and change.

Notes

1. The phrase 'Shakespeare's original text' will no doubt outrage readers
   familiar with the history of textual transmission. Please note that I use it
   only as a term of convenience here.
2. In the production I directed for the Shakespeare Festival of Arkansas in
   2001, I found a third option: one actor played both Dromios, while a set
   of actual identical twins played the two Antipholi. This strategy really
   kept the audience guessing.
3. Dario Fo, *The Tricks of the Trade*, trans. Joe Farrell (New York: Routledge,
   1991), 34 and note.
4. A snippet of the performance can be viewed online; see 'Comedy of
   Errors – Texas State – Clip 1', YouTube video, 3:10, https://youtu.be/
   bx3f6cLV5Aw (uploaded 20 July 2017).
5. William Shakespeare, *The Comedy of Errors*, in *The Norton Shakespeare*,
   3rd edn, ed. Stephen Greenblatt, Walter Cohen, Suzanne Gossett, Jean
   E. Howard, Katharine Eisaman Maus and Gordon McMullan (New
   York: W. W. Norton, 2016), I.i.39–41.
6. Shakespeare, *The Comedy of Errors*, I.i.119–20.

STAGING A BILINGUAL *COMEDY OF ERRORS* IN TEXAS 177

7. *The Comedy of Errors*, II.ii.198, 200.
8. *The Comedy of Errors*, V.i.300.
9. *The Comedy of Errors*, V.i.308–11.
10. *The Comedy of Errors*, V.i.406.

Part IV: Translating Shakespeare in Ashland

17

Creating a Canon of Latinx Shakespeares: The Oregon Shakespeare Festival's *Play on!*

Trevor Boffone

Oregon Shakespeare Festival's (OSF) 2019 production of *La Comedia of Errors*, a bilingual adaptation by Lydia G. Garcia and Bill Rauch, isn't like any other production of *The Comedy of Errors*, one of Shakespeare's most well-known plays.[1] Something is different. Here, the two sets of twins are divided by the US–Mexican border – Antipholus and Dromio of the United States, and Antifolo and Dromio of Mexico. Once grown up, the twins in Mexico head to the United States to find their missing brothers. *La Comedia* seamlessly interweaves English and Spanish throughout the play, with some scenes being performed entirely in Spanish. The heart of the play is about acceptance of different cultures and perspectives. In many ways, the play is an ideal tale to stage a conversation about empathy and difference, a topic just as important now as when the play was first staged. *La Comedia* exemplifies how OSF has become a site to reimagine the work of William Shakespeare, specifically positioning Ashland, Oregon, as an epicentre in the development of a growing canon of Shakespeare remixed through a Latinx aesthetic. These so-called Latinx Shakespeares take what was once old and make it new again, opening up conversations about how the Latinx community engages with the Eurocentricity of Shakespeare.

Garcia and Rauch adapted their text of *La Comedia of Errors* from a translation of Shakespeare's play created by Christina Anderson for OSF's *Play on!* project, a multi-year venture that saw thirty-six contemporary playwrights translate the Shakespeare canon into contemporary English. In an article about this project, dramaturgs and theatre scholars Martine Kei Green-Rogers and Alex N. Vermillion ask, 'What does it mean to make a "new" play out of an "old" play? Why do we need to make a new play out of an old one?' Moreover, they add, 'Has something changed about our society and the way we view the older version of this story that needs to be addressed for the story to resonate with contemporary audiences?'[2] Green-Rogers and Vermillion argue that 'for the continued relevance and survival of some stories, those stories must be changed and updated as language shifts and evolves'.[3]

Given the United States' demographic shift into a definitively Latinx country, coupled with the increasing necessity to build a theatre ecosystem that appropriately reflects this diversity, it should come as no surprise that playwrights of colour have taken it on themselves to address gaps in theatre. One recurring source of contestation is Shakespeare. In her landmark article 'From *West Side Story* to *Hamlet, Prince of Cuba*: Shakespeare and Latinidad in the United States', theatre scholar Carla Della Gatta lays the foundation for a new field of Shakespearian studies: 'Latino Shakespeares', or a 'textual adaptation or a performance in which Shakespearian plays, plots, or characters are *made Latino*'.[4] Della Gatta defines Latinx Shakespeares in various ways, focusing on adaptations of the Shakespeare canon for predominantly Latinx audiences as well as 'outreach initiatives' by Anglo theatre-makers who have attempted to explore assimilation through a Latinx lens.[5] Della Gatta rightly points to *West Side Story* as the epitome of Latinx representation in theatre in the twentieth century. That the Bernstein, Robbins and Sondheim musical adapts *Romeo and Juliet* in such a way as to create ethnically different rival gangs only adds to the limitations the musical places on constructions of Latinidad in our popular imagination.[6]

In what follows, I linger on the work of Latinx playwrights as part of OSF's *Play on!* project and question what it means for Latinx playwrights to translate Shakespeare. *Play on!* translations expand the confines of what Latinx Shakespeares can be, effectively updating the dated *West Side Story*-driven narrative. Yet, this work is not without issues and boundaries of representation when it comes to something so canonically Eurocentric as Shakespeare. Put simply: what is gained and what is lost? And, what does it mean for a Latinx playwright to share authorship with Shakespeare? While Latinx playwrights have taken on the task of translating Shakespeare's plays into contemporary English, they are still limited by the rules that *Play on!* has imposed. And yet, the mere act of a Latinx playwright translating Shakespeare is powerful in and of itself. Shakespeare's work can be a source of equity, diversity and inclusion when it is produced through a Latinx theatre aesthetic. This is to say that equitable Shakespeare is more than 'to be or not to be'.

In *Passing Strange: Shakespeare, Race, and Contemporary America*, Shakespearean scholar Ayanna Thompson questions whether 'Shakespeare's plays need to be edited, appropriated, revised, updated, or rewritten to affirm racial equality and relevance'.[7] As this chapter contends, the Shakespearian canon must be remixed through a Latinx lens to create a more equitable canon that not only positions Latinx playwrights as equals to Shakespeare, but also actively pushes against the Eurocentricity of the American theatre, which has systematically disadvantaged Latinx theatre-makers and communities of colour.

Equity, Diversity and Inclusion in Ashlandia

While Shakespeare certainly has his following and remains the most produced playwright in the world, there is no doubt that his work reinforces a
traditional, Eurocentric branch of theatre. Besides the token few characters
of colour such as Othello, most Shakespearian characters are read as 'white'
even if the Bard's plays can be performed successfully with colour-conscious
casting. Moreover, when most theatre companies approach Shakespeare, they
view his work through a lens of whiteness that often reinforces the typical
racial power dynamics at work in the American theatre. To put it simply,
many productions of Shakespeare don't look like the United States in the
twenty-first century.

Enter the Oregon Shakespeare Festival and Bill Rauch. Founded in 1935
by Angus L. Bowmer, OSF is one of the oldest and largest non-profit theatre
companies in the United States. With a season of eleven productions running
on three stages from February to November, OSF is the largest repertory theatre in the world. In 2008, Rauch became artistic director, a moment that saw
a cultural shift in the organisation.[8] Rauch's efforts demonstrate that a theatre
change-maker does not need to be Latinx to prompt – and participate in –
Latinx Shakespeares. Rauch is from a community-collaborative background
largely shaped by Cornerstone Theater Company, perhaps the pre-eminent
US theatre specialising in grassroots, community-based collaboration. Theatre
is a collaborative enterprise, and by embracing the values brought forth by
Rauch, OSF has been able to shape the present and future of the American
theatre.

But Rauch did not do this work alone. Rauch brought in Carmen Morgan
and ArtEquity to evaluate the genetic make-up of the organisation. Through
comprehensive, top-to-bottom equity, diversity and inclusion training under
Morgan's direction, OSF rewrote the narrative of American regional theatre.
The company continues to cultivate new and innovative ways to support this
work. For example, every doorway features a sign inviting *everyone* into the
space. 'WE WELCOME: all races and ethnicities, all religions, all countries,
all gender identities, all sexual orientations, all abilities and disabilities, all
spoken and signed languages. EVERYONE.' This invitation is echoed on
the company's website: 'OSF invites and welcomes everyone. We believe
the inclusion of diverse people, ideas, cultures and traditions enriches both
our insights into the work we present on stage and our relationships with
each other. We are committed to diversity in all areas of our work and in our
audiences.' OSF's Audience Development Manifesto points to the duality
of its mission: to present the works of Shakespeare and to celebrate the rich
diversity of the United States. As such, the manifesto explains, 'we must
pro-actively build an audience that reflects our nation's diversity in its many

expressions'.[9] The manifesto rightly points to the realities that OSF faces in rural Oregon, naming racism and laying the groundwork for how to address it not only within the walls of OSF but also throughout the region.

Naturally, this work of equity, diversity and inclusion extends to theatre programming, including commissions, staged readings, new play development and full productions. After Rauch's arrival in Ashland, OSF began producing fewer plays by Shakespeare and instead shifted to theatre for marginalised groups as well as Shakespeare performance more broadly. While the name Oregon Shakespeare Festival conjures images of a season filled with the Bard's work, on average the company only produces three to four works by Shakespeare per season. This work is supplemented by plays from other classic writers, modern and contemporary works, and world premieres. Some of these new works directly engage with Shakespeare. The 2017 season, for example, saw Lee Hall's *Shakespeare in Love* and Randy Reinholz's *Off the Rails*, which is an adaptation of *Measure for Measure* focused on the 'Kill the Indian, and Save the Man' period. Moreover, OSF regularly programmes full productions of Latinx plays such as *The River Bride* by Marisela Treviño Orta (2016), *Mojada: A Mexican Medea* by Luis Alfaro (2017), *Destiny of Desire* by Karen Zacarías (2018) and *Mother Road* by Octavio Solis (2019).[10] As such, OSF positions contemporary playwrights – and specifically writers of colour – alongside Shakespeare. While Shakespeare may indeed be the main attraction, audiences ultimately engage with much more than the Bard's work when visiting Ashland.

Although full productions remain the crown jewel of any theatre company and the most visible public-facing programming, OSF has been laying the seeds of equity in ways that are not just seen on its stages. With respect to Latinx theatre, we can locate one seed in the Festival Latino, in Rauch's inaugural season. Festival Latino was a five-day tribute to Latinx culture (23–27 July 2008), which saw the company offer open captions in Spanish of OSF's productions in addition to cultural events sprinkled throughout the week. The OSF plaza was adorned with decorations evoking Latinx cultures and was home to free outdoor performances by local and regional Latinx artists as well as students from Guanajuato, Mexico, one of Ashland's sister cities.

Festival Latino ushered in a new era of inclusion at OSF that saw the company make a more intentional effort to engage with Latinx artists and audiences. After several years of producing CultureFest, an extension of the successes of Festival Latino, OSF continued this work with the Latinx Play Project (LxPP), a biennial weekend-long festival that began in 2013 and that has seen theatre-makers from across North America flock to Ashland.[11] The mission of LxPP is 'to develop and present new plays and provide a forum for artists, producers and audiences to discuss and advance Latinx theatre at OSF and nationwide'.[12] This work led to the Brown Swan Lab, an initiative using resources from the LxPP and the Black Swan Lab to bring two cohorts of Latinx playwrights to Ashland to develop new work in a lab setting for two weeks.[13] Aside from hosting festivals and gatherings, OSF also brought in Luis Alfaro as its first playwright-in-residence. Between 2013 and 2019, and supported by funding from the Andrew S. Mellon Foundation, Alfaro served as a strategic liaison to strengthen OSF's engagement with Latinx communities and theatre artists. OSF produced Alfaro's *Medea* adaptation, *Mojada: A Medea in Los Angeles* (2017), supported new work by the playwright through development and staged readings, commissioned him to translate for *Play on!* and backed his community engagement efforts to welcome audiences of colour to OSF in a more authentic way.

Needless to say, OSF has shown more of a commitment to supporting the work of Latinx theatre artists than have most regional theatres. That this work takes place in rural Oregon only adds to the importance of creating Latinx spaces in unlikely destinations. It's no coincidence that the Latinx theatre community often refers to Ashland as 'Ashlandia'.

Play on! Translating the Shakespeare Canon

In addition to programming such as the American Revolutions Series, the Korean Stories Project, the Black Swan Lab and the Latinx Play Project, OSF has engaged diverse communities through its controversial *Play on!* project.[14] On 29 September 2015, the company launched *Play on!*, a thirty-nine-play, three-year project commissioning playwrights to translate the works of Shakespeare. In addition to supporting playwrights, the project has contracted dramaturgs, theatre professionals, advisers and other voices in the field to support the work. The project commissioned a playwright and a dramaturg for each play. *Play on!* was supported by a $3.7 million grant from the Hitz Foundation and was led by Lue Morgan Douthit, director of literary development and dramaturgy at OSF. The project's initial three-year tenure at OSF was successful, leading the project's producing team to form a spin-off not-for-profit company, Play On Shakespeare, also based out of Ashland.

The mission of the project is 'to enhance the understanding of Shakespeare's plays in performance for theatre professionals, students and audiences by engaging with contemporary translations and adaptations'.[15] OSF sees *Play on!* as a way to translate Shakespeare's work into contemporary English, thus creating a new canon of companion pieces to the original texts and, thus, a fresh way for theatre-makers to engage with the Shakespeare canon. The company's goal is for these new plays to be performed, published, read, adapted for the stage and used as teaching tools. While the initiative was met with outcry in some circles, OSF maintains that these translations will not replace the original canon. The original Shakespeare plays are not going away. They will remain front and centre in Ashland and beyond.

Aside from striving to make Shakespeare more accessible to a plurality of audiences, *Play on!* incorporates three core values from OSF: excellence, inclusion and stewardship. According to Rauch, 'We are striving for inclusion, not only in the gender and racial diversity of the artists involved, but in the entire project's purpose to provide more access to Shakespeare's work to the widest possible range of readers and listeners.'[16] Notably, of the playwrights commissioned, more than 50 per cent are women and more than 50 per cent are people of colour, thus bringing voices and perspectives that are often left out of mainstream American theatre, especially when it comes to the hyper-traditional world of Shakespeare. As Della Gatta notes in 'Shakespeare, Race and "Other" Englishes', the diversity factor cannot be ignored as it challenges 'dominant structures to recognise translation of Shakespeare into English, and people of colour as qualified translators'.[17] Speaking of *Play on!*, Douthit claims:

> We began this project with a 'What if?'. There are differences between the early modern English of Shakespeare and contemporary English. What if we looked at these plays at the language level through the lens of dramatists? What would we learn about how they work? Would that help us understand them in a different way? 'Translate' is an inadequate word because it implies a word-for-word substitution, which isn't what we're doing. I'm going for something much more subtle.[18]

To help facilitate this work, OSF gave playwrights and dramaturgs two basic rules. First and foremost, each team had to retain the integrity of the original script. They could not cut or edit the script. Rather, they were charged with translating the play line by line, adapting the play to contemporary English as needed. Naturally, some language would need translating, and some would not. This decision was entirely up to the playwright and dramaturg. Second, playwrights had to be as rigorous with language as Shakespeare was. The playwright had to take into account the metre, metaphor, rhyme, rhythm, rhetoric, themes and character arcs of the original play, while also maintaining the setting, time period and any specific references. In this way, OSF has made it very clear that these translations are *not* adaptations. According to Green-Rogers and Vermillion, 'the goal of the project is to create companion texts to Shakespeare's plays that are meant to illuminate the original text while also standing on their own as pieces of new writing that may be performed'.[19]

Even so, the project announcement was met with a wave of criticism. Many people misunderstood its objectives, focusing on the word *translation* and fearing that *Play on!* would tarnish not only the works but also OSF's and other companies' approach to producing Shakespeare. There was fear that these translations would replace the original canon – at least in Ashland. In an opinion piece in the *New York Times*, Shakespeare scholar James Shapiro claimed that the project set a 'disturbing precedent' that would potentially taint 'the only thing Shakespearean about his plays': the language.[20] In contrast, in the *Wall Street Journal*, linguist John McWhorter pointed to how cultural and lingual shifts negatively affect how audiences hear and, therefore, understand Shakespeare; McWhorter suggested that we 'embrace Shakespeare for real and let him speak to us' in contemporary English.[21] And in the *New Yorker*, literary historian Daniel Pollack-Pelzner placed *Play on!* within a historical context, noting how Shakespeare has been adapted and staged over the centuries. Needless to say, these varying opinions – all by Anglo men of a certain age – demonstrate the ways in which straying from the traditional Shakespeare canon can lead to controversy.

In her article 'Historicizing Shakesfear and Translating Shakespeare Anew', dramaturg Lezlie C. Cross analyses the 'Shakesfears' that have driven criticism of *Play on!*, situating them historically. As Cross proves, anxieties surrounding producing Shakespeare have been commonplace since the Restoration.[22] Despite claims from detractors, dramaturg Martine Kei Green-Rogers claims that Shakespeare did not intend to bewilder or bamboozle audiences through confusing and clever wordplay; rather, Shakespeare 'wrote of subjects familiar to the audiences of his time using both colloquial and very elevated language. The subject and language of his plays were *accessible* to all who attended the plays or could afford a copy of a quarto of his work.'[23] So why not create more accessible Shakespeare in the twenty-first century?

The Shakespeare canon is often polarising: people either love it or hate it. Admittedly, I loathed Shakespeare from the time I was forced to read *Romeo and Juliet* in the ninth grade until I saw a high school production of *Richard III* nearly two decades later in March 2017. *Richard III* changed me. Adapted and directed by Steward Savage at Carnegie Vanguard High School in Houston, this production encouraged me to see Shakespeare's work through a fresh lens. No longer did it seem inaccessible or 'boring', but it spoke to me in new ways that I never imagined possible. I saw it five times. In a fitting end to spring 2017, I made my first trip to OSF. My experiences of these two entities – Savage's *Richard III* and the reinvented OSF – opened my eyes in a way that the American regional theatre had not. Since then, I have been *open* to Shakespeare. All it took was one production to show me that Shakespeare didn't have to be the boring, difficult to understand text that I remembered. It could be something so much more. How could the experiences of Latinx audiences parallel my own journey with Shakespeare, through an engagement with the Bard's work as co-authored by Latinx playwrights?

Latinx Translations of Shakespeare

Typically, when Shakespeare is produced, everyone *except* the playwright is involved. This is contrary to the majority of contemporary theatre-making, in which the playwright's voice is heard beyond the text. Even if the playwright is not involved in the production, the creative team can still draw on the playwright's notes, interviews and the like. *Play on!* is thus groundbreaking in that the project places playwrights at the centre of Shakespeare in a substantial way for the first time since the plays' own era. Eight of the thirty-nine translations were the work of Latinx playwright-translators, each paired with a dramaturg of their choosing: *All's Well That Ends Well* translated by Virginia Grise, dramaturgy by Ricardo Bracho;[24] *Coriolanus* translated by Sean San José, dramaturgy by Rob Melrose; *Cymbeline* translated by Andrea Thome, dramaturgy by John Dias; *Edward III* translated by Octavio Solis, dramaturgy by Kimberly Colburn; *Henry VIII* translated by Caridad Svich, dramaturgy by Julie Felise Durbiner; *Macbeth* and *Richard III* translated by Migdalia Cruz, dramaturgy by Ishia Bennison; and *Richard II* translated by Naomi Iizuka, dramaturgy by Joy Meads.[25]

One of the most powerful aspects of *Play on!* is embodied in how these eight translations situate Latinx playwrights and William Shakespeare as co-authors, with the Latinx name appearing side by side with that of the canonical figure. In other words, these Latinx Shakespeares position both authors as equal, a powerful act given the politics of contemporary US theatre, in which Shakespeare is the most produced playwright while Latinx playwrights remain undervalued. Even if Virginia Grise, say, faithfully translates *All's Well That Ends Well*, she still brings to the process a grassroots, Latinx theatre-making aesthetic, politic and sensibility that cannot be understated. Regardless of the content of the play or the play's textual and visual aesthetics, *Play on!* facilitates a politics of co-authorship and doubleness. This doubleness has redefined Shakspearean performance in the United States, as Della Gatta notes: 'if we do not talk about Latinos onstage, or why they are not onstage, or how Latino culture is being portrayed or being ignored, we are not talking about American Shakespearean performance'.[26]

The doubleness of the playwright credit is a matter of equity. We can see how this doubleness functions if we return to the production of *La Comedia of Errors* from OSF's 2019 season (not listed among the eight above because translator Christina Anderson is not Latinx, although adapter Lydia G. Garcia is). On OSF promotional materials, Garcia, Rauch and Anderson were given as much billing as Shakespeare himself. The difference is only name recognition and cultural capital. But by positioning these names alongside each other, OSF shifts the conversation away from whiteness and instead focuses on the relationship between language and power.

To take one example from among the eight Latinx-authored translations, Migdalia Cruz's journey translating *Macbeth* speaks to the ways in which even a playwright working centuries after Shakespeare, in a completely different sociopolitical landscape, in a country that didn't even exist at the time, and with a host of identity markers seemingly the polar opposite of the Bard, can find power in working alongside Shakespeare. Allow us to briefly examine Cruz's work with *Play on!*. For Cruz, working on a play like *Macbeth* was strategic; Cruz felt the play was the closest to her own 'thematic sensibilities'. Cruz explains, 'I feel a kinship to the themes of this play: mourning, ambition, blood, supernatural intervention, murder, ghosts – and a strong female lead, not so common in Shakespeare's tragedies.' As she began to translate *Macbeth*, Cruz explains, 'As I unraveled the language and did my research about everything from bawdy terms to Elizabethan proverbs to Scottish royal history, I found I could change small things that clarified the plot and the more obscure language.'[27]

In line with the rules of *Play on!* translations, Cruz considered the original metre and rhythm of the work as well as the ways in which Shakespeare uses alliteration. Cruz explains, 'It still feels awkward to think about "changing Shakespeare," but I was determined to only change things that helped to clarify the journey of the characters. It is still Shakespeare, and the audience does still need to listen to his (and my) poetic language and make sense of it in both vocabulary and emotional sense.' Some changes were small, like 'palter' (which became 'deal false'), others more intricate, she says, 'where if I changed a word, then I needed to change the following rhyme so I could keep the rhyme or rhythm. It was definitely a rompecabeza, as we say in Spanish – "a head-breaker" or major puzzle.'[28]

Perhaps the most obvious example of the ways in which Cruz brought her identity to the translation process lies in her use of Spanish. As a bilingual writer, Cruz is able to tap into multiple linguistic systems in addition to the different registers that Spanish and English allow. As far as Cruz's *Macbeth* is concerned, the playwright chose to use 'tú', the informal Spanish word to address people you are more familiar with, to replace dated English words such as 'Thee', 'Thy', 'Thou' and 'Thyself'. In her language notes, Cruz explains that 'tú' is 'how you address: servants, children, lovers & friends'. While this decision may seem minor, it is in fact a change that fundamentally alters the politics of the script. Regardless of the ethnicity of the actor cast in the role, they inevitably become a code-switching bilingual Spanish–English speaker, at least to a certain extent. Further, this choice potentially renders these characters Latinx, especially considering Migdalia Cruz's co-authorship. To gloss over the translation choices that Cruz made and blur the script's Latinidad would be to assume that all renditions of Latinx identities and cultures must be prominently featured in order for the play to be considered

Latinx. A Shakespearean translation with Spanish pronouns penned by a
Latinx author is as much a Latinx play as *Zoot Suit*, *Anna in the Tropics* or *Water
by the Spoonful*.

La Comedia of Errors, Inclusion and Community

In many ways, Bill Rauch's tenure at OSF was much like a game of chess
in which strategic moves took place as the fabric of the organisation shifted
towards meaningful equity, diversity and inclusion work. First, OSF transi-
tioned from diversity initiatives to community outreach. Ultimately, projects
such as *Play on!* helped OSF engage in equity that enabled true inclusion
projects such as *La Comedia of Errors*. While each *Play on!* translation has had
its own unique journey, *La Comedia* is singular in the ways in which it was
used as a vehicle to build inclusion in the local community. As this section
demonstrates, *La Comedia* featured a nuanced community engagement plan
that utilised spaces at OSF and the surrounding Rogue Valley in addition to
digital spaces. These efforts build on each other and push the boundaries of
what a Latinx Shakespeares can be and how the Latinx theatre canon can be
expanded in even the unlikeliest of settings.

While Rauch spearheaded the production, *La Comedia* featured a predominantly Latinx production team as well as an all-Latinx cast.[29] Even though
Lydia G. Garcia is credited as adapting Christina Anderson's translation of
The Comedy of Errors, Garcia's work is that of a co-author and, as such, merits
discussion alongside the work of other Latinx playwrights involved with *Play
on!* That OSF can feature such a Latinx-heavy cast, creative team and production team is a testament to the type of work that OSF has been doing to
foreground inclusion since Rauch's arrival. His involvement is an important
reminder that non-Latinx allies in predominantly white institutions can be
key figures in pushing for equity and inclusion initiatives. It is very possible
that without Rauch, OSF would not be at the forefront of equity, diversity
and inclusion measures in the American regional theatre or in the field of
Shakespeare performance. *La Comedia* is a fitting example of how this work
can organically come together.

While the text and aesthetics of the performance are arguably the most
forward-facing aspects of a Latinx Shakespearean production, *La Comedia* also
expands our understanding of Latinx Shakespeares by foregrounding community engagement. Since *La Comedia* was always conceived of as a project
for the community as much as a production in OSF's season, the organisation
did things for *La Comedia* that are not the norm in Ashland. For instance, *La
Comedia* had a press release and marketing materials in both languages. The
webpage for the production was fully bilingual, with two columns running
down the page, one in English and one in Spanish. In this way, promotion of

the show did not privilege one language over the other. Typically, on bilingual websites information in English appears first with the Spanish translation below, an act that prioritises English-speaking audiences and, as an extension, the values of both the production and the theatre company, values that reveal a non-inclusive bias. Because the languages were placed side by side, *La Comedia* offered equal access to potential English-speaking, Spanish-speaking and bilingual audience members, effectively sending a bold message that this production was for everyone.

Moreover, the production was positioned as both a show in the regular season at OSF and a community-hosted experience for the Rogue Valley and Latinx communities. Whereas typical OSF productions are housed in a single theatre on OSF's Ashland campus, the community-hosted experience is an off-site performance that travels around the Rogue Valley and is co-hosted by local organisations who have a meaningful relationship to specific groups of people – in this case, Latinx and Spanish-speaking peoples. The production is a one-act, ninety-minute adaptation that uses minimal props and costumes; there is no set, lights or recorded sound, making it highly stageable in a variety of performance spaces. OSF partnered with eighteen community organisations to enable deeper collaborations with different communities, and it created space for community members to exchange stories and continue a conversation about themes seen in the play. The production featured a team of Latinx community dramaturgs to facilitate these meaningful conversations before, during and after performances around the Rogue Valley.[30] Notably, these performances were all free and, thus, accessible to all regardless of financial means.

Unlike other OSF productions, *La Comedia* featured a special webpage laying out its community engagement work.[31] The community webpage features artwork specifically designed for this production. As the first thing one sees when opening the webpage, the leading visual serves a fundamental role in setting the tone for the production. The image features one large land mass, representing the original borders of Mexico before the 1848 Treaty of Guadalupe Hidalgo, which saw the United States gain control of much of what is now the American Southwest. The Mexican flag wraps around the land mass on the right side of the image, demonstrating how this land was once and will always be native to peoples of Mexican descent. The US flag lies underneath Baja California as a reminder of the dual nationalities of the characters. The title of the play on the image is also positioned to invoke duality. 'La Comedia' appears above what is now the United States, and 'of Errors' sits alongside what is now Mexico. Finally, dashed lines represent the journey that the brothers in Mexico take to the United States to find their long-lost siblings. The map of their trip speaks to how even man-made borders ultimately cannot separate these Latinx families. Every aspect of the website's art speaks to how the United States is as much a Latinx country as anything else: this land was once and will always be Mexican. As the popular saying goes, 'we didn't cross the border; the border crossed us'. And thus, places such as Ashland, Oregon, remain fundamental sites to perform Latinx identity, something that *La Comedia* highlights at every turn.

Conclusion

In many ways, OSF was an ideal place for this work to originate, given the company's commitment to Latinx theatre over the last two decades. This commitment began with the Festival Latino, the Latinx Play Project and the Brown Swan Lab, and it has continued in the form of an increased commitment to producing the work of Latinx playwrights on OSF's three main stages, as evidenced in recent seasons with new works by Luis Alfaro, Marisela Treviño Orta, Octavio Solis and Karen Zacarías. *Play on!* transcended outreach and diversity initiatives by pushing the boundaries of what defines Latinx theatre, translation and adaptation. As such, this process is a model for other theatres and truly establishes a new ground for equity. This is to say that the movement stemming from 2008's Festival Latino has been outreach, the Latinx Play Project and Luis Alfaro's position as playwright-in-residence have been examples of diversity, and *Play on!*, finally, has ushered in a new era of equity.

According to Lezlie C. Cross, by democratising Shakespeare and making his work more accessible, *Play on!* 'wrests Shakespeare from the hands of the white male establishment with its inclusive array of playwrights and dramaturgs'. Moreover, Cross notes how centring a playwright of colour in a translated Shakespeare text presents the opportunity to bring new audiences to the theatre who might have traditionally eschewed Shakespeare.[32] So, I return to the central question guiding this chapter: What does it mean to have a Latinx playwright translate Shakespeare? First and foremost, commissioning a Latinx playwright to translate Shakespeare is empowering. Shakespeare is the pinnacle of privilege: white and male. When a non-Latinx theatre company's production of Shakespeare is an artistic and financial failure, the company will, oftentimes, continue to produce Shakespeare. When a non-Latinx theatre company's production of Luis Alfaro or Virginia Grise is an artistic and financial failure, the company places the blame on Latinx theatre and, ultimately, reduces future opportunities to engage with Latinx artists and communities of colour. Shakespeare has the privilege to fail; Latinx artists do not. In light of this dichotomy, by placing a Latinx playwright at the centre of a Shakespeare play, by granting Migdalia Cruz or Octavio Solis the chance to become a co-author with Shakespeare himself, *Play on!* destabilises the Shakespeare canon. While Virginia Grise's *All's Well That Ends Well* benefits from a recognisable title and Shakespeare's name, the work is still *hers*. It's a

Latinx play written by a Latinx playwright. It's a Latinx Shakespeares, and that's a powerful act of resistance.

Notes

1. *La Comedia of Errors* ran 28 June to 26 October 2019 at OSF.
2. Martine Keï Green-Rogers and Alex N. Vermillion, 'A New Noble Kinsmen: The *Play On!* Project and Making New Plays Out of Old', *Theatre History Studies*, 36 (2017): 231.
3. Green-Rogers and Vermillion, 'A New Noble Kinsmen', 232.
4. Carla Della Gatta, 'From *West Side Story* to *Hamlet, Prince of Cuba*: Shakespeare and Latinidad in the United States', *Shakespeare Studies*, 44 (2016): 151.
5. Della Gatta, 'From *West Side Story* to *Hamlet, Prince of Cuba*', 151–2.
6. For more on *West Side Story* and the construction of Latinidad in US popular culture, see Brian Eugenio Herrera, *Latin Numbers: Playing Latino in Twentieth-Century U.S. Popular Performance* (Ann Arbor: University of Michigan Press, 2015).
7. Ayanna Thompson, *Passing Strange: Shakespeare, Race, and Contemporary America* (Oxford: Oxford University Press, 2013), 6.
8. At the close of the 2019 season, Rauch left his position at OSF to become the inaugural artistic director of the Ronald O. Perelman Performing Arts Center at the World Trade Center in New York City.
9. 'Audience Development Manifesto', Oregon Shakespeare Festival, 2010. Available at https://www.osfashland.org/-/media/pdf/Company/OSF_Audience_Development_-Manifesto_2010.ashx?la=en&hash=E180F84483738EFEBFBCE6380749192FBCCD554C (last accessed 18 November 2020).
10. Nevertheless, as Della Gatta notes in 'From *West Side Story* to *Hamlet, Prince of Cuba*', when OSF stages Latinx Shakespeares, it does not produce other works written by Latinx playwrights in the same season: 'Plays written by or about Latinos are not mounted in the same year as Latino Shakespeares; the Hispanic/Latino diversity box is fulfilled by either one or the other' (155).
11. Latinx Play Project is supported by a generous grant from the WarnerMedia Foundation. For more on LxPP, see Trevor Boffone, 'The Latinx Play Project: Building a Movement in Ashland', *Theatre Times*, 10 May 2017. Available at https://thetheatretimes.com/latinx-play-project-building-movement-ashland/ (last accessed 18 November 2020).
12. 'Latinx Play Project', Oregon Shakespeare Festival, 2019. Available at https://www.osfashland.org/en/artistic/Latinx-play-project.aspx (last accessed 18 November 2020).

13. The Black Swan Lab OSF invites actors and guest artists to incubate new work without performance pressures. The initiative was launched in 2009.
14. These initiatives began as a result of Bill Rauch's tenure.
15. 'Play On Shakespeare Mission', Play On Shakespeare. Available at https://playonfestival.org/the-details/ (last accessed 18 November 2020). Notably, the initiative and the festival share the same mission statement.
16. Catherine Foster, 'Translating Shakespeare: The Play on! Project', *Prologue*, Spring 2017. Available at https://www.osfashland.org/pro-logue/prologue-spring-2017/prologue-spring-17-play-on.aspx   (last accessed 18 November 2020).
17. Carla Della Gatta, 'Shakespeare, Race and "Other" Englishes: The Q Brothers' *Othello: The Remix*', *Shakespeare Survey*, 71 (2018): 75.
18. Oregon Shakespeare Festival, 'OSF Launches Three-Year Shakespeare Translation Commissioning Project', press release, 7 October 2015.
19. Green-Rogers and Vermillion, 'A New Noble Kinsmen', 234.
20. James Shapiro, 'Shakespeare in Modern English?', *New York Times*, 7 October 2015. Available at https://www.nytimes.com/2015/10/07/opinion/shakespeare-in-modern-english.html (last accessed 18 November 2020).
21. John H. McWhorter, 'A Facelift for Shakespeare', *Wall Street Journal*, 25 September 2015. Available at https://www.wsj.com/articles/a-facelift-for-shakespeare-1443194924 (last accessed 18 November 2020).
22. Lezlie C. Cross, 'Historicizing Shakesfear and Translating Shakespeare Anew', *Theatre History Studies*, 36 (2017): 212.
23. Green-Rogers and Vermillion, 'A New Noble Kinsmen', 233.
24. In an interview on the 50 Playwrights Project, Ricardo Bracho notes that he is dramaturging his 'enemy Shakespeare's *All's Well That Ends Well* for this cray experiment being run out of OSF'. So, if Bracho hates Shakespeare, then why dramaturg Grise's translation? Bracho adds, 'Vicki's is for a cast of black and brown actresses and keyed towards an audience of teenagers. As I hate Shakespeare but love black and brown women and teencentric tv like *Pretty Little Liars* and *Recovery Road*, I feel ideally suited for this dramaturgical task.' See Ricardo Bracho, interview by Trevor Boffone, 50 Playwrights Project, 2 May 2016. Available at https://50playwrights.org/2016/05/02/ricardo-bracho/ (last accessed 18 November 2020).
25. In most cases, *Play on!* chose the playwright and the playwright chose the play.
26. Della Gatta, 'From *West Side Story* to *Hamlet, Prince of Cuba*', 155.
27. Qtd in Foster, 'Translating Shakespeare'.
28. Ibid.

29. The production team included Bill Rauch (director, adapter), Lydia G. Garcia (original Spanish translations), Christopher Acebo (scenic and costume designer), Grant Ruiz (composer), Catherine María Rodríguez (production dramaturg), Micha Espinosa (voice and text director), Antonio David Lyons (community producer), Alejandra Cisneros (community liaison), Derek Kolluri (associate director), U. Jonathan Toppo (fight director), Olsen Torres (production stage manager), Ray Gonzalez (production assistant) and Mark Anthony Vallejo (FAIR assistant director and choreographer). The cast included Armando Durán, Jeffrey King, Mark Murphey, Fidel Gomez, Tony Sancho, Amy Lizardo, Caro Zeller, Cedric Lamar, Catherine Castellanos, Meme García and Grant Ruiz.

30. Community dramaturgs included Martha Carrillo, Ana Cruz, Antonio Cruz, David Malfavon, Donna Malfavon, Michelle Malfavon, Nelly Malfavon, Nuvia Morales, Maria Mosqueda, Mercedes Ramirez, Reynaldo Ramirez and Marco Samano.

31. 'A Community Hosted Experience', Oregon Shakespeare Festival. Available at https://www.osfashland.org/en/engage-and-learn/la-comedia-community.aspx (last accessed 18 November 2020).

32. Cross, 'Historicizing Shakesfear', 225.

18

What I Learned from My Shakespeare Staycation with *Macbeth* and *Richard III*

Migdalia Cruz

The idea: study revered texts by one of the most revered playwrights in the white male Western canon and help them speak to a twenty-first-century audience that includes everyone else – leaving intact the poetry, rhythms, place and characters.

The Oregon Shakespeare Festival's (OSF) *Play on!* project was thought up by Lue Douthit (a dramaturg at OSF) and Dave Hitz (of the Hitz Foundation). The goal was to create a revitalised canon that allowed for a modern ear to understand all of Shakespeare's original intentions without dumbing down the text or poetry.

Cons: Everyone will think you are crazy to do such a thing. Why fix what isn't broken? Why risk the negative press of trying to mess with a white theatrical icon? Why let yourself be compared to the 'Bard?' (A bard is simply a poet – and poets come in all colours, abilities and genders.)

Pros: Answer/echo the work of a master, and from this, learn how to use semicolons and iambic pentameter to emphasise action. Feel entitled to the inspiration of this and any poet. Appreciate how your work can vibrate off another writer's work and help you understand your own work more deeply. As you begin to take one thing apart to rebuild it, you have to believe in your strengths and use them to rebuild. Work on the craft as an artist.

People are quick to criticise anything they don't understand, but that has never stopped me from trying something new. And how delicious, as a Puerto Rican woman from the Bronx, to become part of the Western canon in this subversive way. If it worked, it could mean that people of colour are clearly entitled to these classic works, and, in a deeper way, entitled to poetry without question, explanation or rancor.

The Choice

Macbeth was a natural choice for me – a play about how mourning the loss of a baby, of kingdoms, of country, leads to an inevitable tragedy that is guided by fate. I write about mourning. My first piece of real writing was about the death of my friend who was raped and murdered at age eight. That is how I mourned her. After Douthit offered me other plays to translate for *Play on!* at OSF, I asked to see what hadn't been taken yet and was amazed to see *Macbeth* on that list. That was it. Mourning, ambition, the powerless seeking by any means to become powerful, the fall of people who search for power without remembering the consequences of their actions: this read like a Migdalia Cruz play to me. Yes.

Richard III was a title I inherited from another writer, and I took it on gladly because I saw the direct link between Richard and Macbeth. *Richard III* was Shakespeare's fourth play, the work of a young writer searching for his voice, not completely realised, and leading to *Macbeth*, his twenty-eighth play, which is beautifully crafted and poetically precise.[1] I found that Shakespeare stole lines from himself and placed them into *Macbeth*.

For instance, take the imagery of blood in both plays. In *Richard III*, Richard says before the murderer Tyrell enters:

> Murder her brothers, and then marry her.
> Uncertain way of gain. But I am in
> <u>So far in blood</u> that sin will pluck on sin.
> Tear-falling pity dwells not in this eye.[2]

And from *Macbeth*, Macbeth says after the murderers have killed Banquo, whose ghost appears to him at the banquet:

> All causes shall give way. I am in blood
> <u>Stepped in so far</u> that, should I wade no more,
> Returning were as tedious as go o'er.[3]

Finding parallel lines in *Richard III* gave me insight into the writer Shakespeare would become – from plot-heavy history play writer to a stage poet. I saw how he developed his poetry and gave his characters more humanity. Macbeth helped me understand Richard and enabled me to find a way to humanise him. And so, here are the two passages as I translated them. First, *Richard III*:

> Murder the princes, and marry the princess.
> Unholy way to prosper. But I am

So steeped in blood that sin will pluck out sin.
Tear-dropping mercy dwells not in this eye.

And now *Macbeth*:

Nothing shall halt my way. I am in blood
Stepped in so far, that should I wade no further,
Returning were as bloody as crossing o'er.

Shakespeare made a choice for Richard to be 'Steeped in blood' so Richard
had already been subsumed by his actions, his murders accumulating so much
that he was almost comfortable and proud of the level of blood he had shed.
In contrast, Macbeth had 'stepped in blood', as he fell into his fate rather than
choosing it. Understanding this contrast helped me define the desperation
of Macbeth as opposed to Richard's ruthlessness – ruthless ambition versus
ambition from which there's no turning back.

The Research

I wanted to treat the translation of *Macbeth* as if it were a new play. So I'd
think, 'this is my new play', and somehow I'm shadowing this other writer,
and I'm going to try to take the same journey. Research took me down many
roads. I read several essays, articles and books: from *Bawdy Shakespeare* to
lexicons and scholarly works about semiotics and language. They were often
dense and difficult, but they were necessary to understanding the play as a
whole and respecting all the research that had come before me. Then, I had
to find the character, and I had to spend time discovering Macbeth the man.
To that end, I did some travelling.

Something I do with all my plays is create altars to my characters, a spiritual
place that contains talismans, music, colours and objects. It's not necessarily
something with crosses or any kind of religious symbols. It's about sacred
objects that belong to characters, or a time in my life, or a place that is important to the character or the story. To find items, thoughts and photographs for
my Macbeth altar, I travelled to the Isle of Iona in the Hebrides to find his
grave and pay my respects. In a way, it was also a spiritual journey to my own
thoughts on who he was and what he meant to Scotland and to Shakespeare
as he wrote about Macbeth for James I.

Macbeth, for me, is about the witches. What are they, and want do I want
them to say? For me, they are women of colour surrounding this world,
contextualising it in order to recreate it. Their power comes from their sexual
attraction – this power is scary and powerful and alluring – in particular to
men who think they hold the power. I don't want old hags in the forest.

That witch idea died decades ago. So, what does a modern witch look like? What do powerful women look like? Or women who understand fate and destiny. I wanted to play with them and contextualise the play through them, so I added words for them. But Shakespeare also added words for them, or somebody added words for them; they added songs from Thomas Middleton in the middle of Shakespeare. I thought: 'if he's stealing from other people, he might as well steal from Cruz', so I added intros to scenes, songs and more, making it sound more like a play of mine. From there I began to reconstruct the play as I understood it from a modern woman's gaze.

It was important to choose words that might resonate with a modern audience. There was an openness to the witches, who are outside the play, so I used them to modernise the play. And I thought, 'oh, everybody's gonna hate this'. But audiences appreciated the way that the witches helped bring this play into the twenty-first century. I also made the witches musical, so they sing soul songs from the 1960s. To me that was the point of the project: if you choose a specific contemporary playwright to do this kind of work, they're going to bring themselves to it.

For *Richard III*, I went to Bosworth Field to see where he died and then to Leicester to see where they found his body – in a car park that was once a Catholic church – and then visited his official tomb at Leicester Cathedral. Next, I found Richard's sound track. For all my plays, I find the music of the characters and/or the music I need to hear to write them – music that somehow embodies them. For Richard, it was the Clash, especially the songs 'London Calling' and 'London's Burning'. I saw him as a punky rebel, who effected change by breaking through England's inertia – a hated outsider. Then, I went through videotapes from the Royal Shakespeare Company (RSC) of classes in how to speak iambic pentameter – those John Barton tapes. They're kind of ridiculous, from the 1970s or something. Everyone is smoking, it's like they're talking in a fog. But it's funny, and it's interesting to see how everyone struggles with the language. And part of the struggle with the language is that it's not always clear, and we've forgotten the context for all that language. So we make up context all the time, that's what humans do to make sense of the world. That gave me further permission to refine the text and define it and give it context that was both historical and personal to Richard III, Shakespeare and Migdalia.

The Work

Painstaking, word-by-word analysis and clarification. Sometimes at the rate of one sentence per hour. Together with my intrepid dramaturg, the British actress Ishia Bennison, I combed through the script: with her reading aloud with all her RSC cred and me with my Bronx-bred *coraje*, we put the play together in a way where we both understood all the words, the context and the poetry.

Ishia made sure I didn't change the well-known phrases too much, and I made sure she stepped away from my recreation of the witches.

It was all respectful and collaborative. Together we changed words, syntax and placement, and we tried to keep the best of Shakespeare intact without sacrificing the originality of Migdalia. Ishia as an actress also helped me double-check that the words were speakable for both American and British actors. Two years for *Macbeth*. Six weeks for *Richard III*, because I took him on so close to the June 2019 *Play on!* Shakespeare Festival of readings at Classic Stage Company in New York City, where both plays were presented along with the entire Shakespeare canon – all translated by contemporary playwrights, directors and dramaturgs. Lucky for me that *Macbeth* came first, so I had some short cuts to finding the soul of *Richard III*.

The Productions

So far, I have been blessed with two productions of *Macbeth*. I was surprised that anyone would produce these plays, especially when they can cut to shreds Shakespeare and not pay royalties. Dealing with a living playwright was a tough sell to many Shakespeare companies. Two brave companies stepped up: Actors' Shakespeare Project in Boston and the African-American Shakespeare Company in San Francisco. Both productions were successful in their own ways.

I credit the fact that they both used actors of colour in their casts – for major characters, not just sword-bearers and servants. Both companies addressed my greatest wish, that this play – as with all my plays – be performed by actors of colour. I wanted to create works that could be spoken by, be understood by, and resonate with audiences that may have felt left out of the Shakespeare canon in the past except for minor roles written to make them sound like white British people. A language and a text for all the people, even my own – that was my goal.

The Aftermath

There is so much resistance to touching these texts, particularly from the American Shakespeare studies community, as if the translators are blaspheming a sacred text. Because of this resistance in academia to *Play on!*, I'm always prepared for a fight or some kind of discussion that's such a waste of time in a lot of ways. Scholars and artists come from different worlds. Scholars try to explain the world through rigorous analysis; artists try to explain it by smashing it to bits and putting it back together again. I wish scholars in general would open their minds to different directions that work can go in. They need to be open to the different avenues their scholarship might take and stop trying so hard to make everything fit their theories. Maybe their theories need to move or transform with each production. And we need to understand why people are making certain choices, as opposed to just reacting, 'wow, that was a bad choice'. Maybe it was, but why? Why did they make that choice? What were they trying to do? Why is it negative if it doesn't fit your theory? That kind of scholarship is just tedious because it's reductive.

It's important that scholars understand that this approach – mine, and that of *Play on!* – is different. It's not just some reductive No Fear Shakespeare. I already have a sensibility that is theatrical and unique. I have a specific voice that I'm applying to this translation that means it'll have a different kind of resonance than a literal translation or a translation from a grad student in Shakespeare studies. I'm looking at these plays as a dramatist – not as a scholar. Thereby, I'm enhancing the drama with modern language, not detracting from it.

Shakespeare isn't going away. He will survive all of us, no doubt. His plays have lasted four hundred years and will persevere. I think people need to keep translating and keep adapting so that he can remain present and pertinent in a way that is modern and not based on antiquated ideas about language. When Shakespeare was writing, he was writing for all the people who were there, from queens to groundlings, so that they could hear good stories enacted by wonderful players in a poetic form that was easy to remember and repeat because of its rhythms. He wasn't writing to be studied. Nowadays we treat his plays like they're ancient museum pieces, fun to visit, but audiences don't necessarily walk away feeling like his words speak directly to their own human experience. Good plays should resonate in the soul. I think there needs to be a way to open the field for Shakespeare to continue to be lively and interesting and resonant to society. All writers need to ask questions that fiercely explore and reveal the human condition.

Even translators. Maybe especially.

Notes

1. These numbers can be debated. Current thought is that Shakespeare wrote anywhere from thirty-eight to forty-one plays. The numbers in this chapter reflect the count that OSF used for *Play on!*
2. William Shakespeare, *Richard III*, in *The Norton Shakespeare*, 3rd edn, ed. Stephen Greenblatt, Walter Cohen, Suzanne Gossett, Jean E. Howard, Katharine Eisaman Maus and Gordon McMullan (New York: W. W. Norton, 2016), IV.ii.61–3.
3. Shakespeare, *Macbeth*, in *The Norton Shakespeare*, III.iv.138–40.

19

Willful Invisibility: Translating Shakespeare's
The Reign of King Edward III

Octavio Solis

It takes a great deal of hubris to presume that one can take up the task of 'translating' the eternal plays of William Shakespeare into contemporary American English, much less attempt to make the language of such a genius more accessible to twenty-first-century audiences. The kind of ego it requires is one that I have sometimes lacked, even when approaching my own writing. When I accepted the offer to take on one of the Bard's texts for Oregon Shakespeare Festival's (OSF) *Play on!* project, I felt that ego shrivel up to nothing. Yet, that 'nothing' proved to be my way in.

With *Play on!*, OSF sought to translate the entire Shakespeare canon from Elizabethan English to contemporary English. Thirty-six American playwrights of diverse backgrounds, myself among them, were commissioned to take on the plays. Though it is an audacious undertaking, none of the translations are intended to supplant Shakespeare's own works, which are safely perched at the pinnacle of literature. The challenge was simply to make the works more accessible to new American audiences.

However, as a first-generation Latino whose parents hail from Mexico, and whose English is a rigorously acquired language of which I am not always master, I haven't always been considered quite so American. In discussions of Shakespeare's densely worded texts, I'm often at a remove from this very English domain and have therefore felt irrelevant and invisible. Consequently, I chose *The Reign of King Edward III* from a long list of available plays, a text that wasn't even considered a play of the canon until 2009. I chose it because I hadn't heard of it before, and the chances were good that most people hadn't either, thereby allowing me to work with that same invisibility that I have so often felt. Little did I realise that my efforts at remaining out of sight would become my modus operandi for retooling this little-known work. My 'cloak of invisibility' enabled me to discover on my own terms the marvellous secrets of the world's greatest writer.

I had my marching orders: First, do no harm; if the language is beautiful and lucid, let it stand. Second, honour the metre and verse where possible. Third, don't update the play to subscribe to current sensibilities or faddish expressions or slang. And finally, refrain from cutting or adapting the play for any reason whatsoever. These rules didn't make the task any easier, but at least I knew what not to do.

Originally published anonymously in a single volume, *Edward III* was first performed around 1592, making it one of Shakespeare's earliest works. But because it was not included in the First Folio, doubts about its authorship have lasted for centuries. The play has been attributed to many authors, some singly, some in collaboration, among them George Peele, Christopher Marlowe, Robert Greene, Thomas Kyd and, of course, Shakespeare himself. It wasn't until the play was run through special plagiarism software in 2009 that it was determined to be a collaboration between Kyd (accounting for 60 per cent of the text) and Shakespeare (40 per cent). In the process of line-by-line literal and stylistic translation of this play, I would realise that I was now the Bard's next collaborator, each of us working across the chasm of four hundred years to make his play more resonant to contemporary audiences.

Edward III depicts a vivid period in English history about which I knew little. The Hundred Years' War, which lasted from 1337 to 1453, pitted the English House of Plantagenet against the French House of Valois for control of the French crown. It began when Charles V of France died without sons or brothers to inherit the crown. Edward III, king of England and Charles V's nearest male heir, was declared king by his mother, Isabella of France, but he met with opposition from Philip VI, who claimed the crown for the House of Valois, which would make him King of France as well. This information is dutifully trotted out at the very opening of the play in a conversation between King Edward and Robert Earl of Artois, who has been banished from France. Artois has come to London to relate the events and convince Edward to claim the throne. The text hews closely to historical fact, except for the unaccountable substitution of John of Valois for Philip VI, and it lays out a clear, rational argument for Edward's rightful place on the French throne. There was also tremendous value in the alliterative play of these opening lines, with such words as *rancor*, *rebellious* and *royal* all demonstrably pointing towards the war to come. With the play's opening scene, then, I chose to leave Shakespeare's words largely unchanged.[1] For example, Shakespeare's Artois speaks to Edward of his mother:

> And from the fragrant garden of her womb
> Your gracious self, the flower of Europe's hope,
> Derivéd is inheritor to France.

I retained the sumptuous poetry of these lines, not only because they demonstrate Artois's open flattery of his king, but also because they establish a theme
of planting and gardening that recurs in ensuing scenes. My lines were only
slightly adjusted here:

> And from whose fragrant garden of her womb
> Were you thus born the flower of Europe's hope,
> The sole inheritor to France's crown.

Maintaining the metre was not difficult, though I wrestled for a while with
the line 'Derivéd is inheritor to France'. I determined that this accented word
would cause contemporary ears to stumble, so I rephrased the line in a manner
that kept its metre and still amplified the specific idea on which the entire war
rested. So much for the first scene of the play. Later scenes would bring up
greater challenges in the realm of metre and language choice.

Finding Freedom in the Metre

One reason I wrestled with the metre has to do with my own bilingual upbringing. My first tongue is Spanish, and in Spanish, iambic pentameter is not only
difficult, it's practically impossible. Our Spanish words often end with an *o* or
an *a*. For instance, France translates into Francia in our idiom. It's ingrained in
me to speak in the old rhythms of my family home, which tend to be trochaic,
dactylic and sometimes even anapestic. My solution to the metrical issues that
translation provoked was to alter the line in favour of these other rhythms without disturbing the flow of the content. Again, remaining somewhat invisible.

It was a line late in the first scene of the play that gave me the freedom to
change my strategy with the metre. When he hears that war with Scotland is
breaking out even as he prepares to vie with France, Edward lays forth his plan
to repel the invading Scots:

> KING: First therefore Audley this shall be thy charge
> go levy footmen for our wars in France
> and Ned take muster of our men at arms
> in every shire elect a several band
> let them be soldiers of a lusty spirit
> such as dread nothing but dishonour's blot.
> Be wary therefore since we do commence
> a famous war and with so mighty a nation.[2]

He is direct and assured in his directions, and yet he also cautions his men to
'be wary' because their foe is prodigiously armed. In my translation, I made

the slightest adjustments for the sake of clarity, revising constructions that read as awkward by today's standards while taking care to preserve the metre. 'Elect a several band', for instance, became 'enlist as many bands'. I also wondered about his use of 'famous' as a descriptor for this forthcoming war with Scotland and determined that 'widespread' might better define this conflict.

But the line 'let them be soldiers of a lusty spirit' gave me pause. No matter how hard I tried, I simply could not craft my line that it would fit the iambic pentameter of his play. I parsed his original line once more and realised that it wasn't a pure pentameter. It ended with an additional eleventh syllable on a 'weak' stress. In other words, Shakespeare cheats. And not only once, but often – that is, whenever he deems it necessary. In my translation then, I chose to let the metre carry over from the prior line, creating a kind of internal rhyme between 'band' and 'can':

In every shire enlist as many bands
You can of soldiers of a lusty spirit

Trained as I was in the school of thought that nothing of Shakespeare's comes by chance, I assumed that he must have intended this slight: perhaps he simply preferred the word 'spirit' above all others, and to hell with the metre. The metre enables the actor to remember his lines and deliver them in smooth, unfettered diction, thereby allowing the audience to receive it in the same manner, but often when the rhythm cannot suit the word, the word wins. Whether the line is a sign of his laziness or youth (*Edward III* was likely among Shakespeare's first plays), or whether he simply knew that the audience could not count every beat in his characters' dialogue, the reason does not matter. What is clear is that the metre is only meant to be a guide, not a hard and fast rule. A colleague of mine reminded me that in Shakespeare's most famous line of all, he violated his own rule by ending on the extra syllable: 'To be or not to be, that is the question.'

Within the same speech of Edward's, Shakespeare transgresses yet again by ending on six iambic feet, or twelve syllables: 'a famous war and with so mighty a nation'. The work of my translation became easier with this realisation; if the Bard could slyly cheat on his own verse structure, then so could I. I almost used the word 'land', which would have made the line scan perfectly in iambic pentameter, but I opted for the sovereign weight of the word 'nation'. Ergo, my version of this line rolls in eleven syllables to his twelve: 'a widespread war against a mighty nation'.

Shakespeare's use of language to propagandistic effect added its own unique challenges to the question of metre. *Edward III* celebrates the accomplishments of a vastly popular king who engaged in multiple campaigns that spread the English monarchy across Europe. Edward comes across as fair and level-headed in his dealings with both his captains and his rivals, as is clear even in his early speeches. In contrast, Shakespeare takes pains to make Edward's foes sound ridiculous. For example, in Act II scene ii, King David of Scotland assures the Duke of Lorraine of his loyalty to the French. This speech renders the King of Scotland almost incomprehensible to contemporary ears. He launches coherently enough in the beginning: 'My lord of Lorraine, to our brother of France / commend us as the man in Christendom / that we most reverence and entirely love'. But as he gathers spite and fire, he spouts phrases that delight and yet confound the senses:

> and never shall our bonny riders rest
> nor rusting canker have the time to eat
> their light-borne snaffles nor their nimble spurs
> nor lay aside their jacks of gimmaled mail
> nor hang their staves of grainéd Scottish ash
> in peaceful wise upon their city walls
> nor from their buttoned tawny leathern belts
> dismiss their biting whinyards till your king
> cry out 'enough, spare England now for pity'.[3]

This was a formidable passage to translate, with its 'rusting canker', 'light-borne snaffles', 'jacks of gimmaled mail', 'staves of grainéd Scottish ash', 'biting whinyards', and so much more. I determined that Shakespeare intended him to wax preposterous in his bellicose declarations, and so I kept much of that colourful Scottish vernacular, considering that it may have been comically indecipherable even to Lorraine:

> And never shall our bonny riders rest,
> Nor give their fest'ring blisters time to gnaw
> Their light-borne snaffles nor their nimble spurs,
> Nor lay aside their jacks of gimmied mail,
> Nor hang their clubs of grainy Scottish peat
> So peaceably upon their city walls
> Nor to their buttoned tawny leather belts
> Sheathe their biting whinyards till the king
> Cry out, 'Enough, spare England for pity's sake!'[4]

While retaining the colour of the speech, I adjusted some words for clarity; 'grainéd Scottish ash', for example, became 'grainy Scottish peat' because peat is more familiar as a feature of that northern land. But it was the closing line of David's speech that cemented my lesson about metre. Shakespeare's David concludes his speech with a charge to the Duke of Lorraine:

> Farewell, and tell him that you leave us here
> before this castle, say you came from us
> even when we had that yielded to our hands.

In my version, these lines became:

> Farewell, and tell him that you met us here
> Before this castlekeep; and say you left
> As it submitted even to your will.

David's eleven-syllable closing line is here revised to my own pentametric form. The essential realisation that Shakespeare could vary his metre was the key that set me free. From this point forward, the translation came faster and clearer, as I discerned that his many choices were indeed driven by expedience, but more often by the context of the moments portrayed. I also recognised that the limitations imposed on him by the English language and its rules of tempo drove many of his word choices. Plainly put, I began to understand how he thought.

Rendering the Language for the Contemporary Ear

In my work to 'weed the garden' of Shakespeare's text, certain issues of language were paramount: uncommon accenting ('arméd'), archaic pronouns ('thee', 'thou' and 'thy') and verbs forms that do not conform with current usage ('shouldst'). These are the facets we associate most with Shakespeare, and it pained me to alter them, since that is how we have always heard his plays. But in most cases, especially among those who are not as familiar with Elizabethan drama, these are the cues that most arrest the untutored ear, and thus I altered them to meet contemporary standards. Take, for example, the encounter between King John of Valois and King Edward in Act III, scene iii. John and his two sons, Charles and Philip, are valiant warriors bent on protecting their homeland from the invading armies of England, building alliances against those of the English. When they finally meet Edward and his son, Ned the Black Prince, John fires off a salvo that is replete with archaic phrasing. Here is its opening:

> Edward, know that John the true King of France
> musing thou shouldst encroach upon his land
> and in thy tyrannous proceeding slay
> his faithful subjects and subvert his towns
> spits in thy face and in this manner following
> upbraids thee with thine arrogant intrusion.[5]

I updated the archaic language, but I took it even further, teasing out the intent of the words:

> Edward, know that John the true King of France,
> Appalled by your invasion of his land
> And by your tyrannous propensity
> to slay his subjects and subdue his towns,
> Spits in your face; and in these ensuing terms
> Indicts you for this arrogant incursion.[6]

Translating Shakespeare's sumptuous language into the same forceful terms while refining some of his expressions was difficult but necessary. For instance, the lines 'leave therefore now to persecute the weak / and arméd entering conflict with the armed', which John delivers near the end of the speech, may suggest to some that John is exhorting Edward to depart *in order to* assail the weak, but he actually intends the opposite, employing the word 'leave' to mean 'stop'. Therefore, I rewrote the lines:

> Thus cease your persecution of the weak
> And taste some conflict armed against the armed.

I added my personal flourishes of language, removing the accent to balance 'armed' with 'armed' in these lines, and placing the word 'taste' here to close a metaphor from earlier in the speech: 'thy thirst is all for gold' (or, in my text, 'your thirst is all for gold').

I also chose to keep the theme of gardening that Shakespeare writes into John's speech. Shakespeare's John accuses Edward of transience and thievery, suggesting that he either has no home at all,

> or else inhabiting some barren soil
> where neither herb or fruitful grain is had
> dost altogether live by pilfering

In my text, these lines became:

> Or else, inhabiting some barren soil
> Where neither herb nor fruitful grain can grow
> Survives entirely by pilfering

One of the directives of this assignment was to preserve beautiful language for its own beauty, as well as for the sake of thematic imperatives not immediately obvious to the audience, and these lines, with a minor adjustment, are sustained just so. This aesthetic regard was important to me: in the final analysis, I realised that my goal was to make myself invisible in the process, to coax the audience into thinking that I had done very little to the text at all, and that all they were hearing was Shakespeare at his most lucid. The only way I could accomplish this feat was through the use of the same tropes and techniques that the Bard would employ in his oeuvre. I had to learn to write like him.

Making Shakespeare Sound Like Shakespeare

As I stripped away the archaic underbrush of the text, I came to see that my primary task in translating Shakespeare was to make him sound more like himself. I turned to techniques that he used in his later plays in order to bring this one to life for contemporary viewers. I wanted audiences to feel like they're only really listening to a clear rendering of his play. The text that is incontestably self-evident remains unchanged, while the text that hinders this experience is stripped away.

This work of stripping away debris was particularly important to a scene between Edward and the countess of Salisbury in the second act. This scene exemplifies the theme of vows that runs throughout the play, which explores promises, oaths, contracts, allegiances and marriage vows from a deeply humanistic perspective, examining the complexities that pit men against their king, against each other, and even against their own wills. The scene takes a detour from the battles of the Hundred Years' War to depict the one dark stain on Edward's storied career as England's sovereign. It was long rumoured, even in Elizabethan times, that Edward had raped the countess of Salisbury or had at least used his royal privilege to enjoy an illicit affair with her. But a legend had also grown that the countess had freely bestowed her love on him (this version is part of the story of how the chivalric Order of the Garter was created).

Shakespeare knew that in recounting the glories of Edward he had to depict, if not resolve, this nettlesome rumour, and so he constructed a powerful narrative in which the king breaks the siege on the countess's castle, for which she repays him with a feast. Naturally, he instantly falls in love, tumbling headlong into the language of amorous conceits. His speech begins:

> She is grown more fairer far since I came hither
> her voice more silver every word than other
> her wit more fluent.[7]

She is more comely than he remembers, and the king wonders whether her imprisonment and trouble have enhanced her beauty. It is a beautiful passage, but I sought to employ some of Shakespeare's own later techniques of repetition and chiasmus to clarify it, and recalling how the Bard himself would later structure his comparisons in more elegant lyric, I dared to imitate his own commanding verse. My version began:

> She was fair before, but fairer since I've come,
> With every added word her voice more silver,
> Her wit more witty.[8]

As 'wit more fluent' became 'wit more witty' and as 'more fairer far since' became 'fair before but fairer since', I realised how, in translating these verses, I was concealing my own voice with the Bard's gorgeous constructions in his later works. Again, the power of invisibility. Even with lines that began with trochaic feet, with the stress on the first syllable, I found a way to form a more 'Shakespearean' flow in the thought expressed. For example, Shakespeare's Edward marvels about the countess:

> Wisdom is foolishness but in her tongue
> beauty a slander but in her fair face.

And in my translation:

> Wisdom is folly on any tongue but hers,
> Beauty a crime on any face not hers,

The end result is still Shakespeare. And to the contemporary ear, it's arguably *more* Shakespearean than the original. Such was my goal.

Of all the issues that a contemporary audience faces in Shakespeare's works, his frequent allusions to now-obscure ideas, objects and activities are what make the call for translation most necessary. Too many such references have unfortunately muddied the poetry of Shakespeare's plays. Specific references to weapons of war, animal husbandry and heraldry, old jokes and obscure passages in ancient literature can sometimes illuminate the characters' dialogue, but they may also leave glazed-over expressions on the faces of contemporary spectators.

One passage in the first act was particularly difficult for me to make sense of. In conversation with the countess, Edward hints at the pain that his love for her is causing him, characterising it as some sort of betrayal:

> COUNTESS: Far from this place let ugly treason lie.

> KING EDWARD: No farther off than her conspiring eye
> which shoots infected poison in my heart
> beyond repulse of wit or cure of art.

Now in the sun alone it doth not lie
with light to take light from a mortal eye
for here two day-stars that mine eyes would see
more than the sun steals mine own light from me.
Contemplative desire, desire to be
in contemplation that may master thee.[9]

This is one of those passages that made me consider that my upbringing as a young Mexican American would never permit me to fully understand Shakespeare. But I realised that the passage is dense and impenetrable not only to me but also to so many others. I was especially jammed on 'to take light from a mortal eye': does it mean death, or blindness? I did some research among the many annotations to this play and learned that in Shakespeare's day it was commonly assumed that in total darkness, the human eye had the natural capacity to project its own light, as in a lamp, to see by. This 'emission theory' was thought to explain our pupils' adjustment to the dark. Edward is saying that even in the blazing sun, her shining beacons of light (the 'two day-stars' that are her eyes) have utterly blinded him. But since he uses a defunct concept for his metaphor, this passage's meaning is lost.

The question became how to serve the purpose of the passage and still employ the same notion. It's the signature Rubik's Cube of the play, one in which language, rhythm, metaphor, meaning and dramatic emotion all have to click into place. Here is my attempt at this passage:

COUNTESS: Far from us may this ugly treason lie!
KING EDWARD: *(aside)* Yet no farther than her treasonous eye
Whose glancing poison quickening the pulse,
Sparks that which wit nor feeling can repulse.
If eyes to see by render their own light
And light of day itself expands my sight,
Then gazing here I should but cannot see,
For her twin suns steal my own light from me
Oh contemplation of desire, desire me
To contemplate a course of apt sobriety.[10]

The trick lies in the word 'if' in the king's fourth line, which creates the suggestion of a theory of light emission in the eyes to make the feeling true. It makes an elegant kind of sense, too, since lovers are often blinded by the glow in their paramours' eyes. I am largely pleased with the result, particularly in the reformulation of the chiasmus that takes place in the final couplet (with the repetition of 'contemplation' and 'desire', which also keeps the rhyme intact, albeit with different words.

Elsewhere in the play, Edward references what is now a little-known myth about the nightingale while describing the sharpness of his sword:

KING EDWARD: Fervent desire that sits against my heart
is far more thorny-pricking than this blade
that with the nightingale I shall be scarred
as oft as I dispose myself to rest
until my colours be displayed in France.[11]

He refers to the belief that the nightingale's song is sweetest when it tears its breast open against the thorns of the briar. But as no one today knows this myth, I interpret the passage in a different way:

The longing that presses against my heart
Is sharper and more vexing than this blade
And like the nightingale's penetrating song,
will cut the fiber of my sleep to shreds
Until the English flag is raised in France.[12]

It is different, but it expresses the same emotive idea in a way that discards a myth that no longer touches on our consciousness. And yet, still embedded is this notion of cutting oneself open for the sake of poetry, in 'the nightingale's penetrating song'.

Still other passages allude to older texts that may be somewhat obscure today. One refers to a tale from Ovid's *Metamorphosis*, citing Hero, Leander and the Hellespont. And, from the Old Testament, there is a reference to Holofernes and Judith. I could not bring myself to excise these references, since I find them scholastically valuable beyond the scope of the immediate play, and such allusions feel distinctly Shakespearean anyway. Perhaps they might induce some to conduct their own research into these timeless fables.

Bringing to Life the Battle Reports

Shakespeare has a proclivity for giving some of his greatest speeches to commoners, soldiers and villagers – characters who appear once and then are seen no more. In *Edward III*, we see this happen with a speech given to a mariner in the third act, who recounts in vivid detail (and across forty-four lines) what appears to be the 1340 Battle of Sluys in the English Channel.[13] For example:

These iron-hearted navies
when last I was reporter to your grace
both full of angry spleen of hope and fear

hasting to meet each other in the face
at last conjoined and by their admiral
our admiral encountered many shot

It is a vivid and fiery speech, filled with the horrors of combat in the open sea. Its detail and scope capture both the epic nature of the battle and the personal cost to the men who perished in it. Still, there was much work to do. Here is my iteration of the above snippet, which brings the action more into focus for a contemporary audience:

These hostile iron-hearted navies,
When last I was reporter to your grace,
All full of anger, hope, and fear, and men
Hasting to meet each other hull to hull,
At last faced off, and from their flagship
Our flag incurred substantial cannon-shot.[14]

The mariner's eyewitness report fires the imagination with its recounting of wholesale gore. In translating it, my goal was to intensify this feeling while mitigating points of confusion in the language or the imagery.

One such point of confusion occurs early in the mariner's report about the naval encounter. He states, 'by this the other that beheld these twain / give earnest penny of a further wrack'. These lines are a reference to the guarantee of greater conflict in the initial face-off between the two opposing flagships, the 'earnest penny' being the down payment on this conflict. So I translate the lines thus: 'On cue, the others that beheld these ships / Transact a pledge of further ruin'. By employing the idea of a 'pledge', the passage now calls up the overarching theme of vows and promises kept and broken, while also playing on the original passage's allusion to a financial transaction.

And yet, so many passages remain untouched, lines that still throb with the richest metaphors, such as the potent description of cannon fire, from which 'smoky wombs' the warships 'sent many grim ambassadors of death'. Even the most graphic description of human butchery is so poetically and vividly rendered that I kept the lines intact and unchanged:

Here flew a head dissevered from the trunk,
There mangled arms and legs were tossed aloft,
As when a whirlwind takes the summer dust
And scatters it in middle of the air.

Of course, there is also much that I transposed in the mariner's speech: Shakespeare's 'compulsion' for my 'conscription'; his 'purple the sea' for my 'sea all crimson'; his 'foeman's side' for my 'opponents' side'. These and other changes had to be selected carefully and made with enough discretion to offer some clarity and familiarity to the listener without sacrificing the tenor of Shakespeare. Even as I aimed to become invisible in the playing of the work, I felt some permission to carry this 'translation' further than perhaps some of my colleagues, if only because *Edward III* seems ripe for the kind of revision that the Bard himself might have applied were he alive today. Which is presumptuous of me to say. There is no doubt that the changes I have offered have marked this particular play as my own creation, but I prefer to regard myself as simply his newest collaborator on the work, one whose chief task is to enhance his gift for expressive language.

Solving the Puzzle of Shakespeare's Text

One of my chief diversions is solving crossword puzzles in the *New York Times*. The true satisfaction comes not from solving the puzzle but from learning to read the mind of the enigmatologist. A good puzzle is at first very difficult to solve, but once a few squares are filled in and a theme is established, the rest of the answers fall into place. I know there are only so many blanks per clue, and I know the answers can't be too esoteric or depend on arcane knowledge or the puzzle will lose the solver. With these tools, it's thrilling to intuit what wry wordplay will drop next.

I suspect that Shakespeare tackled *Edward III* in the same manner. There are only (mostly) ten syllables per line, and they need to express a specific idea or emotion; they must (more or less) conform to the beat of the iambic foot; nothing esoteric or arcane can be delivered to the audience without some more conjoining metaphor to ground it. He was his own enigmatologist, solving his own puzzle as he was writing, finding the perfect word and placing it just so within the rhythmic framework of his dialogue. The unity of the original text feels as though it had only one mind devising its code, and therefore I assert – regardless of the computational findings on percentages and authorship – that the play is wholly Shakespeare's. The many tropes he uses in *Edward III* correspond to those we find in many of his plays in the canon, and the Bard's expansive spirit which confers all his characters, friend and foe, major and minor, the same generous humanity is found in this work; but it is the essential flow of the language, the complex music of the work, that ultimately felt 'Shakespearean'. If the play is a result of writer collaboration, it exists between the younger, cockier actor-writer and the mature master dramatist he will become in later years. I also have to admit that any remnants of Kyd or any other dramatist, any language and stylistic choices that may have been attributed to him, have been thoroughly reconfigured in this translation to resonate more with Shakespeare's. In other words, my translation has crowned Will as the sole author of *Edward III*.

Edward III is, in turn, his puzzle for me. As I begin to understand his choices, I sense the poetic workings of his mind. I gradually intuit something vital about him that helps me in my translation. I see why the music of the spoken idiom is so important to him. It's the bridge between the poet and the playwright: one mind fixed on the purity of the verse, the exacting nature of language, built on the foundations of a thousand years' tradition of poetry; and one mind bent on putting on a ripping good show, working to depict a king and an entire world of subjects in a time of war, each possessing their own particular needs and intentions, each with their own historical context. This balance between intellectual rigour and theatrical bravado is what defines Shakespeare and what permits him to take liberties with his own rules.

But it is also what makes me suddenly more visible. I take the same approach and seek the balance between honouring the language and metre and crafting new expressions for our contemporary sensibilities. At times, this approach means strictly adhering to the rhythms and tropes already present in the work, a rigorous choice in itself; and at other times, it means taking special pains to alter the language and the metre just enough to make the work a little more distinct and theatrically satisfying. Remarkably, at a recent live reading of *Edward III*, I was heartened to see Shakespearean scholars listen to the performance with side-by-side versions of Will's play and mine to compare and contrast, and to see how deftly we managed our collaboration.

Here's the final revelatory aspect of my work. I had the American Heritage Dictionary, Roget's Thesaurus, countless online lexicons all over the Web, and the entirety of Shakespeare's canon to help me. There have been more than 420 years' worth of words added to the English language since *Edward III* was written. Shakespeare had none of this. He worked without the benefit of any lexicon, and yet he's credited with adding over 1,500 words to the Oxford English Dictionary. When he didn't have the right word to fit the metre for his purposes, he simply invented it. In Eric Sams's edition of *Shakespeare's Edward III: An Early Play Restored to the Canon*, which was the chief volume I used for my work, I found many annotations in the notes that began with the phrase 'first recorded use of this word'. The genius required for this kind of massive undertaking, not only on *Edward III*, but over his other plays and volumes of poetry, is unmatched. No other writer has accomplished anything like this before or since, and I had no pretentions about trying.

So it was this humility, this *Will*ful invisibility, that enabled me to approach the translation of this great work, and whether or not my version finds itself onstage sometime in the future, I remain proud to have become more intimately acquainted with the genius of this man, and immensely indebted to the *Play on!* project for ultimately making me feel *seen* as a writer worthy of sharing his inkwell with the Bard himself.

Notes

1. These two scenes appear, respectively, in William Shakespeare, *Edward III*, ed. Eric Sams (New Haven: Yale University Press, 1996), I.i.17–19; and Octavio Solis, trans., *Edward III* by William Shakespeare (unpublished script), 1.
2. Shakespeare, *Edward III*, I.i.145–52.
3. Shakespeare, *Edward III*, I.ii.204–12.
4. Solis, *Edward III*, 7–8.
5. Shakespeare, *Edward III*, III.iii.1368–73.
6. Solis, *Edward III*, 52–3.
7. Shakespeare, *Edward III*, II.i.377–9.
8. Solis, *Edward III*, 15–16.
9. Shakespeare, *Edward III*, I.ii.310–19.
10. Solis, *Edward III*, 13.
11. Shakespeare, *Edward III*, I.i.114–18.
12. Solis, *Edward III*, 4–5.
13. Shakespeare, *Edward III*, III.i.1192–7.
14. Solis, *Edward III*, 46–7.

20

Diálogo: On Performing Shakespearean Characters as Latinx

Alejandra Escalante and Daniel José Molina
Facilitated by Carla Della Gatta

In this conversation, Alejandra Escalante and Daniel José Molina tackle the nuances of portraying Shakespearean characters as Latinx actors. Although currently living in New York, they have both worked extensively for the Oregon Shakespeare Festival (OSF), and they met when starring in the lead roles of OSF's *Romeo and Juliet* in 2012. They shared the stage again at OSF in *The Tempest* (2014) and in *Henry IV, Part I* (2016). Their onstage relationships soon took on an offstage life, with the two marrying each other in 2018. They have both performed Shakespeare in Spanish in various roles. In this dialogue, they discuss their background with Shakespeare, the process of translating his work into Spanish, and their history with performing in plays written by Latinx playwrights.

Carla Della Gatta: How did you get involved with Shakespeare?

Daniel José Molina: My favourite college professor very frankly said to me, 'Molina, you can't sing, and you can't dance. You might want to pick up Shakespeare.'

Even though I completely agreed with him on my limitations, it wasn't until many years later I understood how wise and practical his advice was. Before that moment, Shakespeare only brought up memories of that interminable and dull semester in junior high. Maybe [that professor] just wanted to keep me busy. Maybe he was savvy enough to know that regional classical theatres are a great first step for a young non–equity actor.

Even if I didn't go on to steadily work in productions of Shakespeare's plays (going on eleven years now, which blows my mind), [this professor] had offered me an invitation into an entire dimension of history, performance and art I otherwise might not have discovered. He might have just thought it would keep me busy. In those early days it was just lexicons and plot synopses and monologues, but very quickly that evolved into spear-carrying in actual summer stock productions and, before I knew it, an acting career.

But if I ask myself why I've stuck with it? It would be a very glib combination: people keep offering me jobs and, very luckily, I can't get enough of it.

Alejandra Escalante: My first role was Lady Macbeth in high school, when I was seventeen. I had done scenes from Shakespeare before, but that was my first full production, and weirdly enough, that was the show that got me to love Shakespeare, whatever that says about who I am as a person. I remember being seventeen and not necessarily understanding word for word what I was saying, but I understood something, those murderous intentions. That was my first experience of loving it. Now I love to dissect and discover the words, rhythm, and verse.

Carla: Does your process for engaging with Shakespeare differ from your process with other playwrights?

Alejandra: In a sense. Working on a script by Shakespeare I tend to work on the language in a very specific way. I need to understand the language backwards and forwards to feel confident that I have a hold on the character as well as know that the audience understands me. On more contemporary pieces I don't tend to rip apart the language and put it back together in the same way.

I definitely approach a script of Shakespeare's very differently than I do a contemporary script. Sometimes I like to say it's the same thing, but it isn't. I found out quite early on, being one of the younger people in a cast, à la *Romeo and Juliet*, and being around these people who had been doing this work for years, I realised I needed to actually know what I was saying. And to not embarrass myself when we go through first reads and I am pronouncing everything wrong. So I am really meticulous now about [approaching] the script and writing down every single word. I will translate it into modern English; if there's a phrase I can understand word by word but I can't really intellectualise it, I will translate it into a way I can understand it or a phrase I can understand. I have to do that for every single word in a Shakespeare script. Whereas I think there's a lot more interpretation and ease with something that is more contemporary. If I understand what I'm saying, hopefully the audience will too.

Daniel: It does, but only in the technical sense. Those first few read-through or table work days might be my favourite when working on a Shakespeare play. Picking apart the giant knot of rhetorical parenthetical subjects, proper nouns, historical references, and terribly unfunny and archaic Elizabethan jokes with a group of intelligent artists/dramaturgs/directors is some version of my ideal Sunday. All this is to say, Shakespeare earns himself maybe a couple extra table work days to make sure everyone comprehends every word in that script.

And (hot take), the difference between working on Shakespeare and [working on] a new play honestly ends there. I am most moved by Shakespeare when it is performed by actors hungry for truth, not style. Flawed, three-dimensional, breathing, all-too-mortal characters is the way for me, baby. I remember working at a theatre in my earlier days and getting chewed out by a director for not respecting the elevated language by not behaving onstage in a . . . well . . . elevated manner. Presentational. Stylised for stylisation's sake. Unplaceable transatlantic accent. That was the wave at this particular venue.

I didn't have a comeback then, but now I would just throw Hamlet's speech to the players at him. All this is to say: do I want every audience member to hear and follow every single one of my character's specific, poetic, timeless thoughts? Absolutely, diction IS important! But am I going to perform my [role] any differently than a real human being onstage simply because the play is historic? No thanks.

Carla: Both of you are bilingual, but were you trained to act in Spanish? What are the biggest challenges to being in a bilingual or semi-bilingual production?

Alejandra: Spanish was my first language. I learned English through school, once preschool started. I did not receive training in acting in Spanish. I'm not sure there are too many challenges. When it comes to Shakespeare, I think it's important to have a great translation. I will go through the verse to find emphases and things I learned in school, for sure, particularly if I get stuck on something that sounds weird, and then I work with Daniel through it. But other than that, it's kind of been a mash-up of what I've put together. The wonders of Shakespeare appear in his language, not necessarily in his plots, so an evocative translation is really necessary. Just putting the words into Google Translate does not work! I promise!

Daniel: My acting training did not include any Spanish. I've had two recurring challenges when I've been in bilingual and semi-bilingual productions. One of them is, sadly, I've never been in a semi-bilingual production with a fully bilingual cast. Every time, the non-Latinx cast members learn beautiful Spanish. But I've wondered what would happen if it were a full cast of Spanish speakers that have grown up and have an emotional connection with those palabras.

My second problem is when a Latinx story in a play in English feels the need to translate words within dialogue. You know what I'm talking about? When a character will say a line that goes something like 'My favorite food is an Aguacate! An avocado!' Who are you translating for? If all these characters speak Spanish, why are you translating? If it's a scenario where the characters are all speaking their native language, but it is just translated for the audience's sake, then what is happening in that moment? That's just a pet peeve of mine.

Carla: Alejandra, you played Julieta in the 2011 OSF *Measure for Measure* set in a border town, and you were the only monolingual Spanish-speaking character. How did speaking the lines in Spanish affect your character? What did it mean to be linguistically segregated from the other characters?

Alejandra: It was definitely the first time I had worked on a production that was almost entirely set within a Latinx community. I found a lot of happiness and excitement in being able to represent that part of myself. It was very cool to have a commonality with some cast members. To be honest, a small percentage of the cast was actually Latino/a/x. Four of about fifteen speaking parts were played by Latinx actors. I found a great sense of stakes in Julieta only being able to speak in Spanish. I felt her frustration and urgency in trying to communicate. I really had to do very little acting because the desperation came so naturally. I remember not being confident with my English when I first started school (preschool), and the fear I had of speaking up. Here was Julieta, pregnant, with her fiancé in prison facing death, and she can barely plead her case. It was very moving.

I was also in Tanya Saracho's plays *The Tenth Muse* (some Spanish) and *Songs for the Disappeared* (partially in Spanish) at the Goodman, and when I was younger, I did *Blood Wedding*, and that was entirely in Spanish. Most of it was in Spanglish. There was also a lot of Spanish in *2666* at the Goodman.

Carla: Daniel, you played Romeo in (mostly) English in the OSF production in 2012 and then in Spanish with the Neruda text in a staged reading for The Public. Aside from the different scripts, what were the differences you noted in playing the role in two languages?

Daniel: Honestly, it's very difficult to compare the experiences since OSF was a full production while The Public was just a reading. But Romeo's track felt both similar and dissimilar. Much of that I attribute to Neruda's decision to translate Shakespeare's play line by line rather than editorialising. So every single one of Romeo's thoughts was uttered, but since they were in Shakespeare's order, there was no rhythm, and certainly no rhyme. To be frank, I expected so much more from the adaptation. A discovery was made of the stark contrast between adaptation and translation. It was like a bad cover of an incredible song. But I loved the experience both for that discovery and the new friends I made on that project.

Carla: What about translating?

Alejandra: Most of the directors I have worked with, although they are Latinx, don't speak Spanish, or I have played roles where I was speaking Spanish and maybe there were Latinx elements to the play, and some that weren't Latinx at all. In terms of the language, I started doing a lot of that on my own, kind of fairly thrown in the deep end. When I came in to do *Measure for Measure*, nobody told me that I was only speaking in Spanish. At the first read-through (it was a different time, and things have gotten better), it was very clear that it was a Google translation, and it didn't make any sense at all.

That day, I switched some words around. Then I approached Bill and asked if I should translate it, and it was put on the back burner. So I translated it myself. That was the first time, of several, that I have done that. And I don't mind it. I really like the work. It's a weird way to use your brain, to try to translate poetry. It is challenging and really fun, and fun to ask my mom if I read it to her this way, how does she interpret it. In terms of the acting, I never found it to be any different or approached it differently.

I have definitely looked at Spanish translations before. Once I got to *Romeo and Juliet*, Dan and I would spitball back and forth, because there was Spanish thrown in here and there, so we had to go over that. For example, should he call her 'Mi cielo' or 'Mi sol'; we would go back and forth in that way. For the most part, I like to do it on my own, and what feels evocative to me, especially if I am the one saying it, I might as well make it work for me. I do like to run it by my mom, Dan, anybody just to see not only does this make sense, but more so, does it give you the sense of what it means in English, does it inspire you to see and hear that same imagery?

Carla: You starred opposite each other at OSF in *The Tempest* and later shared the stage in *Henry IV, Part I*. What was the difference in your experiences in these non-Latinx/Spanish-themed productions and *Romeo and Juliet*? How was the process and/or product different?

Alejandra: I don't think there was any particular difference in how the process came to be. Of course, every production is so different because of the cast, director, story, etc. At the end of the day I am still a Latinx body performing all of those different roles.

Daniel: If we're completely honest, not too much, if anything, changed in our processes. Our approach to character building is not dependent on what language the dramatis personae carries in their mouth. Pretty please don't misunderstand that to mean we don't care! Perhaps the experience of performing that role is a deeper, personal one. If us being Latin is a diegetic element in the productions that we're in (i.e. *Romeo and Juliet*, *Water by the Spoonful* or *The Tenth Muse*), it's a real privilege. We can contribute in some small way to the story of our respective cultures. Which means that, conversely, if a play never brings up the fact that we are Latinx, both Alejandra and I cherish that opportunity. Sometimes the representation is enough. It is good to know that tokenisation is not the only way to tread the boards as a Latinx performer.

Carla: Have you ever been asked to perform Latinx identity in a way that made you feel uncomfortable? How did you modify the characterisation?

Daniel: Sadly, yes. Of course I won't name the theatre or the production but it was a role that was a part of an ensemble of clowns. The rehearsal period was incredibly brief, and really much of the characterisation work was done in one conversation at the beginning of us getting on our feet. This was earlier in my career, and I was still in college and very green. I saw smarter, more experienced actors enhance or grow aspects of themselves to an appropriate clown scale almost effortlessly. And regrettably, the only feature I thought I could exaggerate about myself was that I was the only Latino in this motley crew. Ridiculous accent and broad stereotypes and all. The worst part of it is I remember them being the biggest laughs I had ever gotten at that stage of my career. Thankfully, much has changed.

Alejandra: For *Romeo and Juliet*, Dan and I were asked on the first day, for the first read-through, to read with accents, which none of us knew, none of us knew we would be doing this, including our voice and text coach. So that was the first time he was hearing it too. As you can imagine, David Carey, definitely not being Latino, was quite shocked. That whole idea kept getting tossed out, mainly really, because of Dan and me. Me crying, and asking, 'Please don't let us do this. It's going to be really bad. Please don't make us do this.' For lots of reasons, but mainly it was that we didn't want to seem like a weird, stereotypical story, and because there wasn't the research into what this accent would be, the style that it would sound like. The first day we were told, 'Something Spanish', and we thought, Spanish from 1847 from Spain? I have no idea what that sounds like; I have no frame of reference. 'Flavour', 'spice', 'fiery' – any of those words are such trigger words for me now. I never want to hear them again. It was just so much time spent. [. . .] I would definitely hope that those things were going to get more specific as time goes on. And I have worked with a good number of Latinx dramaturgs, which is really great.

Carla: Have you ever tried to change your Spanish accent for a role?

Alejandra: Yes, there has been some direction. In *2666* (at the Goodman), I played a German character too, but mainly a Mexican character and then a Spanish character. I definitely worked on a Spanish accent because she spoke entirely accented English, and then I was supposed to speak in Spanish. That was an easier change to make because the rules were simpler than that versus being Mexican and changing it to more of a Colombian sound, because I am less familiar with those subtle differences. I have definitely been asked to sound more Mexican, which is interesting because I find what people usually think is that more Mexican is more LA, a more Chicano accent; people often say to talk a lot slower. I've heard the direction, 'You've been working out in the field all day so you're tired. [. . .]' [ironic commentary]. So that's the direction that you get to get to where they want. [. . .]

Carla: Actors (and directors) often establish themselves by demonstrating mastery with Shakespeare. Conversely, some feel that they might be pigeon-holed if they engage too much with Latinx theatre. Were you ever reticent to take on any roles? Why so?

Daniel: I have hesitated to accept roles before for various reasons. Have I done something too similar to this before? Will I really be challenging myself in this? And conversely, can I pull that off? More of those kind of doubts. I consider myself lucky in that I have never felt particularly pigeonholed or stereotyped onstage. All the Latin roles I've performed (with the exception of that show with the clowns) I remember as being multilayered and human. Again, I know that is not every Latin actor's experience, and I say again, lucky.

Carla: Have there been any other types of theatre you took to?

Alejandra: The play that I read that I will never forget that showed me what theatre could be is *Topdog/Underdog*. And just from reading it – I had not yet seen it – I was completely transported. I was completely shaking afterwards. In terms of practice, I got really interested in physical theatre and things that maybe didn't use language quite as much, which is funny coming from someone who loves Shakespeare. I had an amazing teacher named Elaine Vaan Hogue, who taught physical acting, the Grotowski method, and that opened up a whole other part of my brain. I had been a dancer before, when I was much younger, so I think that was also something that made me realise how to bridge this gap and get out of my head and fully in tune with what I was actually saying and doing.

21

What's with the Spanish, Dude? Identity Development, Language Acquisition and Shame while Coaching *La Comedia of Errors*

Micha Espinosa

I was eighteen and had just returned from theatre school to my native Arizona. It was Christmas Eve in the Espinosa household, and the tamales and posole smelled so good. After church, the custom was for the family to gather, the mariachis to play and the cousins to reunite. During these gatherings, the majority of the family spoke Spanish. My Spanish was rusty, but feeling confident from my studies and travels, I tried to engage with confidence. Doing my best to be humble from a minor mistake, I proclaimed, 'Estoy embarazada?' From the puzzled looks from my family, I knew I had done something wrong. No one corrected me, but they laughed and laughed and laughed. I ran from the room and locked myself in the bathroom. Did I have food in my teeth? Had I spilled food on myself? Embarazada – embarrassed – what was so funny? I later found out that I had told everyone that I was pregnant. The word for 'embarrassed' is vergüenza, not embarazada. How did I get it mixed up? Spanish became my false friend. The next time I was asked to speak in Spanish was for a performance in a play. I hesitated. My body froze and my mind fogged; memories of being put in the corner at school for speaking Spanish, my embarrassing moment, and the pressure of getting Spanish 'right' for the play all hit my nervous system at once. Even though I grew up speaking Spanish, I had trouble learning my lines. In my mind, I felt there was something wrong with me.

Fast forward thirty-two years, and it is spring 2019. I have spent years studying my body's reaction to this freeze sensation (with research interests in identity development, language acquisition and shame), I have reclaimed my Spanglish identity, and I am the visiting voice and text coach at Oregon Shakespeare Festival (OSF). One of my assignments for the season is *La Comedia of Errors*, a bilingual adaptation by Lydia G. Garcia and Bill Rauch of a *Play on!* translation by Christina Anderson. The *Play on!* project was created in alignment with the equity and inclusion initiatives at OSF to engage and inspire audiences. A total of thirty-six playwrights were commissioned to translate thirty-nine plays using modern English to increase understanding and connection to the work.

I was deeply honoured to work on the world premiere of *La Comedia of Errors*, which was artistic director Rauch's last production at OSF. It had long been a dream of his to offer a bilingual production. This ninety-minute production, in which Spanish and English were spoken equally, was staged in the round and was actor driven. The play follows Shakespeare's *The Comedy of Errors* in a new cultural context. All classic characters are represented, and the story follows the same plot. There is the classic mistaken identity, puns, rhyme, verse, twins, stock characters and, of course, the amazement and wonder of physical comedy. But the play is now set in a fictitious town in the United States. Two actors play the two sets of twins, and these two sets are geographically split, with one set having been raised in the United States and the other in Mexico. Egeon, the father of the twins, searching for his family, now faces deportation instead of execution, and the play has an important new character called La Vecina. La Vecina, which translates as 'the neighbour', is the bilingual, chatty, opinionated, telenovela-loving, noisy witness who sits in the audience and helps narrate and interpret events, awakening us through her testimony. This new character, La Vecina, uses her wicked sense of humour to interpret for the audience. The passage that follows takes place soon after the Mexican twins' arrival in the United States. The confused jeweller, having already given the twin, Antipholus of Mexico, the necklace for Antipholus of USA's wife, has just approached Antipholus of the USA about payment for the necklace. This interaction takes place entirely in English. La Vecina observes the action and then steps in to remind Antipholus of the USA of the theatre audience and to narrate the action for Spanish-speaking spectators:

LA VECINA
Whoa, that's a lot of English. ¿No que esta obra es bilingüe? What about mis vecinos? Who's taking care of them?
ANTIPHOLUS OF USA
Whatchu mean? We speak American in America.
LA VECINA
Oh, is that how it is? You know what, I got this.
(to audience)
Este señor es el joyero encargado del collar que la esposa celosa deseaba. Y parece que este patrón por fin encontró al hombre que le pertenece. Pero están hechos vueltas sobre quien le pegó a quien.
(to ANTIPHOLUS, dabbing)
American.[1]

La Vecina is not afraid to challenge Antipholus of the USA and his mono-lingualism. The text dives headfirst into the politics of language. The play's contemporary reimagining and border crossing (both US–Mexican and US–Canadian) also highlight the treatment of immigrants, the reunification of families, and the urgency of empathy in our political times.

In the programme notes for the 2019 season production, Rauch asked, 'How do we reveal the comedy of errors, the misunderstandings, the whole extra lens – the profoundly political and aesthetically thrilling lens of lan-guage? Who speaks Spanish? Who speaks English? Who speaks both? How are characters connecting and conflicting because of language and through language?' As a fourth-generation Sonoran Chicana artist, I fell deeply in love with this script and the concepts Rauch offered his audience. At the beginning of the play, Antifolo de México reflects on his journey after arriving in the United States:

En el mundo soy como una gota de aqua,
Buscando orta gota en medio del mar –
I to the world am like a drop of water
That in the ocean seeks another drop – [2]

When I read La Comedia of Errors, I immediately felt like my thirst had been quenched. I've always spoken Spanglish, and I think in both languages. However, I had never worked on a production of Shakespeare that so fully embraced the spectrum of Latinx identity and language.

The success of the play's language blending is primarily due to Garcia and Rauch's writing. The adaptation benefited from the brilliant Spanish trans-lations of Garcia, which reflect her understanding of language politics and her years of equity and diversity work. The show was created in 'workshop' over many months in tandem with a group of diverse actors/players in the company. The intersectionality of the players and their relationship to lan-guage made this production unique. In addition, OSF is fiercely committed to the local Latinx community. Community organisers Antonio David Lyon and Alejandra Cisneros spearheaded outreach efforts and engaged in radical welcoming, inviting community members to serve as cultural experts during pre-production, and bringing the show to local community centres (often with tamales), school gyms and OSF's rehearsal hall. Through their presence in the room, the community knowledge holders offered a situated perspective to the writers during the rehearsal and adaptation process, as well as an oppor-tunity to gauge how the material would resonate with audiences who might be new to OSF's work.

As the US Dromio so eloquently puts it in the play's first scene, 'What's with the Spanish, Dude?'[3] This play features a variety of Spanish speakers –

Puerto Rican, Guatemalan, Costa Rican, Mexicano, Gringo, Spanglish – as well as English speakers, with and without accents. The printed text of the play is multicoloured: red indicates text spoken in Spanish; blue indicates text in which a native Spanish speaker is speaking English; green indicates text in which a native English speaker is speaking Spanish; and black indicates when the text is spoken in English. It was exciting, refreshing and terrifying to approach a text that allowed for this level of cultural bumping. This type of experimentation can be seen throughout *La Comedia*. The following early exchange between sisters Luciana and Adriana, narrated by La Vecina, reveals how the levels of mixing, code-switching and Spanglish move the story forward:

LA VECINA
Por la gran púchika, cree que su esposo tiene una novia.
LUCIANA
¡Los celos matan! Tsk, smack jealousy away.
ADRIANA
Unfeeling fools can with such wrongs go play!
Hermana, you know he promised me a chain;
Would that alone be a token he's detain,
So he would keep right faithful to his bed!
El quiere otra mujer, yo estoy entre espada y pared:
Since that my beauty cannot please his eye,
I'll weep what's left away, and weeping die.
        (singing as she exits)
'Y Volver, Volver, Volver
A tus brazos otra vez . . .'

Adriana's song here is a classic ranchera about returning to a lover: 'To return, return, return to your arms once again'. Still, I heard this familiar refrain as a reclaiming of language and cultura. To hear the nuance of the accented English of the native Spanish-speaking character Luciana was deeply meaningful to me. The sounds were of someone who lives in two worlds, ni de aquí, ni de allá, sounds that represented my family and my community. I could think of no other time in my career where I had been part of a professional production where crossing sonic borders was welcomed and embraced. My relationship with language and identity has always been complicated. Linguistic strategising has been a means of survival. Spanglish has been an assertion of my political identity and my relationship to borders has been the fulcrum of my research and performance.

Thus, I felt uniquely qualified to serve the play and the players. In 2005, I published a study, 'Insights into the Challenges Latino Students Face while

Training in Theatre', in *Shakespeare around the Globe*.[4] The chapter was the first of its kind and has since led to numerous articles and publications. In preparation for *La Comedia*, I revisited the work. In the study, I used phenomenological inquiry to examine linguistic identity. I specifically look to George Kitahara Kich's scholarship on developmental stages for bicultural identity formation to better understand language acquisition.[5] I offer the steps now through my lens of actor training. They are as follows:

> *Stage one*: this stage can be emotionally painful, when the subject/actor realises they have an accent, or when their cultural voice is markedly different from the way others perceived them or their phenotype. Different-ness, the feeling of not belonging, can lead to feelings of self-negation, rejection and shame.
>
> *Stage two*: the subject/actor might find themselves emotionally unstable. The subject's feelings might fluctuate between an understanding of their beliefs in the context of their social and political world and the possibility that a situation could be triggering, and thus the unhealthy feelings return.
>
> *Stage three*: this last stage of development brings stability. The subject can be expressive rather than be defensive. The subject/actor actively seeks and takes joy in their cultural or linguistic identity.

As a vocal coach, I found myself going through these same stages of acceptance. I feared that my skills would not be enough; I had grown up under the English-only movement and had not had a formal bilingual education. Would my Latinidad serve the play and players; would my intermediate Spanish level II skills and 'border crossed over me politics' be enough? How was it, after years of study and significant life experience, that I still had to go through the process of reclaiming my right to cultural competency and linguistic dexterity?

In my years of teaching bilingual/bicultural workshops and researching the experiences of Latinx actors, I have witnessed that second-language learners of both English and Spanish share in the same process of acceptance of self. I have experienced and seen the debilitating effects of shame and shame memory. To take Spanish as an example: some people speak better Spanish than others. Some people can speak Spanish but cannot read or write it. Some studied in school but have never performed while speaking Spanish. Some can speak Spanish and English, but only within the context of where they were raised, with only local rhythms and pronunciations. Others do not speak Spanish at all but need to do so for work or social acceptance because of their phenotype and cultural background. Lastly, there is the fear of judgement from the experts in the room, those who speak Spanish with greater fluidity, proper grammar and pronunciation: this fear dramatically increases the possibility of the freeze response in the body. Language ability is deeply tied to one's identity, as exemplified in the first scene of *La Comedia*:

THE ACTOR WHO PLAYS DEPUTY
The first scene of our play picks up somewhere in the United States. . . .
And we begin with:
EGEÓN
El padre, hecho un cautivo, que solo habla español.
DEPUTY
(interpreting)
The father, now a captive, who only speaks Spanish.
SHERIFF SOLINUS
A sheriff, who only speaks English.
DEPUTY
Un sheriff, que solo habla inglés. And a deputy, who will do his darnedest to interpret.[6]

This moment nicely sets up the rules of the world and reveals how central language ability is to the characters' identities. The actor playing the deputy, the talented Mark Murphy, took the last line above and brilliantly encapsulated the struggle of speaking a second language. The joke was not played for laughs; rather, the actor gestured his arm with earnest enthusiasm and shared his truth with the audience by allowing them to see in his eyes the feeling of relief that came from returning to his mother tongue after successfully translating in effortful Spanish.

Towards the latter half of the play, Emilia, the abbess and long-lost wife of Egeon and the mother to the separated twins, reunites with her family and community. Emilia is an expert code-switcher, and she reveals her true identity by speaking completely in Spanglish, a reflection of her two lives united:

Nuestros queridos vecinos,
And all that are assembled in this place,
That by this sympathetic one day's error
Have suffered wrong,
Please come with us into the chapel here
And we shall make full satisfacción.
Thirty-three years have I but been in labor
With you and you, my sons; and till this present hour
My heavy burden never delivered.
Mi comunidad, mi esposo and mis hijos both,
And you the calendars of their nativity,

Go to a baptism feast – un nuevo bautismo – and come with me;
After such long grief, such festivity![7]

These last words – 'after such long grief, such festivity' – struck me to the core every time I heard them. I believe *La Comedia of Errors* will bring relief and festivity. I imagine the many Latinx students and communities that will benefit from producing and seeing the show. I imagine the audiences that will be introduced to verse and Shakespeare and poetry with Spanish, English and Spanglish. OSF is a unique environment where equity and inclusion are at the forefront of the process. Elsewhere, I have seen talented actors not given opportunities because they speak with an accent. Stories of blatant ignorance and racism frequently appear on the Latinx Theatre Commons and Latinx Scholar blogs. Some actors tell stories of directors asking them to be 'more Mexican'; others ask the very real question of *do I belong?* The following post on the Latinx Theatre Commons Facebook page received numerous responses:

> Hello all. First time poster, recently joined. Latinx, obviously. I'm Latinx American tho, brought up without the culture or language. Does that hurt my opportunities being in Latinx Theater, and how can I provide a voice for others in my position? Do I learn and devote myself to a culture I never knew, or can I create something new that is still valid to the Latinx experience?[8]

This question strikes at the heart of the complexity of the Latinx experience with identity and work in the theatre. Latinx Shakespearean projects like *La Comedia* offer audiences and players a more complex representation and thus understanding of who we are as a cultural community. I have seen in the classroom and onstage actors liberated by working in their mother tongue. I have also seen actors who resist and shut down when they are asked to speak in their home language.

In the last act of the play, La Vecina declares, 'You know what, ya basta. I'm done waiting for others to step in and step up.'[9] I concur with her sentiment. As a vocal coach, I am committed to cultural competency and to a recognition of the cultural context and linguistic complexity of the cast/students with whom I am working. An understanding of the stages of identity development and its relationship to shame and to shame memory has helped me develop best practices. I find inspiration in many places, from Erik Erikson's theory of psychosocial development and Brené Brown's resiliency theories, to the growing research on identity and language education, language teaching psychology and numerous studies in second language acquisition.[10] But I am most deeply influenced by the work of Catherine Fitzmaurice, with whom I have studied for over twenty-five years.

The Fitzmaurice method of embodied voice holds at its core the philosophy that the teacher will recognise their own nervous system and the nervous system of the other.[11] I have developed over the years what I am currently referring to as identity-conscious, character-driven voice and accent design. The process begins by creating an environment of trust by using radical listening. I rarely work in groups. I believe that each actor needs time to work individually. I then tailor instructional materials to align with the learning style of the actor to increase autonomy. I try to be conscious of the ways a player could be triggered with shame or shame memory; moments of community involvement put a higher level of stress on the players in terms of their abilities and authenticity. It is at these times that in my role as voice and text coach I serve as an ally, advocating for the time needed for acquisition, serving as a confidant and actively mitigating levels of stress primarily using principles and techniques from the Fitzmaurice 'destructuring' process.

In the fourth act of *La Comedia*, the character Antifolo de Mexico says, 'Este sueño Americano es una pesadilla': 'This American dream is heavy'.[12] As of 2005, just fifteen years ago, bilingual education was banned in three states – California, Arizona and Massachusetts – that, together, as Corey Mitchell details, 'educated 40 percent of the nation's English-language learners'.[13] Generations of actors like myself who grew up under these laws are now reclaiming their language and healing from the demoralising and counterproductive attitudes around language learning. The tide is changing, and many of these laws have recently been repealed, although Arizona's laws remain intact. The play ends on a hopeful tone, with the US Dromio offering to his Mexican counterpart:

We came into the world hermano y hermano;
Let's go, not one before another, but mano en mano.[14]

I am hopeful that more productions like *La Comedia of Errors* will reach audiences, that more opportunities for revisioning and reimagining our narratives will make a difference, that we will continue to fight for a country that embraces its neighbours and that celebrates biculturalism and bilingualism. I love that *La Comedia* uses the artistry of humour yet does not forget the reality of the distribution of sadness in Latinx communities: those migrant/immigrant stories, family separation, Dreamers waiting, waiting, waiting for the day when they will return, return, return, or the day they must leave, or the day when someone will honour and pronounce their names with dignity.

Shakespeare knew it. I believe we all know it. You can only fight back with poetry.

Notes

1. Lydia G. Garcia and Bill Rauch, *La Comedia of Errors*, based on Christina Anderson (trans.), *The Comedy of Errors*, by William Shakespeare (rehearsal draft, 21 May 2019, 30). Translation: This man is the jeweller in charge of the necklace that the jealous wife wanted. And it seems that this patron has finally found the man to whom the necklace belongs. But they are going around about who hit who.
2. Garcia and Rauch, *La Comedia of Errors* (rehearsal draft, 21 May 2019, 15).
3. Garcia and Rauch, *La Comedia of Errors* (rehearsal draft, 21 May 2019, 16).
4. Micha Espinosa, 'Insights into the Challenges Latino Students Face while Training in Theatre', in *Shakespeare around the Globe: Essays on Voice and Speech*, ed. Mandy Rees (Cincinnati, OH: Voice and Speech Trainers Association, 2005), 129–43.
5. George Kitahara Kich, 'The Developmental Process of Asserting a Biracial, Bicultural Identity', *Racially Mixed People in America*, 304 (1992): 317.
6. Garcia and Rauch, *La Comedia of Errors* (rehearsal draft, 21 May 2019, 5).
7. Garcia and Rauch, *La Comedia of Errors* (rehearsal draft, 21 May 2019, 80). Translation: Nuestros queridos vecinos / Our dear neighbours; satisfacción / satisfaction; Mi comunidad, mi esposo and mis hijos both / My community, my husband and both my children.
8. Jordan Rodriguez, 'Hello all. First time poster, recently joined. Latinx, obviously', Latinx Theatre Commons, Facebook, 18 October 2019. https://www.facebook.com/groups/latinxtheatrecommons/permalink/2569996729780686/.
9. Garcia and Rauch, *La Comedia of Errors* (rehearsal draft, 21 May 2019, revised 7.2), 79.
10. For more on where I draw my inspiration, see Brené Brown, *I Thought It Was Just Me (but It Isn't): Telling the Truth about Perfectionism, Inadequacy, and Power* (New York: Gotham Books, 2008); Brené Brown, *Daring Greatly: How the Courage to Be Vulnerable Transforms the Way We Live, Love, Parent, and Lead* (London: Portfolio Penguin, 2013); Peter Costa and Bonny Norton, 'Introduction: Identity, Transdisciplinarity, and the Good Language Teacher', *Modern Language Journal*, 101.S1 (2017): 3–14; Achilleas Kostoulas and Sarah Mercer, 'Fifteen Years of Research on Self & Identity in System', *System*, 60 (2016): 128–34; Sarah Mercer, 'Psychology for Language Learning: Spare a Thought for the Teacher', *Language Teaching*, 51.4 (2018): 504–25; and Sprouts, '8 Stages of

Development by Erik Erikson', YouTube video, 5:19, uploaded 23 April 2017, https://youtu.be/aYCBdZLCDBQ.

11. For further reading of the Fitzmaurice method, see https://www.fitz-mauriceinstitute.org/writings (last accessed 19 November 2020).

12. Garcia and Rauch, *La Comedia of Errors* (rehearsal draft, 21 May 2019, revised 7.2), 50.

13. Corey Mitchell, '"English-Only" Laws in Education on Verge of Extinction', *Education Week*, 23 October 2019. Available at https://www.edweek.org/ew/articles/2019/10/23/english-only-laws-in-education-on-verge-of.html (last accessed 19 November 2020).

14. Garcia and Rauch, *La Comedia of Errors* (rehearsal draft, 21 May 2019, 81).

Index

CPSIA information can be obtained
at www.ICGtesting.com
Printed in the USA
LVHW082325220621
690914LV00002B/69